ADVERTISING CREATIVITY
Techniques for
Generating Ideas

JAMES L. MARRA
Temple University

PRENTICE HALL, Englewood Cliffs, New Jersey 07632

Library of Congress Cataloging-in-Publication Data

Marra, James L.
    Advertising creativity.

    Bibliography:
    Includes index.
    1. Advertising.   2. Creative ability in business.
I. Title.
HF5823.M266   1990   659.1   88–36388
ISBN 0-13-015009-6

HF 5823 .M266 1990

Marra, James L., 1943–

Advertising creativity

2 4 5 3 2 6

Editorial/production supervision
    and interior design: **Mary Kathryn Leclercq**
Cover design: **Wanda Lubelska Design**
Manufacturing buyer: **Carol Bystrom**

© 1990 by Prentice-Hall, Inc.
A Division of Simon & Schuster
Englewood Cliffs, New Jersey 07632

Printed in the United States of America
10   9   8   7   6   5   4   3   2   1

ISBN   0-13-015009-6

Prentice-Hall International (UK) Limited, *London*
Prentice-Hall of Australia Pty. Limited, *Sydney*
Prentice-Hall Canada Inc., *Toronto*
Prentice-Hall Hispanoamericana, S.A., *Mexico*
Prentice-Hall of India Private Limited, *New Delhi*
Prentice-Hall of Japan, Inc., *Tokyo*
Simon & Schuster Asia Pte. Ltd., *Singapore*
Editora Prentice-Hall do Brasil, Ltda., *Rio de Janeiro*

CONTENTS

PREFACE

Those interested in learning more about advertising creative strategy and executions (copy or art) have plenty of insightful and informative books from which to choose. The belief prompting the research and writing of this book, however, is that those interested in learning more about how to generate creative advertising ideas have relatively few books from which to choose. There just aren't that many around. This scarcity is a bit baffling, given how vital the creative idea is to the overall effectiveness of any ad. Whatever the reason for this scarcity, this book assumes there is a need for identifying usable techniques to help in idea generation.

This book is not restricted to copy or art. It assumes that a creative idea can begin in many ways—with a word, with a remembrance, with an accident, with a smell, and especially with an image. The key is to form connections among and between the many stimuli the world has to offer, the problem being confronted, and ourselves.

A guiding premise to the three-part structure of the book is that believing in our creativity precedes our being creative and having creative ideas. The three-part structure also relies on the fundamental stages of the creative process, beginning with preparation, moving to incubation, then to illumination, and ending with verification or elaboration. Overall, the three parts concentrate on the incubation and illumination stages.

Part I of the book contains three chapters. Chapter One discusses creativity apart from advertising, including profiles of the creative process, the creative personality, the act of connective thinking, and creative ideas. Chapter Two argues that all of us have the potential to generate creative ideas since all of us are naturally creative. If we don't believe we're creative, it's because that belief has been doused or hidden somewhere along the line. What needs to be done, then, is to revive it or bring it out in the open. A first step to doing that is in believing it's okay to be creative or different. Chapter Three discusses why it's okay, especially in advertising.

Part II of the book also contains three chapters. As a group, they are devoted to the preparation stage of the creative process as it pertains to advertising. Chapter Four describes what constitutes creative advertising ideas. It introduces the acronym, ADNORMS, an easy way to tell if your idea has the potential to be the *Big Idea*. Chapter Five outlines the basic steps in communication and persuasion. These steps are outlined in the context of real-life situations. Those situations are then used to deepen understanding of how advertising communication and persuasion tend to operate. Chapter Six introduces a Creative Prep Sheet and Creative Plan. These are the guide and map the creative individual can use in preparing to generate ideas.

Part III of the book contains six chapters. Part III is where Parts I and II were heading. Chapter Seven offers tips for finding and holding on to your creativity. It focuses on the importance of fearlessness, nonjudgment, quantities of ideas, empathy, alertness, individualized rituals, and playfulness. Chapters Eight, Nine, Ten, and Eleven offer a number of idea-generation techniques, ranging from *associations* to *opposites* to *clocks and calendars*. These techniques are exemplified in a variety of ad ideas shown and discussed in each chapter. Each of these chapters includes exercises. Chapter Twelve explains how six of those ad ideas came to be. It steps backward into the strategy and planning stages, and then forward into the inceptions of those ad ideas.

My hope is that you find this book interesting, perhaps unique in its presentation of a new slant, a new look at creative advertising ideas and advertising creativity. My greater hope is that you find it helpful. If it does what it's supposed to do, it should help you get in touch with your creative spirit. It should help you generate ideas more quickly and more fluently. And it should help you believe in your creativity and individuality.

ACKNOWLEDGMENTS

Every book is a collaboration of sorts. Since I'm the author, my name is given ample notice. As a result, it would seem that this book is a noncollaborative effort. That, of course, is not the case. On the contrary, there are many collaborators, many individuals, companies, and groups to whom a debt of gratitude is owed. Their influence on and support of this book should not go unnoticed.

My thanks go out to students, past and present, from Texas Tech University and Temple University. They have made my teaching a joy and challenge. And they have reaffirmed my faith in the creativity, vigor, and eagerness of today's young people.

My thanks go out to the kind folks at Prentice Hall, especially Mary K. "Katy" Leclercq and Steve Dalphin, for their encouragement and professional guidance during the research and writing of this book.

Thanks also go out to the book's reviewers: Neil Alperstein, Loyola College; Timothy A. Bengston, University of Kansas; Bob Carrell, University of Oklahoma; Deborah K. Morrison, University of Texas at Austin; Richard Tino, University of Bridgeport; and Carla Vaccaro-Lloyd, Syracuse University. Their thoughtful and perceptive comments have helped to reshape and reword many key passages and topics. I only wish there were more time to include more revisions based on what was suggested.

Thanks also to colleagues and friends, some of whom have been one and the same. Throughout the years they have supported my efforts, and their wit, insights, challenges, and friendship have helped me in the classroom, at the processor, and in life. In no particular order, I would like to acknowledge Billy Ross, Alex Tan, Jon Wardrip, John Schweitzer, Hower Hsia, Leon Higdon, John Runden, Kirby Hoke, Bob Strada, and Tom Eveslage.

Thanks to those advertising and corporate professionals whose creative ideas and insights you'll meet between the covers of this book. They have been very helpful and cooperative. Without their ad ideas, surely this book would not exist.

Thanks to Jay and Faye because they understand and still like to play.

Thanks to parents because wherever we go, they're right beside.

And a special thanks to Mary Ella, a talented artist and teacher, and by far the most important individual to the completion of this book.

                                                                    J.L.M.

1
CREATIVITY: AN OVERVIEW

Imagine this. We're sitting across from one another, and I ask you the question, "What does it mean to be creative?" What do you answer?

Do you immediately begin to pull together what you know of advertising or any other specific field and include it in your answer? If so, I would argue that you're being too narrow, too confined. I would argue that in order to understand creativity, you need to think of it beyond any specific field, advertising included. To understand it, you need to think of it as embracing many fields, perhaps all fields and even life itself. You need to think of it as a type of generalized, all-encompassing phenomenon which really knows no boundaries, at least as far as a specific field is concerned. And you need to think of it as reverberating outward and upward beyond any one discipline, any one individual, or any one answer.

What you are confronted with here, then, is a book on advertising creativity that begins by saying, forget advertising for the moment and think beyond it. It says this because that's a good way to learn more about how advertising works, including how its creativity works as well. In other words, this book begins by saying that if you understand creativity now—the phenomenon to which advertising ideas and individuals belong—then you will be better able to understand advertising and advertising creativity later. This book's beginning supposes that the best way to tap into your creative advertising potentials is first to tap into creativity. It also supposes that the best creative advertising individuals are creative individuals first and creative advertising individuals second.

So, back to our question, "What does it mean to be creative?" Volumes seeking to answer that question have been written at least as far back as Plato. One of the consistent answers is that it all depends on what part of creativity you're talking about. Are you talking about the creative process? The creative personality? Creative ideas? Each comprises an important aspect of creativity. As a result, when we seek to answer the question, we are inevitably drawn into several aspects of what turns out to be a very large and reverberating word, creativity. Even including consideration of these aspects, however, there is one common thread, a single word and concept that can serve to knit things together: *connections*. It is a key word for the remainder of this book's pages.

RIGHT AWAY, PRACTICE THINKING CREATIVELY IN ORDER TO UNDERSTAND WHAT IT MEANS TO BE CREATIVE

A large part of creativity is the creative individual's ability to think by connections, many times by analogies or metaphors: Something is like or suggests something else. And this connection provides the spark for creative ideas.

Just from those few words, you should immediately be able to discern something important about the aspects of creativity. For example, creative ideas are a matter of connections originating from individuals with the ability to connect. They use this ability as they weave their way through the creative process, itself a matter of connections. This can be synthesized into the following. To be creative is to connect. Since all connections aren't necessarily creative, however, this synthesis is not enough. Let's add qualifiers. To be creative is to connect something with something else to produce a new and relevant idea. That's closer to it.

Now, imagine I again ask you the question, "What does it mean to be creative?"

You might be inclined to give an answer like, "To be creative is the ability to connect something with something else in order to produce a new and relevant idea."

That is certainly a concise and solid answer. It is a very uncreative answer, however. Think about answering creatively. For instance, could you answer by completing the following statement: "To be creative is to be a fisherman because _____." Think about what has to be included in that answer. Think of all the things, the equipment and such, that you need to fish. Think about water. Think about fish. In fact, think about giving creative meaning to the following: water, a boat, weather, a map, fishing gear including bait and tackle, and fish. Remember what you're trying to do, though. You're trying to describe what it means to be creative and, in the process, expand your understanding of creativity.

What is the water? Can it be the world of reality? Our sensory world of experiences and memories?

What is the boat? Can it be our drive to solve a problem? The motivation?

What is the weather? Can it be positive forces encouraging us to be creative? Negative forces encouraging just the opposite?

What is the map? Can it be the plan we follow to reach certain goals? Knowledge?

What is the fishing gear? Can it be our powers of observation? The powers of imagination? The powers of consciousness or subconsciousness?

What are fish? Can they be creative ideas?

If you connect these possible answers, what do you have? Perhaps this.

To be creative is a matter of skimming along our world of reality, our sensory world of experiences and memories waiting to be caught and connected into ideas by our powers of observation, imagination, and consciousness or subconsciousness. To catch and connect these realities, experiences, and memories, we must be open and ready to dip and probe below the water's surface. But first we must skim, and we manage to do that by means of our drive to solve problems. We're allowed or not allowed this opportunity by positive or negative reinforcement from those around us or from ourselves, and our goals and knowledge guide us in this quest.

In connecting these answers you should feel your base of understanding of creativity broaden. But why is that?

In all likelihood, this broadening is due to the notion that one of the best ways to see something clearly is not to look at it too directly. Often it's better to look at it indirectly, in this case by association and connection. This gets our mental engines chugging. Images and concepts begin to occupy multiple tracks in our minds. More mental space is taken up by those images and concepts, and we become more actively involved in connecting them.

Think of looking at the sun as an example. If you look at it directly, you really don't see much. You're blinded. But if you look at it indirectly, obliquely, perhaps by peripheral vision, then you get a clearer and even fuller insight into what the sun is and what it does. Often that's how it goes with trying to understand something and its workings.

As you think about looking at the sun and even fishing, you're actually thinking creatively in order to better understand what being creative means. You've been asked to branch outward and upward beyond something literal to something else entirely. You've been asked to think of creativity according to fishing. And you've been asked to think of thinking and understanding according to looking at or not looking at the sun. This is how we will approach many concepts during the parts of your book.

Right along, you will have to connect, to think creatively. For now, consider the sun and fishing as warm-ups, especially for the essential third part of your book on idea generation.

THE CREATIVE PROCESS

It certainly would be nice if creativity restricted itself to a pat answer expressed in one or two lines, but it doesn't. Instead, it reverberates, reaching outward to include many aspects. One of these is the creative process itself—the procedural movement of how we arrive at creative ideas. By procedural movement we mean a pattern, a kind of stage-by-stage evolution of thought and emotion which culminates in the birth and elaboration of creative ideas. And to understand that pattern is to take a large step toward the understanding of what it means to be creative.

There have been a variety of models proposed seeking to explain the creative process. Despite this variety, however, most models explain the process by reference to similar steps or stages. The similarity is clear in three models that have endured for some time now. Two were proposed by advertising giants, one of whom is Alex Osborn, the O of the BBD & O advertising agency, a founding father of The Creative Problem-Solving Institute at the State University of New York at Buffalo, and author of the pioneer book, *Applied Imagination*. The other giant is James Webb Young of the Young & Rubicam advertising agency. He is the author of the influential and concise little book, *A Technique for Producing Ideas*. The third model is really the base, the origin, for the Osborn and Young models and others as well. It was proposed in 1926 by Graham Wallas in his book *The Art of Thought*.

The three models possess strong similarities to each other. Wallas's model, however, was the forerunner for the others. For Wallas, the process was a matter of stages the creative individual passes through in a quest to solve problems. He identified the four stages as preparation, incubation, illumination, and verification.[1]

The preparation stage includes the individual's orientation toward a problem and the gathering of information needed to help solve that problem.

The incubation stage includes the period prior to the discovery of an idea or problem solution. This stage is typically known as a waiting period. But don't be misled—this doesn't mean it's a period of inactivity. To the contrary, a lot is going on during this stage, both consciously and unconsciously.

The illumination stage is the emergence of an idea or solution. This stage has had many names throughout history, one of the most common being "Eureka!" "Eureka" is a term derived from the Greek, Archimedes, who discovered a method for calculating a metal's composition based on the amount of water it displaces. He discovered it while taking his bath, at which time he leaped from his tub and ran naked through the streets shouting "Eureka!"

The verification stage includes the actual working up of the idea or solution. It is a kind of elaboration of the idea so that the idea is made ready for introduction to the real world. For example, for advertising writers and artists, it's the stage when creative ideas are written and designed according to how they will be seen or heard in the various media such as newspaper, magazine, radio, or television.

From preparation to incubation to illumination to verification. According to Wallas, these are the stages the creative individual passes through in the juggling and playing with the various ways and means of solving problems. For both Osborn and Young, these stages remain fairly well intact, though they are either elaborated or described differently.

For Osborn, the elaboration of the Wallas model includes several new stages such as an orientation stage proceeding the preparation stage. Before gathering material to help solve a problem, the creative individual orients the self toward the problem to be solved. In effect, the problem is crystallized. Then, the individual prepares by gathering appropriate information and material. This leads to an analysis of that information and material, followed by the generation of various ideas as alternative ways to solve the problem. From here, the individual incubates in a kind of selective processing of those ideas until a synthesis occurs. The synthesis determines what is needed as a workable idea. Finally, the individual evaluates the idea based on various objectives and goals.[2]

For Young, the focus is not so much on elaborating the Wallas model, but more on renaming the stages in the model. For instance, Young refers to the incubation stage as a period for digesting food or turning the problem over to the unconscious. He also refers to the illumination stage as a period of idea appearance and the verification stage as a period of adapting the idea to reality. Overall, Young relies on a tight, unwavering focus on the Wallas model.[3]

Despite the Osborn and Young variations of the Wallas model, notice how all three models are strongly similar. All include a preparation stage when information and material are gathered. All include a kind of hiatus period, a period when the information and material are left to percolate in the mind. All include a period of insight, the "Eureka" illumination stage. And all include a verification stage when the idea or problem solution is elaborated and brought to reality.

What this brief look at the creative process should tell you is that if you expect to be creative, then you had better be prepared to experience the various stages in the process. Not only that, you had better be prepared to connect them, since getting stuck in one stage invariably means you are unable to move to another and thus create or actualize an idea. This doesn't mean all of us go through the stages in the same way, at the same speed, or even in the same linear, straight-and-narrow order. It does mean, however, that we all go through them, regardless.

In a sense, going through this creative process is a bit like fishing. As you set out to fish, you'll guide your boat through the water to your destination. Sometimes you'll skim easily over the surface. Sometimes you won't. Instead, you'll buck waves and currents along the way. This, too, is a lot like our own psychological and emotional reactions to the stages in the creative process. There will be ups, and there will be downs.

THE UPS AND DOWNS OF THE CREATIVE PROCESS

Like the creative process, reactions to it also follow a pattern based on stages. No doubt, the best way to understand both of these patterns is to remember an instance of your own creativity. Remember a situation when you solved a problem with a creative solution. Since creativity is certainly not restricted to the creative arts as we may know them and does in fact include many of life's activities, then perhaps you remember creating an exotic meal or a special gift for a special someone. Let's take the special gift as an example. What happens when you create a special gift idea?

First, you sense a problem. A special day for your someone is fast approaching, and you're intent on giving a cherished gift. But what should it be? To solve that problem, you think about your someone's likes and dislikes and finally go shopping. This is your preparation stage. During this stage you gather information and material.

Next, you take all the information and sit on it. Just like a chicken sits on an egg, you sit and wait for the birth of an idea. This is your incubation stage. Should I get this? Should I get that? What if my special someone doesn't like it? You wrestle with all these nagging uncertainties. As in giving birth, you're not comfortable, not in the least. There's tension, anxiety, and perhaps an occasional bout with morning sickness. So, in typical fashion you wriggle and squirm psychologically and emotionally, unsure of what your special gift will be.

As you wriggle and squirm, you sense the realities of gift possibilities floating into your mind. You begin to connect them. You begin to expand the possibilities. You may even include creating a gift for your special someone. Your excitement mounts. You begin to feel yourself lifting up. Then, there it is—the *Big Idea*, a special gift for a special someone made with tender loving care by your own hands. This is your illumination stage. This is "Eureka!" This is what Rollo May describes as the "encounter," the period marked by the highest "degree of absorption, the degree of intensity."[4]

Immediately, you just know your someone is going to love the gift. You can feel it, and you're certain. You're absolutely, positively convinced this is it. You're also absolutely, positively aglow with the prospects. So, you rest easy, a kind of self-satisfied gleam in your eye.

But what goes up must come down. You think about the idea overnight. When you wake up, you think about it again, only now it doesn't quite have that sparkling star quality it had the day before. This is your entrance to the verification stage, when the idea is elaborated and completed into a reality. As Young puts it, it's a stage signaled by an awareness of the "cold, grey dawn of the morning after."[5]

Filled with mixed feelings, you set out making your gift. But you're troubled. What if the gift isn't right? What if this? What if that? Like the incubation stage, this stage can be an uneasy one. Still, as you toil away with your gift, you begin to relocate some of those grand feelings you experienced during the preparation and illumination stages. Before you know it, you're working feverishly, convinced again that your gift idea is absolutely the right one. No doubt about it.

Then, whoops. The slide once more, probably right after you complete the gift. You feel uncertain about it all. You even seriously consider a last minute trip to a nearby department store to pick up a gift certificate for your special someone. Well, don't. Don't bother with the gift certificate, because chances are your special someone will just love the gift. Even if your special someone doesn't, chances are you'll never know about it.

Still, why all this turmoil? Why all the ups and downs as part of the creative process?

The reason for the ups and downs is that the creative process and creativity generally are growing, living organisms. They are cyclical in nature, just like other growing, living organisms. As such, they involve pain and anxiety. Think about it. Is giving birth easy? Any birth? Ever watch a hen sitting on an egg? Does she ever look uncomfortable? You bet. For a plant to be born, a seed needs to break through the ground. Do you think that's easy? Do you think it's easy for two people to connect into a growing creative relationship? Probably not. But is it rewarding in the fullest and most complete sense? Probably so.

The point to remember here is that the creative process and your up and down reactions to it are quite natural. There are waves and currents to be bucked. There are pushes and shoves along the way. During the preparation stage, you get excited, and that pushes you on to the incubation stage, when you feel uneasy and uncertain. To rid yourself of those nagging feelings, you create ideas and solutions (it's either that or continue to feel anxious, or just forget the whole thing). When you enter the illumination stage, you feel euphoric. Eventually, that too fades during the verification stage.

So you come down. But, once again, coming down gives way to rejuvenation and paves the way for reentering the creative process all over again as you tackle a new problem.

And so it goes. Just like giving birth. Just like interpersonal relationships of worth. We could even say all of it is just like fishing.

It's important to understand that the entire process and your reactions to it are very much an individual matter. Indeed, the very word, *individuality*, is central to creativity as a whole. Even with the process and its reactions, your individuality shapes how, when, and for how long you remain in various stages. For some, the incubation stage may last longer than for others. Or, for some, the illumination stage may be a matter of many ideas rushing in at close to the same time, while for others it may be a matter of fewer but more complex ideas rushing in at various times. Similarly, some may experience greater heights and depths in the way of emotional reactions than others will. Whatever the case, the process and reactions are yours. They evolve and you experience them as a consequence of your own individuality.

THE CREATIVE PERSONALITY

No doubt, individualized differences in the creative process and the reactions to it derive in great measure from differences in individual personalities. As much as personalities differ, however, when it comes to describing creative personalities, there is also much that is the same. Notice, for instance, the similarities in the creative personality descriptions found in Figure 1–1. These descriptions have been extracted from a selection of works by some of the leading researchers and theorists in creativity research and thought.

Character or personality traits such as independence, nonconformity, courage, self-assertion, openness, curiosity, spontaneity, and empathy form the nucleus of the creative personality. In all probability, these traits aren't very surprising to you. Surely, each of us has known creative individuals who exemplify most of them: an eccentric uncle whose basement is glutted with weird whittlings of tiny circus figures; a friend whose nights are taken up composing remorseful poems about a love gone wrong. We have all known people like this, and, if pressed, we may be inclined to describe them as independent, nonconformist, or spontaneous.

Unfortunately, in classifying and generalizing as we have done here, one of the problems is that we open ourselves to the dangers of stereotyping. At the same time, creativity research suggests that such commonality of traits exists. Often, however, the commonality shifts because it is one dependent on individuality and difference. A kind of paradox exists here. On one hand, creative personalities are similar. On the other hand, their

FIGURE 1-1   Character/Personality Traits of the Creative Individual

From Abraham H. Maslow:
 —spontaneous, expressive, less controlled and inhibited, unfrightened by the unknown, boldness, courage (pp. 85, 94)
"Creativity in Self-Actualizing People," in *Creativity and Its Cultivation,* ed. Harold H. Anderson (New York: Harper & Row, Publishers, 1959), pp. 83–95.

From Frank Barron:
 —prefer complexity, independent in judgments, self-assertive, reject suppression (pp. 208–209).
Creativity and Psychological Health (Princeton, NJ: D. Van Nostrand Co., Inc., 1963).

From Morris I. Stein:
 —need for curiosity, persistence of motive, independent, autonomous, rejects repression, open to feelings and emotions, intuitive, empathic (pp. 58–60).
Stimulating Creativity, Vol. I (New York: Academic Press, 1974).

From Donald W. MacKinnon:
 —independent, nonconforming, open to experience (inner self and outer world) (pp. 125, 129).
In Search of Human Effectiveness: Identifying and Developing Creativity (Buffalo, NY: Creative Education Foundation in association with Creative Synergetic Associates, Ltd., 1978).

From Carl R. Rogers:
 —openness to experience, internal locus of evaluation, ability to toy with elements and concepts, play spontaneously, juggle elements (pp. 299–301).
"Toward a Theory of Creativity," in *The Creativity Quest,* eds. Albert Rothenberg and Carl R. Hausman (Durham, NC: Duke University Press, 1976), pp. 296–305.

similarity is their individuality and difference. What we have then are personalities that are different, and these differences make them similar as a group.

No doubt, it's one thing to list personality traits as we have done here, but it's quite another thing to understand how those traits manifest themselves when it comes time for being creative. In this respect, imagine that we have a composite creative personality containing many of the traits we have listed. Make this composite personality a kind of Every Creative Man or Woman—you. You be that individual. See yourself as having those traits. Now, imagine you're put into a challenging position where you need to be creative and generate an exciting and original advertising idea. Using your traits as a base for your decisions and actions, how would you respond to the following situations?

> Before you even think of an advertising idea, one of your respected peers tells you there's no sense in trying to be creative with the idea since the powers that be will never accept it. Does this stop you from being creative? Or do you continue in your efforts? Why or why not?

An idea occurs to you, but you believe it's fairly new and different. Do you pursue it, or do you scrap it and go on to something else? Why or why not?

Assume you pursued that idea, but it gets shot down. It just won't work. Do you get discouraged? Or are you still confident you will find an acceptable and workable creative idea? Why or why not?

As you diligently work away trying to find ideas, your perspective gets clouded. You begin to lose your bearings. Things get muddied. The problem seems much more complex than it originally seemed. Do you get frustrated to the point where you are impotent? Or do you relish this loss of perspective and see it as a challenge? Why or why not?

A supervisor visits and asks you to come up with many idea possibilities. Plus, the supervisor gives you another problem needing creative ideas as solutions. Do you again feel frustrated to the point of impotence? Or do you continue confidently on your way? Why or why not?

Your supervisor shows you various ad ideas and asks you to think of something similar. Do you? Or do you continue to search for something new? Why or why not?

During a leisurely moment, you're seized by a potentially exciting and innovative idea. Do you show an emotional reaction? Or do you inhibit that reaction and carry on as before? Why or why not?

Now, think of how you related to the situations and answered the questions. Did you apply your stereotypical traits? If so, then you probably found yourself relating and answering in the following ways.

Despite the fact that others tell you not to bother doing something in a particular way, you tend to challenge what you're told. You may take their comments and criticisms to heart. But you will also remain steadfast in your quest for creative ideas. This is because you're an independent sort. You're also willful. If you want to be creative, you will be, regardless of whether others think it's valuable or not.

You tend to pursue ideas others don't. This is because you're observant and curious. You tend to notice things others may overlook. You're also open and willing to veer off a designated path in order to experience and create something new.

Despite having your idea shot down, you're not deterred. You may see it as a temporary setback. But you remain courageous and self-confident overall.

Losing your perspective and facing a puzzling situation have little negative influence on your creativity. To the contrary, you often relish ambiguity and challenge. For you, things are not nearly as black and white as they are grey. You're used to living with grey. You're used to living with indeterminacy. You remain undeterred and confident in your ability to create.

As a creative individual, you're flexible and able to juggle several things at one time. You're also capable of generating ideas from many different angles. You're fluent with those ideas, and so the prospect of having much to do is not all that disturbing. Once again, you continue confidently on your way.

You're willing to try new things. You're a risk taker. You're open and curious. You're not closed to new ways or new ideas. When asked to come up with something similar, you will probably nod your head, yes, and then continue to search for something new. Again, you're independent and different. You may even pride yourself on those qualities.

You do respond to your emotions. Childlike, you're spontaneous, playful, and emotive. If anything, you lack inhibitions or at least are bothered by them. For you, natural, emotional responses are the rule, not the exception.

When we talk about the creative personality, we invariably talk about the strengths of will, empathy, individuality, and difference combined with the carefreeness of openness, spontaneity, curiosity, and playfulness. A creative personality tends to manifest itself through these traits, which become the driving force behind idea discovery. And they become the driving force behind the creative individual's ability to connect with the world in order to stimulate that discovery.

CONNECTING

Just based on your general view of the creative process, its ups and downs, and the creative personality, you should be able to see how a definition of what it means to be creative ripples outward and expands beyond a simplified, direct, one or two-line statement. You should also be able to see how that expansion is very much dependent on the individual.

Creative individuals weave their way through the creative process in individual ways. The common ground to their personalities is also based on individuality. The same will hold true when we talk about how creative individuals find their creative ideas. Yet, despite these similarities of individuality and difference, there is that one important concept which unifies the diverse aspects of what it means to be creative. The concept is *connections.* Perhaps above all else, creative individuals are able to form connections that are new and relevant. Often this is what most distinguishes their ideas and work from the ideas and work of others.

As you think about this ability to connect in new and relevant ways, think about this as well. The personality traits we have briefly discussed contribute significantly to this ability. For instance, to be open to the world and experience means you allow yourself to connect with all the expansiveness of that world and experience. You don't shut anything out. Likewise, to be curious or spontaneous or impulsive means you allow yourself to make the same connection. Again, you don't shut anything out.

Try to see all of this as a means of connecting or integrating yourself with the world. This doesn't mean you integrate yourself with the world according to how others think it should be done. Remember, creative individuals are independent. It does mean you integrate yourself with the world according to how *you* think it should be done. You connect or integrate with those things in the world providing you with the material for actualizing your creative drives, and to do that you need to be open and curious to what the world has to offer. You cannot be closed. This means you're alert to the world and you pay attention to it—close attention. Then your alertness and attention yield many observations based on connections—penetrating observations.

Connecting Through Observation

When we talk about connecting through observation, we're really talking about more than the sense of sight. We're talking about being in tune with the world of realities as it offers diverse stimuli through our senses, our experiences, our memories, and our emotions.

In any given day we are bombarded by countless realities. Generally, these enter us through our senses. We hear an alarm clock ring in the morning. That's a reality. We smell coffee brewing downstairs. Another reality. We shower and preen ourselves. Other realities. And on it goes throughout the day and night. Combine these sensory realities with the realities of our own experiences, memories, emotions, thoughts, and conversations, and during each day we have crossed a virtual sea of realities. What is important for actualizing our creative potentials, however, is how good we are at observing, truly observing, these realities and then connecting them with our problems in order to create ideas as potential solutions. This is what is meant by integrating or connecting the self and world.

There is little or no coincidence to the contention that highly creative people are among the best observers. This is because they rely on their observations to form the connections yielding creative ideas. Take the well-known American artist Georgia O'Keeffe, for example. Reknowned for her large flower paintings, O'Keeffe exemplifies how the creative personality manages to observe and then integrate and connect with the world. She offers this insight into her work:

> In the twenties, huge buildings sometimes seemed to be going up overnight in New York. At the same time I saw a painting by Fantin-Latour, a still-life with flowers I found very beautiful, but I realized that were I to paint the same flowers so small, no one would look at them because I was unknown. So I thought I'll make them big like huge buildings going up.[6]

Notice O'Keeffe's powers of observation and connection. Dipping into the world of reality, she observes huge buildings, the skyscrapers of the 1920s in New York City. As an artist, she is also in touch with the work of other artists, in this case Fantin-Latour's flower still-life. Realizing she needs a unique presentation in order to be noticed, she connects her observations into a creative idea.

Now, what are the personality traits revealed in this example? What we have is a sensitive artist with an openness to the world of realities surrounding her. She refuses to shut those realities out. Instead, she either absorbs them or is absorbed by them. She integrates and connects herself with them. In addition, she is independent and courageous. She is willing to take the risk of connecting her observations into an innovative, original form of creative expression. Openness. Absorption. Connection. Courage. Without these personality traits as driving forces behind her creativity, she would have been less inclined to be so innovative and original with her large flower paintings.

This same kind of keenness of observation and willingness to connect—to dive right into the world of realities and connect them in order to actualize one's creative potential—are inseparable from what it means to be creative. Consider writers, for instance. Writers write about observations accumulated through their experiencing of the world's realities. In short, they write about life. In their book *Creativity and the Writing Process*, Olivia Bertagnolli and Jeff Rackham comment on just this view: "We cannot separate writing from life, from being alive, from the life we have lived. The process we are talking about is an 'organic' one."[7] This organic process is a matter of integrating one's self with the world. It's a matter of absorbing and being absorbed. It's also essential for creative expression and creative ideas.

For the creative individual, there is no such thing as a kind of routine numbness or trancelike nonexperiencing of life. Open, curious, and sensitive, creative individuals are great observers of the world, of life. They take the time to probe and be aware. They know that if they avoid the scent of flowers, then far be it for them to write a sensitive and endearing ode to a rose or an appealing and appropriate headline for FTD.

To be creative means you must be prepared to pay this kind of open and diligent heed to what the world has to offer. It also means you must be prepared to sweep your observations to the centers of your problems. You must be able to store those observations and then connect them together as solutions to those problems. But none of that can be accomplished unless you're open and ready to observe. The playwright Neil Simon has this to say about the importance of observation for actualizing creative potential:

> I always picture myself as that person at a cocktail party standing in the corner and watching. And I've always felt, and I think this is very true of most writers that I know, we are observers rather than participants. . . . When I am sitting and having a conversation with a friend, I hear the conversation. I become a third person at the table listening to the two of us.[8]

Of course, to experience the dual roles of observer and participant simultaneously is no easy chore. But a creative individual can do this. A creative individual can form a persona of the participating self, a kind of other person, who steps out from the role of participant to log the key observations gleaned from the role of observer. This is what Georgia O'Keeffe did when she participated in the world by walking down New York City's streets, studying Fantin-Latour's painting, and then simultaneously observing and logging these realities from the point of view of her own creative drives and work.

Connecting Through Individualized Rituals

Beyond the powers of observation and integration or absorption, to be creative also means you're able to connect with yourself. You know what you need in order to get you going creatively. And you make certain to place yourself in situations allowing that to happen. Of course, this again is an individual matter. Creative individuals work differently. But each individual develops a customized ritual peculiar to the self.

To see how diverse, individualized, and even eccentric rituals can be, let's skim over some examples from the lives of well-known creative people who devoted themselves to pursuing and often attaining their creative goals. These rituals can be divided into time, place, and work habits and production.

Let's consider time and place first. In the writing field, for example, the famous nineteenth-century American writer and philosopher Ralph Waldo Emerson would leave his family and rent a hotel room to gain the solitude necessary to generate and elaborate his ideas.[9] Another famous American writer, Ernest Hemingway, would organize his work efforts around the early morning.[10] While living in Key West, Florida, Hemingway would rise early in the morning and take his customary walk across a footbridge to the studio behind his home. There he did his writing, finding the morning hours compatible with his creative drives. Hemingway would also leave his writing while he still had something of importance to say, believing this would prevent his facing creative blocks when he returned the next morning. As is well known, Hemingway's nights were times for carousing and gleaning those observations to be used in his fiction.

Like Hemingway, many creative individuals tend to organize their work efforts around certain times, particularly morning and night. As a "borderland between sleep and full awakening," morning and night are conducive to the kind of uninhibited thought required for creative production.[11] The hustle and bustle of the day hasn't quite begun or has mellowed out in a sense. So, as opposed to rushing around frantically to meet schedules, appointments, and the like, we tend to settle in. The pressure is off, and we can relax, dream, and create.

The French philosopher René Descartes was another writer who found such times conducive to creative expression. For him, the early morning was particularly suitable for generating ideas, mostly while in bed. The

British writer Sir Walter Scott believed the half-hour between waking and rising was especially friendly to any task of invention.[12] And, on the P.M. side, Pablo Picasso was notorious for working through the night into the early morning hours, only then to fall asleep until midafternoon.[13]

It is those twilight times of morning and night that appear to be important times for creative individuals. The problem in advertising, of course, is that it demands a kind of nine-to-five existence. Still, this doesn't mean a large part of creative thought or production is restricted to the regimen of that existence. To the contrary, since being creative is a great part of their lives, creative individuals tend to take their creative responsibilities with them whenever and wherever they go.

You can see this kind of independent ritualizing occurring in each of our brief examples from the lives of creative individuals. Notice, however, how the rituals cluster around the morning and night hours. Notice, too, how on occasion they tend to cluster around the bed, a place where we can be prone. In his interesting little book, *Lying Down*, Marco Vassi presents his view of the individual's relationship with the world. For Vassi, to be vertical is to be in combat with the world. In contrast, to be horizontal is to be in harmony with the world.[14] It is an intriguing perspective, legitimized to an extent by Albert Einstein, who formed his space and time theory while sick in bed, and James Brindley, a well-known engineer, who would go to bed for days until he managed to solve a problem.[15]

To lift all of this out of the trivial, however, the point to remember is that to be creative requires a connection with the self and how the self relates to both time and place during creative periods. As individualized as the time and place may be, the creative individual connects them with the self in order to actualize the creative drive. In a large way, time and place act as cues for being creative.

Beyond connecting with themselves and their creativity through the rituals of time and place, creative individuals also connect through the rituals of their work habits and creative production. Though it is difficult to tell whether these rituals aid inspiration or simply exist as a result of individual personalities, the fact remains that they do exist and thus are an important part of the creative individual's means for being creative.

To understand how individualized, yet necessary, these rituals become for the creative individual, let's again skim over some examples from the lives of prominent creative people. For instance, the writer Rudyard Kipling could not write with a lead pencil.[16] Both writers and philosophers Marcel Proust and Thomas Carlyle created in soundproof rooms or chambers.[17] Another writer, Emile Zola, pulled the shades at midday in order to simulate the night. Still another, Ben Jonson, needed a cup of tea, the purring of a cat, and the odor of an orange peel in order to create, while Honoré de Balzac wore monkish clothing to inspire the creative muse.[18]

In the field of musical composition, anecdotes of such peculiar rituals among individuals are plentiful. Schiller bathed his feet in ice water for inspiration. Mozart exercised before creating.[19] Leonard Bernstein dedicated some of his works to dogs; perhaps they served as inspiration for his compositions. Debussy and Beethoven claimed they needed nature for inspiration, a not uncommon claim among many creative individuals, since nature is an extremely fertile source for creative ideas.

These diversities in the rituals of work habits carry over to actual production as well. For instance, Schubert used a regimented work schedule, 9:00 A.M. until 2:00 P.M., to create. However, another composer, Rossini, detested regimented schedules. For him only absolute necessity prodded his creativity. His writing of the overture to *Othello* took place only after he was locked in a room by the producer, given a plate of spaghetti, and told he would not be allowed out until he had finished his work. In contrast, Schubert composed eight songs in one day, Beethoven wrote over two hundred variations for the finale of his famous Ninth Symphony, and Wagner wrote over nine thousand pages of music during his lifetime.[20]

Even beyond the field of musical composition, the situation remains fairly well the same. Charles Darwin, for instance, hit upon the idea of evolution at the age of twenty-nine. He spent forty-four more years devoting himself to the idea's verification and elaboration. Similarly, a fledgling student, Copernicus, working from the knowledge base of Pythagoras, played with the idea of the sun as the center of planetary motion. As with Darwin, he spent the remainder of his life verifying and elaborating this core idea.[21]

Once again, to lift everything out of the trivial, the point to remember is that being creative involves honing and using your ability to connect. On the one hand, to be a creative individual you need to be open and ready to connect with what the world and experience have to offer. On the other hand, you need to be in touch with yourself, your creative self, so that you can connect with those rituals individualized and customized to you.

No doubt, a large part of this ability to connect will be dependent on the strength of your creative personality. At times you will have to fly in the face of adversity and negative feedback. But the strength of your individuality and confidence will go a long way toward making the flying easier. At times you will have to fly in the face of anxiety and worry. Again, however, the strength of your individuality and confidence will go a long way toward making the flying easier. Ultimately, the powers of individuality and belief in yourself motivate you to connect—to connect the stages in the process, the downs with the ups, the world of reality with your problems, and your creative work with your individualized rituals.

A + B = CREATIVE IDEAS

The end result of being creative is ideas. Not just ordinary ideas, however, but ideas that are new and relevant. Creative ideas are very dependent on these qualities of newness and relevance. For us, ideas that have one or the other of these qualities are not complete creative ideas. They are only one-half creative ideas.

Together, newness and relevance comprise a tandem of prerequisites for creative ideas. Still, as much as they can act as criteria for recognizing such ideas, they cannot provide an explanation for how creative ideas come into being. In this respect, we need to identify the generative spark to ideas, that process which actually ignites them in the creative mind. Here, we can again turn to the process of connection for that is the dominant action and spark igniting creative ideas. Of course, given all we've discussed in this chapter, you shouldn't be surprised by the importance of connection. Creative individuals connect. It's no wonder then that their ideas are based on connections.

To understand the importance of connections to creative ideas, recall the large flower paintings by Georgia O'Keeffe. One reality, the skyscrapers of New York City, was connected with another reality, the flower still-life of Fantin-Latour, in order to create a new reality, the creative idea behind O'Keeffe's paintings. Notice how connections are central to that idea. Acting as sparks, the connections spur the creative mind to think beyond existing realities. When the mind thinks that way, as O'Keeffe's surely did, creative ideas are ignited. Whether in art, advertising, or elsewhere, these ideas then signal a change from one or more realities to something else entirely, namely new and relevant realities.

Put simply, what we have then is this. Creative ideas are new and relevant realities resulting from the innovative connections of old realities. Often, this is the byproduct of analogical or metaphorical thinking. To understand it more simply, however, think of it as a simple formula of $A + B = C$. Creative ideas, C, are new because A and B have been connected to the point of being blurred out of existence, at least in terms of what they typically mean or represent on their own or even together in the everyday, status quo world of reality. These same ideas become relevant when they serve a function, generally that of meeting needs or solving problems. Overall, creative ideas exist when part or all of A and part or all of B are connected, fused, perhaps even destroyed or transformed in the process in order to ignite C.

This simple formula of $A + B = C$ is the generative spark for creative ideas. Think back again to Georgia O'Keeffe's large flower paintings. New York City skyscrapers $= A$. Fantin-Latour's flower still-life $= B$. O'Keeffe's flower paintings $= C$. Though the formula can be modified to include more realities in combination, the core of $A + B = C$ remains the foundation for sparking a creative idea. The creative mind takes one reality, connects or associates it with another, and a new and relevant reality, a creative idea, is formed.

An additional point to bear in mind as you think about the $A + B = C$ formula is that many times the old realities of A and B may appear detached or dissimilar from one another, especially to the uncreative mind.

For instance, just how similar are skyscrapers and flowers? One could argue that they're not very similar at all. The point, however, is that one of the functions of the creative mind is to find similarities, even when they may appear to go against the grain of everyday reality. As the reknowned poet Robert Frost said, "Let's put this straight. The coupling that moves you, that stirs you, is the association of two things that you didn't expect to see associated."[23]

If we take Frost's words to heart, we can understand that creative ideas may often result from connections or associations between realities which don't appear to belong together. This is an important part of what makes them creative because this is what often makes them new. If we stop and think of what we know of creative ideas and accomplishments, we can see these dissimilar realities connected together in our A + B = C formula. Some examples would be Alexander Graham Bell's connection of the construction of the human ear (A) with its vibrations (B) to create the telephone (C); Mary Shelley's connection of a futile attempt to bring a piece of macaroni to life (A) with the gothic novel (B) to create her classic work, *Frankenstein* (C); Lorie Anderson's and David Bowie's connections of theatrics such as dance and song (A) with the world of art (B) to create the newness of performing art (C).

To these significant creative ideas we can add many more simply by looking at the world around us. For example, how many creative ideas derive from a connection with electricity? Lamps. Guitars. Pianos. Knives. Toothbrushes. Indeed, look into almost anything, and you will probably find creative ideas inside. Tap dancing. Helicopters. Velcro. Submarines. Clock radios. Cruise control. Music synthesizers. The theory of relativity. The list goes on, perhaps forever. But what such a list tells us is most important. Creative ideas are the new and relevant realities resulting from connections, often unique and unexpected connections between and among very commonplace realities.

Examples of Creative Thinking and Ideas

As we did with individualized rituals, let's roam far and wide, this time through examples of creative thinking and ideas exemplifying the important qualities of connection, newness, and relevance. We can begin with another retreat, this time to the eighteenth and nineteenth centuries in England when creative individuals were teeming with imaginative thought.

In the midst of the Romantic revolution, poets and philosophers were captivated by theories of creativity and the imagination. Their works reflect their devotion to those theories. Among those works, Samuel Taylor Coleridge's *Biographia Literaria* is one of the most complete philosophical treatises on the topics. In it Coleridge used a variety of connections to explain the creative process. In their own right, those connections exemplify creative ideas.

As with many of the other poets and philosophers during his time, Coleridge turned to nature as a source for his creative ideas, in fact, as a source for his theories on creativity and the imagination. For example, he viewed the imagination as a variety of river currents flowing into each other. When they do, the currents mix and fuse together to create a totally new composition of their fused elements. He termed this process "esemplastic," meaning it possesses a reconciling, unifying power able to connect, fuse, and consolidate the elements.[24]

This theory of river currents and the imagination is an example of the new reality known as a creative idea. In taking one reality (river currents) and connecting it with another reality (the imagination), Coleridge created a new reality, a metaphorical, conceptual theory of the imagination. In the process, both river currents and the imagination were transformed. River currents as A no longer existed as A. The imagination as B no longer existed as B. Connected, they became C, the new reality, a theory of the imagination.

Many of us might be inclined to say that river currents have little, if anything, to do with creative ideas. But that is a very literal and limited interpretation of the potential river currents hold for the creative mind. For that mind, worldly realities such as river currents and the imagination can be more than they appear to be. They can be vehicles for creative insight. They can become, as Robert Frost said, "the two things you did not expect to see associated."

In thinking by means of these associations, the creative mind forms connections between the realities. To be considered creative, however, these connections must be new. And to be new means they have not quite been thought of or expressed that way before. Take a grain of sand, for instance. Imagine you observe it on a beach. Is it just that, a grain of sand? If so, that's a literal and limited interpretation of a worldly reality.

For the creative mind, in this case the mind of William Blake, a grain of sand can be any one of a number of possibilities if it's connected innovatively and relevantly to something else. For Blake, for a grain of sand to be the core of a creative idea it needs to be connected upward, somewhere along his "stairway of vision," the highest step of which is supreme creativity and imagination.[25] This means it cannot be mired in the lowest level of its worldly reality as a grain of sand. It needs to be lifted from that level. For example, what happens if you connect the grain of sand (A) with life (B)? Can the C be a single lifetime measured against the trillions of lifetimes on the beach of human existence? If so, and if that thought is shaped into a new and relevant form of creative expression such as a poem, then you may have the essence of a creative idea.

Imagine it's autumn. Imagine you're walking down a street. Imagine, too, that there are winds swirling and blowing fallen leaves in front of you. Is that what those realities are, winds and leaves? For Percy Bysshe Shelley they were more. The winds were tyrants swirling and blowing the leaves. The leaves were the oppressed peoples of the world.

At one time or another, haven't we all observed river currents flowing into each other? Haven't we all climbed stairs or played in the sand? Haven't we all walked along an autumn street and seen leaves blown about in front of us? But did we see or think the same things Coleridge, Blake, and Shelley did? If not, isn't the difference a matter of their ability to form unique connections from very plain and observable realities? Aren't their creative ideas representative of those unique connections?

To bring this matter of creative ideas as connections closer to home, consider a series of lightning bolt connections in a creative idea from the mind of Ben Franklin. The idea was that of conducting electricity. Franklin was stymied by the construction delay of a spired building in Philadelphia. The spire was to serve him as an experimental testing site for actualizing and verifying his theory on drawing electricity down from the sky. In its own right, this theory was certainly creative. As it turned out, however, it could not be actualized into a purposeful and relevant idea unless he made connections between very observable realities.

One of the connections Franklin made was of thunderclouds and Leyden jars, which are jars lined with tin foil and used to conduct electricity. In his mind, Franklin connected the thunderclouds with Leyden jars. If you've ever seen Leyden jars, you know how much they resemble the shape of thunderclouds. Franklin connected the two realities.

Another connection began with that of a finger as an electrified body able to draw a charge or spark such as what we experience when we scuff our feet on a carpet and touch someone's shoulder. Franklin noticed that a finger could draw a spark from a Leyden jar. He connected this with drawing a spark from a thundercloud. But he needed a fingerlike object to do so. He formed another connection, that of a finger and the spire. Unfortunately, the construction of the spire was delayed. So here he was stymied. What did he do?

As a young boy, Franklin would swim on his back while being towed by a kite in the wind. The memory of this experience led him to consider the possibility of using a cedar wood kite in his experiment. In his mind, the kite was connected with the spire which had been connected with the finger. As separate, everyday realities, a kite, spire, and finger are distinctly different. For the uncreative mind, they are what they are and nothing more. But for Ben Franklin they were more. They were the means for reaching out and up to something else. When connected with a thundercloud, they could help him solve his problem and bring his creative idea to completion.

With the spire and finger out of the question, Franklin was left with his boyhood memory of a kite reaching out and up to something else. He reasoned that if you could connect something with the kite, as he was connected while he was swimming, then you might be able to bring whatever you wanted down to wherever you wanted it. This is where his key came into play. Sure enough, in June of 1752 thunderclouds swept over Philadelphia, and the rest, as they say, is history.[26]

Creative ideas everywhere and throughout time evolve in just this manner. A need or problem exists. Creative individuals wrestle with it, bringing to bear all they have experienced and observed. Then they connect, and the connections become the generative sparks behind their creative ideas to meet needs or solve problems.

Take the case of Clarence Birdseye, for example. He had the problem of finding a solution for rotting food. He observed that when he threw scraps of food outside, they didn't rot as long as the ground remained frozen. Connecting this observation with his problem, he went on to market the famous line of Birdseye frozen foods.[27]

As evident in the most creative ideas, those of Clarence Birdseye and Benjamin Franklin included, recognition of their creativity means the ideas cannot exist in a vacuum. They need to be functional in some way, if even as a salve for emotional wounds as in the case of confessional poems or as a vehicle for communication or persuasion as in the case of advertising. This is what is meant by relevance. One of the difficulties in discussing relevance, however, is that the concept has many shadings and sides to it. For instance, creative ideas can be relevant to a small and specified group. Or they can be relevant to almost everyone. Or they can be relevant solely to their creators. Regardless of where the relevance is found, however, it must exist. For creative ideas to be creative ideas, they must function relevantly, and generally this means they should meet needs or solve problems.

Think back to the creative ideas we have discussed and notice how each contains this quality of relevance. For instance, Georgia O'Keeffe's large flower paintings were relevant to the fulfillment of her personal creative vision. So, too, were the published theories or poems of Coleridge, Blake, and Shelley. Once actualized into art or literature, these ideas met specific needs or solved specific problems for their creators. In those respects, they were relevant, if even for single individuals.

Still, beyond their relevance to the needs or problems of their creators, these ideas also became relevant for larger audiences, either in art galleries or libraries. Once actualized into art and literature, they could meet some of the intellectual and perhaps emotional needs of a larger group.

This same dualism of relevance also holds true for Ben Franklin's string of creative ideas culminating in one giant creative idea. They met his needs and helped solve his problems. But in the end, they also met the needs and solved the problems of many others. The same can be said for Clarence Birdseye's idea. Even those ideas actualized as technological and cultural advancements (the telephone and performance art) illustrate how creative ideas are bound to some form of influential and functional relevance.

Taken together, the qualities of newness and relevance are inseparable components of creative ideas. In many ways, they become so inseparable they begin to overlap and superimpose themselves on each other. For instance, as receivers of those ideas, we begin to notice the newness simply because it is expressed as relevant to us, and we notice the relevance because it is so new. This combination serves to energize creative ideas. It helps them rise above other, less inspired ideas and soar beyond the ordinary and mundane.

Even in contemporary rock music terms, we can see how these inseparable qualities of newness and relevance work in tandem. For example, in the 1960s and 1970s the new musical ideas of social commentary by The Beatles changed the way a large part of society listened to music. In the 1980s, the music and music videos of stars like Michael Jackson and the Talking Heads accomplished similar ends. At once new and relevant, these musical advances changed perceptions and, in some cases, behaviors as well. The same is true of most creative ideas. After we come in contact with them, we tend not to see certain things exactly the same way again. In this sense, creative ideas advance thought in new and relevant ways. They catapult things ahead. As a result, they are often synonymous with change, change as expressed by their creators and change as experienced by those of us on the receiving ends of the ideas.

CONNECTIONS BACK

Imagine this. We're sitting across from one another, and I ask you the question "What does it mean to be creative?" What do you answer?

Of course, at this point your answer should be broader and fuller than it would have been pages ago. It may even hedge a little bit. Perhaps you would answer by hitting the ball back in my court and asking me "Do you mean the creative process? The creative personality? Creative ideas?" And if I answered "Yes, all of those things," what would you say?

Assuming you said a lot in your answer, what would you say if you were pressed to give one word, one concept, that summarized more than any other what being creative means? Would you give the word "connections"? After all, connections are at the root of the process, the personality, and the ideas. But could you put the word to work and connect process, personality, and ideas? For instance, if I asked you to take one isolated example from this chapter and weave it through the chapter's three main divisions could you do it? Could you do it with fishing? Could you do it with Georgia O'Keeffe? Could you do it with Ben Franklin?

Can you imagine Ben Franklin gathering information as he wrestled with his problem? Can you imagine him incubating by bringing to bear what he knew of worldly realities and what he remembered of his experiences? Can you imagine him connecting one reality with another with another and so on? Can you feel his excitement at the exhilarating prospect of successfully reaching to the sky? Can you feel his uncertainty as to whether it could actually be done?

He did it, though. He actualized his vision. What was there in him that led the way to accomplishment? Do you think he may have been told along the way that he was loony? Did that stop him? Do you think he was open to the world? Do you think he was a penetrating observer capable of integrating himself with the world of reality in order to actualize his own creative vision? Do you think he was like everybody else? For instance, while he stood in the stormy night sailing a kite to the clouds, what do you think others were doing?

What was the core of Ben Franklin's string of creative ideas culminating in one giant creative idea? Was it connections or some variation of A + B = C? Did this produce something new? If so, was that newness enough? Or was there something more? Did those connections produce something relevant?

Do you think Ben Franklin could have created what he did if he saw reality as something definite and unalterable? Do you think he saw reality as something lacking depth or the potential for being something other than what it was or seemed to be? Or do you think Ben Franklin created what he did because he saw his own reality, a new reality blending his needs, wants, and problems together with the realities of old?

Certainly there is mystery and intrigue to creativity. As you can tell, it's not always so black and white. Often, it's grey. This makes it a big reverberating concept. But, that doesn't mean it can't be understood for its greyness, and it doesn't mean that greyness is indefinable or unapproachable.

What we have done in this chapter is attempt to define and approach the grey. It should be clear, however, that as much as we have bandied about concepts and examples, when it comes to being creative there is one true resource you can rely on—yourself. You control the connections. You control your creativity. This doesn't mean they are always under control, far from it. But, it does mean that being creative can only come from within. Since it does, each of us must accept responsibility for it. If that caveat of self-responsibility in being creative is discomforting, take comfort in this perspective. Being creative is really a matter of tapping into what has always existed in each of us. The creative potential is there. It always has been. The idea is to make use of a certain state of mind and temperament for tapping into it.

2
TO BE CREATIVE IS TO BE

Since this is a book mainly for the young and young at heart, some of whom are intent on thriving in a creative career, let's talk about you as a creative individual.

When it comes to creativity, you may believe you are in another world altogether, a world beyond Mother Earth, beyond understanding, beyond even yourself. You may believe it is a magical and mysterious world, a world inhabited by only a few. Maybe you see those few as strange, out of the ordinary, or, at the least, too eccentric for you to begin to understand. Musicians. Artists. Writers. Inventors. Sure, they have creative powers. They may think in odd ways. But you're not sure you have the same powers and can think in the same ways or perhaps even want to.

In my experience, even among those of you who seemingly believe you have creative ability, there is a kind of anxious uncertainty about that belief. It may even be a kind of wishful thinking, one that's unsure about your ability, let alone whether it's the right one to have.

In either case, for those of you who believe you aren't creative and those of you who believe you are, there is uncertainty about where you fit in personally with this creativity business. So, you may shrink a little bit when it gets mentioned or when you're asked to come up with creative ideas. If so, then it's important to get this straight right away. You *are* creative. All of us are. All of us have creative powers. Let's also get this straight. You can nurture and increase those powers.

Unfortunately, despite the fact that all of us have creative powers and they can be nurtured and increased, we still continue to hear these kinds of words: "I'm just not creative, that's all," or "Either you have it or you don't, and if you don't, there's no way you can get it." These are deceptions. Don't believe them. Because the fact of the matter is all of us have creative powers. This doesn't mean all of us can be Georgia O'Keeffes, Benjamin Franklins, or, in the case of advertising, William Bernbachs. But, it does mean we can think creatively and generate creative ideas.

WHY WE BEGIN TO HAVE DOUBTS ABOUT OUR CREATIVE ABILITIES, OR STORMY WEATHER ROLLS IN

Did you know that by the time we're forty years old, we're only a fraction as creative as we were at five years old? The percentage may even be as small as 2 percent.[1] Two percent! Why is that?

Imagine you're in a supermarket standing by the fresh produce section with all those red, green, and gold fruits and vegetables piled high to the back wall. Imagine, too, you see a little tyke, say five years old, standing eye-level at the base of a mountain of oranges. All those round balls of golden fruit, each perched precariously on top of the other and stretching out of sight are tantalizing to that little tyke, and not because they promise to taste juicy and sweet.

Hands clasped behind his back and rocking heel-to-toe, he can't take his eyes off those oranges. Finally, his curiosity gets the better of him, and he plucks an orange out from the base of the mountain. Sure enough, a dozen oranges are set free, bouncing and rolling their way along the floor. A commotion surrounds our little tyke when around the corner, shopping cart straining on two wheels, Mom and Dad bolt to the scene. Bam! They let him have it. On the fanny if he's lucky. Across the head if he's not. Either way, it's a step toward the dousing of curiosity, one of those traits essential to the creative personality and temperament.

As another example, how many of you can remember something like this? You loved to experiment during your early years in school. Maybe you tried writing left-handed. Maybe you even tried writing with your toes, or writing big, bold letters and words that crossed over the barriers of lines and margins. Then you were given lined paper and asked to stay within those lines and margins. Worse, your pencil was put in your right hand over and over again by a well-intentioned soul despite your persistence in trying to write with it in your left hand or between your toes. Again, the dousing of curiosity.

As another example, take a young man, any young man, regardless of whether he eats delicate quiche or hearty charbroiled steaks. Put him in a movie theater with his date or wife. Let the movie be a real tearjerker, especially at its close. Imagine the movie ends, the credits begin to roll across the screen, and the house lights snap on. What does our young man do? Sure, he may feel as though he's just tried to swallow an orange whole. But what does he do? Chances are he bucks it up. He swallows hard, real hard. Maybe he turns away. Maybe he even says he's catching a cold or he's allergic to hairspray. The question is, Why does he react that way?

Our young man reacts that way because he's been desensitized. He's fallen prey to a stereotype of what a man is and is not, what a man should be and cannot be. And he has responded or not responded accordingly.

Meanwhile, do you recall how important empathy is as a characteristic trait of creative individuals? Creative individuals are capable of integrating themselves with the world, including the captivating world of filmed emotions or plights of others. This integration or empathy is to be in touch with a wellspring of creativity. A young hulk of a man whimpering over the make-believe sorrow of a spoiled love just doesn't cut it in some circles. A young man laughing or shaking it off does.

Of course, figuratively we can't have millions of people running around pulling oranges out from the base of society's mountain. It would be chaos. And literally we can't have millions of people insisting on writing with their toes or millions of strong young men whimpering in movie theaters across the country. All of us know that, so we conform, at least to a degree. Then we do our part to maintain the status quo.

But, this kind of behavioral conformity, and many times mental and emotional conformity as well, also means that dampers are put on our creativity. We begin to lose our curiosity, our childlike playfulness, maybe even our self-confidence in the belief that it's okay to be a creative individual. We begin to lose all those very important characteristics for realizing our creative potentials, which then become submerged beneath the regimen of the status quo.

The point is that as we journey in time and experience through the world, the world has a way of letting us have it—across the fanny if we're lucky, across the head if we're not. In time, the strength of our creative spirit withers and wanes. Just like our little tyke, we begin to learn there are some things we can do and some things we can't. Some things are okay. Some things aren't. Often, the things that are okay belong to the status quo. The things that aren't okay belong on the fringe, outside somewhere, in places we shouldn't like to go. It's a kind of don't-rock-the-boat guideline to much of what we do, think, and feel.

This is what is meant by "stormy weather." The winds blow. The waters of reality churn and darken, perhaps to the point where the realities needing connection in order to solve problems blur or escape our observation completely. And ultimately the fishing for creative ideas is terrible.

Creative theoretician and author Charles H. Clark relates an interesting anecdote as an illustration of stormy weather. An advertising salesman once recommended to a Hookless Fastener executive that a zipper would be a unique and practical replacement for buttons on the flies of men's trousers. To that creative recommendation, the executive replied, "I like trousers the way they are ... we could get into trouble." This is what Clark terms a "killer phrase." Others such as, "So what else is new?," "We tried that two years ago," or "What are you? Some kind of nut?" are no doubt equally murderous.[2]

When our Hookless Fastener executive tells our advertising salesman, "I like trousers the way they are," it's like the world letting the salesman have it or a storm blowing in to ruin the fishing. When someone tells you, "Do it my way, not your way," the world is letting you have it as well, and that same storm threatens your fishing. One day you might get it from a friend. Another day it might be from a teacher or co-worker. Still another day it might be from yourself, your negative self intent on pulling your positive self right down with it. And each time you get it, your creativity is forced further and further beneath the surface. Gradually, over time, it may begin to seem like you never had creative ability in the first place. Or if you did, then it is gone forever.

Again, think of it like this. Those storms that get in the way of your creativity are the status quos of the world, things like rules, regulations, authorities, regimens, codes, and unbreakable, unbendable practices. Creativity theorists and researchers refer to these storms as perceptual, cultural, or emotional blocks to creativity.[3] We all experience them at times. For instance, the status quo is to perceive trees as right side up and green. But if we portray them as upside down and purple, we may have a problem. Right-side-up, green trees don't churn against the perceptual status quo. Upside-down, purple trees do.

In addition to being bound perceptually, we're also bound to the various codes and mores of our culture, whether national, local, family, or even peer. When we butt up against them, we may have a problem. Emotionally, we are bound to class, sex, and social roles, just like our young man at the close of a tearjerking movie. When we violate those roles, we may have a problem.

Paradoxically, as important as overcoming perceptual, cultural, and emotional blocks is to creativity, we also know that living within them is a key to survival in the real world. We can't have chaos. We can't have total abandonment of structure and organization. We can't totally manufacture our own realities. Above all else, we must live in the real world. But that creative side of us can still maintain a kind of independence and difference balanced against that conforming side, the one keeping us productive and positive in the real world.

WILL, BELIEF, CONSTRUCTIVE REBELLION, AND NOT PASSING THE BUCK

What can you find that is common to each of the following four examples from the lives of successful creative individuals?

> Albert Einstein failed his first geometry class.
> Thomas Edison was sent home from school one day with a note pinned to his shirt. The note read, "Keep this boy at home. He is too dumb to learn."
> Pablo Picasso would stand and stare out a classroom window in spite of the protests of his well-intentioned teacher.
> John Lennon would practice his guitar until his fingers bled in spite of the protests of his well-intentioned aunt.[4]

Think about these four examples. What do they have in common? Is persistence common? Without a doubt. Do you think courage and energy are common? Certainly. Can you understand how the creative visions of these four individuals were willful and unalterable? Can you also see those visions persisting despite the stormy weather that may have been encountered along the way? No doubt.

As you can see from these examples, tapping into one's creative abilities is a kind of self-fulfilling prophecy. This means that the will and belief go a long way toward producing the result. Unfortunately, when you encounter storm after storm, you may tend to feel discouraged. You may grow weary of the struggles. This is why will and belief are so important to actualizing your creative potential. As the examples illustrate, once you're focused, entirely focused on your creative vision, the vision grows and matures into a reality. One becomes the other. That's because you start from a position of will which feeds and nourishes your belief and, ultimately, your creativity.

You should have recognized another important common denominator in the four examples: rebellion. Don't misunderstand, however. It's not rebellion for the sake of rebellion. It's rebellion for the sake of a constructive pursuit. Call it constructive rebellion. Purposeful. Independent. Different. And positive.

At this point, of course, you really should not be surprised by the importance of will, belief, and constructive rebellion to actualizing creative potential. Think back to Chapter One and the personality traits of creative individuals. Those traits were important then for your understanding of what it means to be creative. Now they are even more important, since you're asked to believe you are or can be creative.

Indeed, those traits are even more important now because you're being asked to accept the bulk of the responsibility for that creativity. There can be no shifting of responsibility here. Sure, many times the storms of the status quo make it difficult to be creative. But those of us who lambast the status quo and hold it responsible for our own unwillingness to keep after our creative visions are only passing the buck. It should be clear that our visions demand a singleminded devotion, one that begins and ends within ourselves. In this sense, we are creative because that's where we get our satisfaction. Extrinsic end goals, whether of money, status, or prestige, remain secondary to the overriding, compulsive drive of thinking, working, and existing creatively.

Think of it like this. The journey is its own compulsion. You're responsible for it. You control it. And you drive the boat. Ultimately, it is this compulsion in the traveling that yields its own fulfilling rewards.

A LARGE REASON FOR BELIEVING YOU ARE CREATIVE

Let's get grandiose.

Perhaps the greatest reason for believing you're creative is a cosmic one, one dealing with the entirety of life, birth, and death. As a connective process paralleling the creative process, life is demonstrably creative.

With a vital part of the essence of creativity being the matter of connections, our birth mirrors that essence. Two people connect to create an embryo of life. The embryo connects with its mother and grows into a baby until it is ready to be born. Once born, the baby again connects, this time with its world. While growing from baby to youth to adult, this one life continues to connect with its world and, in fact, often connects with another life to create still a third life, a new baby. As with all babies before and after it, this new baby carries with it all the connections accumulated from past generations. It, too, grows, and the entire process repeats itself. Indeed, looked at largely, cosmically, life as a whole can be seen as a process of connections.

The same holds true for death. When death comes, some say we're returned to our original state, again a connection. Others say we're fused, connected with some form of great universal being or consciousness. Possibly, we connect as part of the vast food chain. Or perhaps we're consumed into the cosmos of fire from which the world originated. We may even connect to a new life in a new place and time.

Of course, we don't want to get too philosophically thick here. But, the point is that existence—creation, birth, life, death—is fundamentally a matter of connections. As we well know at this point, so is being creative and thinking creatively.

In large, cosmic terms, there is an appealing kind of circularity to it all, a kind of harmonious and whole essence of existence as we know it. Even in more concrete terms, all of us have borne witness to this essence. For example, consider how similar babies are to older individuals, senior citizens, fortunate enough to have lived out a long life. Take a baby, two years old, and take an adult, ninety-two years old, and notice the similarities. Notice how they play alike. Notice how they may even think alike.

Haven't we all had a grandmother and grandfather who seem forgetful? Are they really forgetful, or are they simply their own people, detached enough from the status quo that they are resolved to remember only what they want to remember? To us, they appear to be regressing. But regressing to where? Childhood, perhaps? Maybe they are connected back to the innocent curiosity and playfulness of childhood, when to pull an orange out from under a mountain of oranges provided all the playful joy and mystery life had to offer.

Is it possible that young children and old people are the most creative of us all? For both, the storms the world hurls their way may be less important than for those of us in the throes of consciously having to try to master or control those storms on a daily basis. Maybe in this way the young and the old are in closer connection with their creative selves.

In fact, we can even shrink the years of that connection from a lifetime to a single day. Recall, for example, our discussion in Chapter One regarding peak creative times, typically the beginnings and ends of our days. Both are particularly fertile times because the world of status quos recedes for those moments. As a result, we tend to be left with ourselves, our essence, the creative spirit. The beginning of day and the end of day are like the beginning of life and the end of life. They are like childhood and old age—connected to the peak of creativity.

THE SIGNS OF CREATIVITY IN YOUNG PEOPLE

What we have then in a large, cosmic sense is that connection binds creativity and life together. But, for some, creativity pulses and thrives with life, while for others, it may need to be revived. It's always there because it's part of living. It's just that it may be dormant, perhaps hiding out somewhere to shelter itself from those storms that push and shove. Despite the fact that creativity may be tucked away in hard to reach places, there are clear signs that the young and young at heart still have it.

One sign is that they're not that behaviorally far from five years old. They still like to play. To an extent, they're still innocent, naive, and spontaneous. They're relatively untainted and unscarred from combat in the real world. If the urge strikes, they'll give a friend a piggyback ride. In short, they'll play. Young people might even laugh or cry so hard they let their emotions show. In other words, they haven't quite given up their childhoods

yet. And, as you know from Chapter One, childlike playfulness is inseparable from the creative personality.

Another important sign is that they're still curious—maybe not as curious as they were at five, but it is there. They still want to know how things
work and why they work the way they do. Sure, they are probably also intent
on securing a "good job." And often that's a big reason for serving appren-
ticeships in school or at work. But for those who also go beyond the "job"
motive and study or work because they feel themselves growing and learning, the creative spirit brightens and pulses inside.

Still another important sign is that they're independent. For many of
them, their years at school or work are years for spreading wings. And for
most of them that probably feels good, though it's certainly not without
its pain and uncertainty, of course. Perhaps growing never is. Still, they're
growing. Take yourself, for instance. Can you remember a visit to family
back home only to discover you had formulated some opinions and views
that sometimes ran counter to those you love and care for? What happened
was that you were growing. You were beginning to individualize yourself.

For the young and young at heart, their growing independence also
relates to a form of constructive rebellion. In spreading wings, they're learning to fly their way. This may not always be the way others want them to fly.
And it may not be the way they will fly in the future. But it's still their way.
They're building a method for flying that's individualized to themselves. By
its very nature of formative individualization, this is a form of constructive
rebellion.

Playing. Curiosity. Independence. Constructive rebellion. Each of
these signs suggests that young people and the young at heart have not lost
their creative drive, not yet, anyway. And, there are other signs as well.
Things like their occasional or even frequent openness to experiences, risk-
taking, their ability to focus when they have to, or their energy, spontaneity,
and impulsivity. Taken together, all of these signs should suggest to us that
those who are young in age and spirit are creative or at least have the potential to be so.

YOUR CREATIVITY CAN BE NURTURED AND INCREASED

If creativity is inherent to living, then it stands to reason we can nurture it
along the way. After all, it's not like we're trying to impose something upon
ourselves that's not there to begin with. To the contrary, we're only trying
to increase or revive something that has been there all along. Yet, the very
issues of whether creativity can be taught, nurtured, or increased have
sparked considerable debate between skeptics and believers.

The major issue seems to be whether creativity can actually be taught.
On the skeptics' side, the argument centers on this idea of teaching. Gener-

ally, it's an argument claiming that what's not there to begin with can't be put there. For example, at a 1985 meeting of the New York Ad Club, a debate among five advertising agency creative directors led to the conclusion that creativity "could be nurtured, but not implanted."[5] Unfortunately, what is not being considered in that conclusion is that creativity doesn't need to be implanted. It needs to be revived. That is quite a different story. In this respect, it's a matter of providing the tools, methods, and even the frame of mind and temperament needed to revive it.

Quite simply, based on research findings, there can be no doubt that the tools, methods, frame of mind, and temperament can in fact be taught and taught successfully. What this means, of course, is that they can be learned. Perhaps the most glittering example is that of Synectics, a unique creative problem-solving method (now an institution in its own right) begun over forty years ago and still going strong today.[6] Relying on the irrational rather than the rational and encouraging psychological chances, analogical thinking, and playfulness, Synectics is well known for its innovative, problem-solving successes in a host of industries and professional fields. Indeed, the idea for Silkience shampoo emerged from Synectics when Sandra Lawrence, a director for new ventures at Gillette, imagined herself as a strand of hair.

Don't be misled. Synectics isn't the only example of a successful creativity program. The Creative Problem-Solving Institute at The State University of New York at Buffalo is another. The successes at the Purdue Creative Training Program have been well documented.[7] And what with a dramatic surge of interest in the 1970s (it stands to reason, given the rebellious nature of the latter half of the preceding decade), by 1980 there evolved more than seventy creativity programs in the United States.[8] They range from universities such as Stanford to corporations such as General Electric. And they are often responsible for innovations in a variety of commercial and noncommercial ventures. The idea for Pringles potato chips, for example, evolved from a formal creativity program.[9]

Beyond these specific examples of programs, if you also consider the raw number and diversity of educational programs devoted to nurturing creativity—programs in advertising, art, writing, media, philosophy, science, and technology, to name a few—it seems outrageous to conclude that creativity is unteachable or unapproachable from a learning or nurturing standpoint. Still, skeptics insist that this is the case. The success and durability of a wide range of creativity programs suggest otherwise, however.

CONNECTING BACK

Unlike the goal of our first chapter, which was to provide a bird's eye view of some important aspects of creativity, the goal of this second chapter was to provide a telescopic view of you as an individual with creative potentials.

Some of you believe those potentials are actualized as daily realities. Others of you may actualize them but are unaware of it. Still others of you believe you don't have those potentials. Whatever the case, there should be several important concepts you take from this chapter.

Because we tend to live day to day within the status quos of the world, we either begin to have doubts about our creativity or it gets pushed deeper and deeper into hiding.

In order to revive our creativity or bring it out in the open, we need to be willful and persistent, perhaps singleminded in our vision and pursuit. Keeping at it goes a long way toward actualizing our creative potentials.

Keeping at it means thinking independently, thinking beyond the status quo. This is a form of rebellion. Most important, however, is that this rebellion be constructive and positive.

If we don't have the will, belief, and persistence in actualizing our creative potentials, then to a large extent we have no one to blame but ourselves. This demands courage on our part—being different or thinking differently always does.

We can find self-confidence, self-comfort, and self-belief in the realization that everyone is creative because creativity is life. There are certainly degrees of creative powers or abilities, but just the idea that we live means we're creative. To deny our creativity (self-denial or denial from others) is to deny what is quite natural as a part of life.

The young and young at heart reveal signs of creative potential. They're playful, open, curious, independent, risk-taking, and energetic.

Our creativity can be nurtured and increased. This doesn't mean it can be implanted. It doesn't have to be. It's already there. But it may need to be revived or allowed out in the open.

Of course, lingering in the background of all of this is the realization that being creative means being independent and different. We have spanned centuries and many examples pressing this point. Only infrequently, however, have we referred to advertising. In this regard, can it be that advertising creativity is excluded from what we have discussed up to now? Does it demand something else? Sameness, for instance? The point-blank answer is "No."

3
WHY IT'S OKAY TO BE CREATIVE IN ADVERTISING

When the storms of the status quo begin to blow, creative individuals search for safe harbors. One of those is advertising. Advertising welcomes the creative individual because much of its success and power is moored right smack on the word, creativity. Without creativity to carry its messages, advertising has a good chance of getting lost in a marketplace overflowing with parity products and services. When this happens, advertising's success and power begin to disintegrate. When creative advertising ideas are new and relevant, they help prevent this disintegration. This is why advertising is one of those environments more friendly than unfriendly to the individuality and differences of creative individuals.

Don't expect, however, that advertising is all that friendly to strictly "idea" people who are not talented craftsmen and strategists. It isn't. Besides, strictly "idea" people don't exist in advertising. Creative advertising individuals do, writers and artists among them. When it comes time for generating and executing creative ideas, the responsibility generally falls on the shoulders of advertising's writers and artists.

Yes, those writers and artists are "idea" people. There can be no doubt about that. With an even more emphatic "yes," though, they are also talented and compulsive craftsmen and strategists. Their craft is to generate creative ideas and then communicate them through the words and images we see and hear in ads in the various print and broadcast media. Their strategy is to shape and tailor pointed messages in ways that evoke some form of positive intended response from a particular target audience. Ultimately, it's this combination of ideas, craftsmanship, and strategic communication that separates strictly "idea" people from the creative individuals in advertising.

As we have discussed in our first two chapters, to be creative in advertising also means being new and relevant with your ideas. This means you cannot drift out to the ad-making sunset with some of the wackiest, wildest ideas ever, which also happen to be totally irrelevant, grossly misleading, or pointlessly distracting. That's not what being creative in advertising is all about. Instead, it's about being as creative or different with your ideas as you want to be, as long as that creativity or difference is anchored firmly to sound goals and objectives.

Right here, it's important to make that distinction because allowances for advertising creativity expand or shrink depending on a host of variables. Often, these variables relate to the communication mix, including the advertiser, the message, the medium, and the target audience. Often, too, they relate to economic conditions. For example, when economic times are good, there tends to be more allowance for creativity. When economic times are bad, there tends to be less allowance. But if your creativity or difference is anchored to solid considerations based on strategic thinking—in other words, if it is relevant—then it continues to be effective and needed in good times or bad.

Through all of this, the point to remember is that in advertising it's okay to be creative with your ideas. This means it's okay for you to create ideas that are new and different, as long as those ideas are also relevant. In fact, it's not only okay, it's imperative.

As you know, however, creative ideas originate from individuals who tend to be apart from the mainstream. They tend to be individualistic and different. They tend to be more curious, observant, independent, spontaneous, open, empathic, and nonconforming. That can be a rare and difficult combination to find, let alone embrace, especially if one is inclined to believe that advertising expects its creative individuals to be otherwise. Fortunately, it doesn't. Advertising can be very democratic that way. Often, it embraces individuality and difference because it understands them as necessary parts of being creative.

Because advertising is a business as well as an art, it also understands the meaning of the bottom line. That understanding alone means advertising will respect and nurture individuality and difference. There is a catch, however, and it is this: Advertising will respect and nurture those qualities only as long as they are central to impressing and, more often than not, selling the customer. To accomplish that, creative individuals use their individuality and difference to find creative ideas that are both new and relevant. Before use comes belief, however, and to that extent, before putting their qualities to work in finding creative ideas, creative individuals must believe it's okay to be creative in advertising. This means it's okay to be an individual, and it's okay to be different. What follows explains why.

ADVERTISING CLIENTS EXPECT AND WANT CREATIVITY

Creativity is one of the big reasons clients solicit or otherwise work with advertising agencies. And since clients pay the bills, agencies tend to pay heed to the clients.

In *Advertising Age,* William M. Cowan discusses how advertising agencies win accounts from clients. He bases his discussion and conclusions on the comments of over 150 clients during the past ten years. From the client's point of view, prior experience in the client's line of business is vital to the final selection of an agency. But "creative capabilities," "creative experience," "creative concepts," and the "creative team" are also vital components in the decision-making process.[1] Other *Advertising Age* articles lead to the same conclusion.[2] In fact, in its regular "Agency Watch" column, *Advertising Age* itself uses creativity as a central variable in assessing a client's satisfaction with its agency.

What this should tell you is that creativity is essential, regardless of whether it's the pitching, winning, or holding of an advertising account. Stan Richards, principal of The Richards Group (a "hot" Dallas-based agency), puts it this way. "You don't have to sell the client or convince him that creativity is a top priority. He came to you because he wanted that."[3] Of course he did, and chances are he will stay with you if he can see his vested interest secured by a solid, workable advertising plan, a choice part of which is the promise of an exciting creative idea. That's a large part of why he will be with you and not somebody else. That's also a critical point in understanding why it is important to be creative and different. Many times, it's what clients expect and want.

ADVERTISING GIANTS EXPECT AND WANT CREATIVITY

Beyond clients, you can also look to the heavyweights, the giants of advertising, for support that it's okay for you to be creative or different. By and large, they tend to agree that creativity is more than an incidental to effective advertising. It is a necessity.

When you turn to those giants, you must turn to William Bernbach of the original Doyle Dane Bernbach advertising agency. Bernbach has been described as "the hero of the creative fraternity" by another giant, David Ogilvy of the Ogilvy & Mather agency.[4] In the following quote, notice the importance given by Bernbach to words like "fresh" and "original." Clearly, when we speak of originality, we speak of creativity and difference.

> So the most important thing as far as I'm concerned is to be fresh, to be original—to be able to compete with all the shocking news events in the world today, with all the violence. Because you can have all the right things in the ad, and if nobody is made to stop and listen to you, you have wasted it.[5]

Bernbach's words from 1969 are no doubt as relevant today as they were then, and they summarize to a large extent the thinking of one of advertising's most successful and respected spokesman. Fighting against clutter and attention-grabbing news headlines, advertising needs to be creative and different in order to get noticed.

Another advertising giant, Ed McCabe of the Scali, McCabe, Sloves agency, offers similar advice when he says, "If you look at something and say 'I want to do something like that,' you're already lost. When they do all pictures, I'll do all words."[6] There can be no misinterpreting what McCabe is saying. Look at what those around you are doing and do the opposite, do something different.

Still another advertising giant, Jerry Della Femina of Della Femina, McNamee, WCRS, Inc. is one of the best known models of creativity and difference in the advertising business. His book, *From Those Wonderful Folks Who Gave You Pearl Harbor,* is an enduring (and endearing) symbol of the advertising creative revolution during the late 1960s and early 1970s.

In his book, Della Femina ranges far and wide through the good, the bad, and the ugly of advertising practices and people. He also reveals the qualities of individuality and difference inherent to advertising's creative individuals, himself most certainly included. For example, the book title was originally his brainstorm of a copy line spoof for Panasonic as it sought to make headway in the American marketplace. Della Femina then became known as "the Pearl Harbor guy at Panasonic."[7] Can you imagine being a corporate officer for Panasonic and listening to that copy line spoof?

Suppose you started an advertising agency with three partners. Suppose things got rough and two of the partners quit. Suppose, too, you had only $11,000 in the bank. Suppose your bills were about $2,000 a week. Suppose you had no business coming in, no revenues. What would you do? Would you do what Jerry Della Femina did? He took $3,000, sent out over 1000 invitations, and threw a wingding of a Christmas party. The next day his agency landed the advertising business for a large insurance account. The day after that brought in another big account.[8] Of course, those accounts had been represented at the wingding Christmas party.

Would you say what Della Femina did was risky? Different? You bet. Would you also say it was risky and different with a pointed, strategic purpose in mind? No doubt.

Examples such as these are testimony to the fact that advertising offers safe harbor for the creative individual. It's important to understand that the examples here aren't exceptions to the rules of the advertising business. They are the rules, at least as far as the creative sides of writers and artists are concerned. In fact, since the late 1970s, if you want to get ahead in the advertising business, a rule of thumb is to work your way through the creative hierarchy. During the past decade, for example, more and more chief executive roles at major agencies have been filled by creative directors. In addition, during the late 1970s and into the 1980s, the amount of creative people employed per $1,000,000 in advertising billings nearly tripled from previous figures.[9] Even today, the trend continues to hold, with the call from top-flight agency professionals reminding us of Bernbach's own call years ago for "originality."

Of course, referring to creative stalwarts such as Bernbach, McCabe, and Della Femina for support of advertising creativity is a bit like referring to former President Reagan for support that you should be a Republican. Still, even among those advertising giants who are more guarded or skeptical regarding creativity or difference, there is the acknowledgment of creativity's importance. For example, most of David Ogilvy's qualifications for the *Big Idea* center on creativity. For him, the *Big Idea* makes you gasp (surprising, unexpected difference can do that). It makes you wish you had thought of it yourself (don't all unique and yet relevant ideas make us wish that?). And, it's unique (what else is unique besides being original and different?).[10]

This acknowledgment of creativity's importance holds true, too, for other great names in the field such as Claude Hopkins ("doing admirable things in different ways gives one a great advantage"), Rosser Reeves (the U of his famous USP formula stands for unique), and Leo Burnett (he suggests ruffling the grammar or scrambling the rhythm).[11] Though not bowing at the altar of creativity as readily as the Bernbachs, McCabes, and Della Feminas do, the Ogilvys, Hopkins, Reeves, and Burnetts do not abandon creativity. They acknowledge it as playing a vital role in effective advertising as long as it avoids the everpresent danger of upstaging the selling message.

The core advice from each of our advertising giants, enthusiastic or guarded, is that creativity or difference is needed as long as it doesn't overshadow the selling concept or what the product can do for a consumer. This brings us back to the beginning of our chapter and the term relevant. To be different is simply not enough in advertising. As Leo Burnett says in quoting an old boss of his, "If you insist on being different just for the sake of being different, you can always come down in the morning with a sock in your mouth."[12] That just won't cut it. There needs to be more. In this respect, we can turn again to our creative hero, William Bernbach, who says, "You are not right if, in your ad, you stand a man on his head just to get attention. But you are right if you have him on his head to show how your product keeps things from falling out of his pockets."[13]

There is the key. Yes, put a man on his head. Great. First, though, make sure the product keeps things from falling out of his pockets. And second, make sure that's what your target audience needs or wants from the product. This is what is known as relevance.

ADVERTISING PROS AND EDUCATORS EXPECT AND WANT CREATIVITY

In colleges and universities across the country, advertising education has been growing steadily for over a decade. Assuming the general economy remains stable at worst or grows at best, the future looks bright for advertising in the classroom. This is mentioned, of course, because as a young person in college or beginning in the field, you can assume that the competition for jobs will grow and not decline. As a result, it's wise for you to know just what it is the advertising community expects of you.

The Medill School of Journalism at Northwestern University is actively involved in both the educational and professional workings of advertising. Recently, it hosted a symposium attended by five personnel recruiters from major advertising agencies. The recruiters were there to discuss how to teach creativity. They were also there to exchange insights with educators regarding college and university advertising majors. Generally, what they concluded is that students have "too few new ideas."

You might want to read that quote again. Students have "too few new ideas." That's what they said, "Too few new ideas." Other things they had to say should also interest you.

From Jan Diamond, DDB Needham advertising agency: "A sense of playfulness has disappeared. . . . I don't think your students understand that we're looking for innovators, people who can see things through new eyes."

From Marlene Calders, Foote, Cone & Belding advertising agency: "We want to see work that surprises, amuses, that breaks the rules."

From Flinn Dallas, Leo Burnett advertising agency: "Make them brave. Tell them to try anything and everything."[14]

These same kinds of advice are found in the writings of many of your professors as well. For example, take a look at some of the textbooks pertaining to advertising creative strategy. Though they don't focus exclusively on the many aspects of creativity the way we're doing here, they will tell you the importance of being creative and different with your ideas. Even in terms of putting your portfolio or "book" together, educators offer similar advice (your portfolio or "book" shows a prospective employer layouts and copy to illustrate how you think, create, and write). John Sweeney, for instance, offers these words for budding copywriters, "It[your book] must be daring, risk-taking, innovative, original yet personal. . . . More and more, the reason to hire new talent is to get fresh thinking."[15]

Overall, the message from both the advertising professional and educational communities is very clear. Be creative. Be innovative. Be different. To play it safe is not the way to go when it comes to creating ad ideas, especially for your "book," that image of creativity you present to an employer. What that employer expects and wants from you is something creative and different. Perhaps some words from David Fowler, a former student and now a successful young copywriter, tell the story. In addressing an auditorium full of aspiring advertising young people, Fowler told them, "As students or beginners you really have nothing yet. So, take a chance. Because you really have nothing to lose."

ADVERTISING'S RESPONSIBILITY TO NURTURE AND SUPPORT THE CREATIVE SPIRIT

Let's get grandiose again.

As a potential copywriter or artist, you have the opportunity to help advertising fulfill its social obligation as a creative force and form of modern day communication. In this respect, advertising has a bit of a mission. It needs to do its part to nurture the creative spirit which, in many ways, is also the spirit of growth, individuality, determination, democracy, and the acceptance of difference. By nature of its creative existence, advertising should exemplify the belief that the creative spirit is an inseparable part of economic mainstream activity. Perhaps more largely in a true democratic sense, it should also exemplify the belief that without that spirit, everyone loses a sense of our heritage devoted to nurturing the freedom and individuality of life and expression so vital to the lifeblood of our democratic society.

It is because of advertising's visibility and pervasiveness that it can accomplish such broadbased, idealistic goals. Like it or not, because it is so visible and pervasive, advertising is a powerful creative force in our society, perhaps more powerful than many people would like to admit or believe. It can move us deeply, or it can repel us with the same magnitude. It has power, but some of us don't like the prospect of admitting or believing it. Still, with that power comes obligation—obligation to nurture and support important social causes, which, of course, many advertising individuals are fond of doing, and an obligation to nurture and support creativity in order to help guarantee a future for creative expression.

Of course, all of this sounds relentlessly romantic. Advertising as a creative force to raise, ahem, the creative consciousness of the society? Come on! But is it so far from reality? It's not uncommon, for instance, to hear people on the street repeating advertising slogans as they did a few years ago with the Wendy's fast food slogan "Where's the beef?" It's also not uncommon to hear people whistling the tune to the latest Coke or Pepsi commercial. Sure, as time moves on, the slogans and tunes change. And there is always a glazed lightheartedness, a kind of airiness associated with it all. At the same time, however, advertising continues to wriggle its way into the noncommercial consciousness of our society.

In *Advertising Age,* Peter Cornish hit upon just this aspect of advertising's need to wriggle its way into society's consciousness:

> To be called "great," advertising should do something more; it must get talked about. It must be so unique that it becomes a topic of conversation, not just at the agency and the client, but among members of the sales force, the trade, the competition and the general public. It must be so audacious that it gets written about in the newspapers, discussed in supermarkets, worried about in boardrooms or even joked about on talk shows.[16]

Though Cornish emphasizes that there are only a few advertising campaign ideas that get "talked about," he raises an interesting point. Some have done it. Clearly, it's a valuable goal to achieve, both for the bottom line and for the aesthetic appreciation of the creative spirit.

If we ask ourselves what gets "talked about" in reference to various forms of creative expression, all of us can think of examples. What's important is that those examples tend to have a common denominator, that of being different from the mainstream, from the status quo. In the process, they surprise. They may even shock. And, for many, they make life all the more interesting as a result.

As examples from popular culture that were "talked about" because they did something different, something surprising and new, and thus can serve as models for creative advertising ideas, consider the following.

In the late 1980s, the film *Fatal Attraction* made news. Why? It was well-crafted difference. Unlike other films of the period, it plunged into the dark and murky depths of an illicit love affair.

In the mid-1980s, the rock star Michael Jackson made news with his "moonwalk" dance step. Why? It, too, was different for its time.

In the late 1970s, the film *Star Wars* made news. Why? Because it was different, more sophisticatedly different than any space opera preceding it.

In the late 1960s, the film *The Graduate* made news. Why? Again, it was difference that separated *The Graduate* from other films of the period. It was a new genre of film emphasizing America's new antihero. It was a film with a new social message.

In the 1960s, the rock group The Beatles made news. Big news. Why? Again, difference. A different kind of music. A British mystique. Bowl-like haircuts. Social commentary.

These few examples from popular culture simply scratch the surface of what is available to us when we think of creative expressions we remember and which, for better or worse, seep into the very fabric of society.

Naturally, advertising cannot expect to have the impact of films like *Star Wars* or groups like The Beatles. But as a diverse variety of forms ranging from news to entertainment, advertising possesses similarities to film, music, and other vehicles for creative expression. Bear in mind that films are packaged, promoted, and sold, just like products are packaged, promoted, and sold. So are rock stars. In many respects, they are like products complete with packages and brand images in their respective marketplaces.

Yet, films, music, and other forms of popular culture are also creative forms of expression. Because of this alone, they nurture the liveliness, strength, and meaningfulness of the creative spirit. In many respects, advertising is much the same. Its high visibility and pervasive nature mean it's out front and in the open. As such, it has an obligation to both the bottom line and, for society's benefit, the nurturing and support of that creative spirit.

FROM CHAPTER ONE TO CHAPTER THREE

For you, this chapter should be a transition between the first two chapters and those that follow.

From the first chapter you should gain a general understanding of what it means to be creative and what creativity is (and perhaps isn't).

From the second chapter you should gain a belief that you either are creative or can be.

And, from this chapter you should gain an additional belief that it's okay to be creative or different in advertising. Clients expect and want that from their advertising. Advertising giants appreciate it. The advertising professional and educational communities expect and want it from you. And, advertising being what it is, it has a social obligation to nurture and support the creative spirit.

4

WHAT ARE CREATIVE ADVERTISING IDEAS?

Before we can find something, we have to know what it is we're looking for. When it comes to finding creative advertising ideas, we're looking for concepts that are new, relevant, and based on themes. Themes evolve from research findings and creative planning. They tend to cluster around advertiser features, selling points, and especially benefits or problem solutions, particularly in respect to how these terms connect with an intended target audience. Themes are the messages of the ideas. Themes are *what* you want to convey through the ideas. Ideas are *how* you intend to present the themes. The *what* of themes and the *how* of ideas are the matter and manner of ads. Ultimately, they should merge as one in the audience's mind.

Behind every ad you see or hear, creative individuals conceptualized ideas based on themes. Derived from Greek, idea literally means "to see." What creative individuals see is *how* or the manner in which themes will be presented to a target audience. In advertising circles, the manner is often referred to as the creative tactics. Tactics can include a variety of possibilities, such as associations, sense connections, closures, or opposites, all of which will be very important to us further on in the text.

Also derived from Greek, theme literally means "the root." Themes, then, are the roots of creative ideas in that they represent exactly *what* the core messages will be. As such, themes are the actual meanings or matters of the messages. As with creative ideas, themes can also include a variety of possibilities, such as advertiser features, selling points, and benefits or problem solutions.

Ideally, what advertising copywriters and artists seek is a unification of creative ideas and themes. One should become the other so that they don't exist separately or apart from one another. It's a bit like the Irish poet, William Butler Yeats's notion of being unable to separate the dancer from the dance. The ideas carry the themes. But in so doing, they mirror the themes. In fact, in many ways they are the themes, and the result is that ideas and themes become inseparable.

If you recall some of the most memorable advertising creative ideas you have seen or heard, chances are you will find a common ground among all of them. So too, chances are the largest part of that ground will be based on two things: the inseparability of themes and ideas and their relationship to two terms, newness and relevance. Remember, all creative ideas have newness, and all creative ideas have relevance. Remember, too, that newness and relevance must be connected, otherwise you only have half creative ideas.

In advertising, the connection of newness and relevance is very much tied to the connection of themes and ideas. For example, creative ideas should be new in that no one has quite presented the themes that way before. They should also be relevant in that the target audience is easily able to understand the themes at the roots of the ideas. In turn, themes should be relevant to the target audience in terms of what the audience can expect to gain from the advertiser. In fact, it's possible that themes are also new. Rosser Reeves, for example, believed *what* you give to an audience should be unique to your product and not someone else's.[1] He called this the USP. Others might refer to this newness in themes as the differentiating factor (that which separates one brand or product from another).

To understand how all of this works in advertising, let's briefly discuss a few examples of creative ideas most of us can remember. The ideas are for Parkay Margarine, Federal Express, and Charmin bathroom tissue.

You probably recall a Parkay Margarine campaign that featured talking margarine. Whenever someone lifted the lid on a container of Parkay, the margarine spoke the word, "butter." Now, how does that creative idea connect with such terms as newness, relevance, and theme? First off, margarine doesn't talk. At least it doesn't talk in everyday reality. But like seeing a grain of sand as only a grain of sand, nontalking margarine is a literal and restricted reality. The creative mind, however, connects literal realities in order to spark the new realities of creative ideas. In the Parkay campaign, the creative idea is that margarine talks and says, "butter." Here, human speech is connected with margarine to yield a creative idea. Importantly, though, this creative idea is a new reality beyond what we would ordinarily expect reality to be.

As we know, newness isn't enough when it comes to creative ideas. They must also be relevant. In the Parkay case, the relevance is the theme, the message that Parkay tastes like butter. No doubt, research findings led to that conclusion. No doubt, too, that conclusion was deemed important or relevant to the target audience in terms of what the audience wanted (a margarine that tastes like butter) or what the problem was for the audience regarding margarine (it doesn't taste like butter).

As you think about Parkay's creative idea, notice how the theme of margarine tasting like butter is inseparable from the manner in which the theme is presented. The idea or manner of associating margarine with a human voice doesn't get in the way of the theme. It is the theme, and so both the idea and theme become one.

A similar situation exists for the popular Federal Express campaign idea featuring fast-talking characters and fast-moving Federal Express trucks. In everyday reality people don't talk as fast as the fast-talking Federal Express character. Trucks don't move as fast, either. In these respects, the creative idea presents a new reality connecting fast talk and movement with ordinary people and trucks. Notice, however, how that creative idea is relevant in terms of the theme or what Federal Express can provide for the target audience, in this case speed. As with Parkay, also notice how the creative idea doesn't get in the way of the theme. It is the theme, and the idea and theme become inseparable as a result.

With Charmin, the same kind of situation exists. A familiar character, Mr. Whipple, goes blithely through his store admonishing customers not to squeeze the Charmin. Of course, they do. Of course, he does as well. And the reason is that softness or squeezability represents the USP or differentiating factor for Charmin. As a theme, softness is what the target audience wants in its bathroom tissue. But notice again how the theme is inseparable from the creative idea and vice-versa.

Just from this brief discussion of three well known campaigns, notice how those important terms of newness, relevance, and theme are interrelated with the creative ideas. The ideas are new and relevant ways to present the themes. In this respect, the ideas are the themes, and the themes are the ideas. They become inseparable. They are one.

Overall, what we have then when we talk about the characteristics of creative advertising ideas is this. Ideas are new and relevant ways of presenting themes. They are the *how* or manner in which themes are presented. Themes are especially relevant and may also be new. They are the messages, the *what* or matter of the ideas. They evolve from research findings and creative planning. As such, they govern *what* the creative ideas should convey or mean. Both ideas and themes should be connected into one. They should be inseparable.

BEING FIRST (OR NEW) AND BEING RIGHT (OR RELEVANT)

In their pioneer book, *Positioning: The Battle for Your Mind,* Al Ries and Jack Trout elaborated on a new approach for marketers and advertisers. The approach was that of *positioning,* which became a catchword for marketers and advertisers during the 1970s and 1980s. Initially considered a marketing concept, positioning also became a means for distinguishing great advertising from mediocre advertising.

Typically, positioning is thought of as the niche a product makes for itself in the mind of the consumer. Ries and Trout elaborate on that basic understanding by identifying two guidelines for effective positioning, condensed here as being first and being right.[2] Being first means you're new. You're the first one to say or show something. This doesn't necessarily mean you're the first one to have that something, though that may be the case. It may mean you're simply the first one to say or show it. Recall the Parkay case, for example.

To support the importance of being first, Ries and Trout discuss 7Up's "Uncola" advertising campaign. At the time of the campaign, 7Up wasn't the only soft drink not like a cola. There were others. But, the other soft drinks not like colas didn't say it the way 7Up said it. This meant that 7Up was first. This also meant 7Up occupied that particular niche of "not a cola" in the consumer's mind. And since 7Up was the first to do that, it would be more easily remembered and more readily associated with that position.

Ries and Trout also support their idea by asking readers to relate being first to their lives. Who was the first person you kissed? Who was the second? The third? Who was the first man on the moon? The second? The third? More than likely, you're easily able to answer who was first in both instances. It may not be so easy to answer who was second or third, however. The point is that we remember the first, not the second or third.[3]

To see the importance of being first or new in advertising, you can refer to the Parkay, Federal Express, or Charmin examples. And to these more contemporary ad ideas you can add classic ad ideas such as David Ogilvy's man in the Hathaway shirt. The newness was that the man was also wearing an eyepatch. A first. Or, refer to Rosser Reeve's "melts in your mouth, not in your hands" idea for M&M's candy. Similarly, the Volkswagen creative ideas from Doyle Dane Bernbach were firsts. In these you can include the "Think Small" campaign. And Leo Burnett's Marlboro man, as enduring an ad campaign as ever existed, was certainly a first.

The point is that successful creative advertising positioning, or that message niche you occupy in the consumer's mind, depends to a great extent on being first or new. But, that's not all it depends on. You must also be right or relevant. And being right or relevant means *being on strategy*. In turn, being on strategy means your creative theme and idea connect the advertiser and target audience together. Think back to the Parkay example. Relevance. Connecting the theme and idea to what is important to the target audience about Parkay. The ultimate relevance, of course, is ringing the advertiser's cash register. The "Uncola" idea did. We know the eyepatch idea did. The unmessy hand-with-chocolate-in-it idea did. The Volkswagen ideas did. And the Marlboro man idea most certainly did.

These two principles, being first or new and being right or relevant, are as critical to creative advertising ideas as they are to creative ideas everywhere. They're mentioned in tandem because you cannot have one without the other and still achieve the optimum with creative advertising ideas. Creative director Ron Anderson puts it this way: "Advertising based on a sound strategy but executed poorly is as dull as another snowy day in January. Advertising executed brilliantly but based on a weak strategy may be entertaining—but it won't work. So you have to do the whole job, not just half."[4] In other words, you need to say or show what is relevant. Plus, you need to say or show that relevance in a new way. The new way or being first is your manner, or what we have referred to as your creative idea. That which is relevant or being right is your matter, or what we have referred to as your theme. Both must work together as a whole in order to be optimally effective.

In an advertising sense, think of positioning in these two ways of being first and being right. Conceptualize it, too, as a means of elbowing your way out and away from the competition, at least as far as your target audience is concerned. You and your competition are in a very crowded room filled with yourselves and others vying for the attention of a target audience.[5] Unless you're the first to present in a new way what is relevant to that audience, you're sure to get drowned or screened out. This means you should present something in a way that no one has quite presented it before. As we will see with our idea-generation techniques in Part III, there are many means to achieving that end.

CREATIVE ADVERTISING IDEAS ARE CONNECTIONS

Here, we circle back all the way to Chapter One. In our discussion of creative ideas, do you recall how important the concept of connection was to those ideas? Do you recall how important the concept of connection was to creativity generally? Well, it is equally important when it comes to creative advertising ideas. Creative advertising ideas are born through the act of connecting.

Like the creative ideas in Chapter One, creative advertising ideas are new realities. Recall? New realities are formed through connection of A + B = C. In Figure 4–1, you see the first page of a pop-up ad spread for Transamerica. As you turned the page, the spread revealed a pop-up of the Transamerica pyramid building. This ad exemplifies the innovative action of connection.

Here, the connection is one of combining a popular consumer news magazine with the old king and queen storybooks we used to read as children. As a unique approach to magazine advertising, the creative idea connects apparent opposites. Magazine pages are flat. Storybooks are for kids. Insurance companies don't use pop-ups. Adult readers and consumers don't expect pop-ups. These are opposites clashing with one another. The ad reconciles those opposites, however, and unifies them into a creative advertising idea.

Beyond connections of certain realities in order to form new realities, creative advertising ideas also contain connections with their target audiences. Immediately, there is a common ground established, a ground of relevance that links ad ideas with their audiences. You can see this type of connection clearly when you look at the *Communication Arts* magazine ad in Figure 4–2.

Communication Arts is a magazine for people like the one, Lee Clow, you see in this ad. As a reknowned art and creative director, he legitimizes the need for art and creative directors everywhere to subscribe to the magazine. Here, the creative idea governing the ad connects with its intended audience. It shows them someone they can admire and connect with. In effect, it's telling the audience that we, *Communication Arts*, are like you. What we have to say and show is what you want to hear and see. To prove it, look at Lee Clow, and listen to what he has to say.

This kind of connection with the target audience is the means by which creative ideas are relevant to the point of stimulating audience involvement. If the audience can connect with what you say or show, then involvement will occur. Once an audience is involved, they are inside your ad, and your ad is inside them. No doubt, this is a primary goal of all purposeful communication, let alone advertising.

It should be clear, too, that when we talk about connections, we're also talking about the manner and matter of the advertising. They need to be connected as well. In this respect, creative ideas should connect with the themes and vice versa. Neither one should distract from or get in the way of the other. Since a large part of ideas and themes is always the advertiser, then the advertiser must be central to both. This has been called "product-as-hero" advertising. Advertising giants such as David Ogilvy, Rosser Reeves, and Hank Seiden have written books in which emphasis is given to the "product as hero" as a formula for effective advertising.[6]

FIGURE 4-1   A New Idea for TRANSAMERICA. Courtesy of TRANSAMERICA CORPORATION.

To convey the advertiser as a hero obviously requires considerable knowledge of what the advertiser is, what it gives, and what it means to a target audience. What the advertiser is can be identified by reference to features. These are specific characteristics of the advertiser. What those fea-

FIGURE 4-2   A Relevant Idea for COMMUNICATION ARTS. Courtesy of COMMUNICATION ARTS
magazine.

tures give can be identified as advertiser selling points. What those selling
points mean can be identified as benefits or problem solutions. Creative
advertising themes and ideas tend to focus on one or more of these concepts and give special consideration to the last concept, that of benefits or
problem solutions.

As an example to distinguish between the three concepts of features, selling points, and benefits or problem solutions, the theme and idea of Parkay are based on the benefit of being able to enjoy margarine because it tastes like butter. Parkay features would be the ingredients and preparation to make the product what it is. The selling points would be what those ingredients and preparation give to the consumer, in this case buttery taste. But the benefit goes one more step in terms of saying and showing what the selling point of buttery taste will mean to the consumer, in this case, the enjoyment of margarine as if it were butter. For now, understand that features are specific characteristics (usually physical) identifying what the advertiser is. Selling points are what those features give to the consumer (usually appeals that are not physical). Benefits or problem solutions are what those selling points mean to the consumer (again, usually not physical).

To center creative ideas on these concepts, especially benefits or problem solutions, helps connect your target audience to your advertiser. It also assures you of making the advertiser central to the themes and ideas. In this respect, the advertiser and what it can deliver to the target audience should be the matter and manner of the advertising messages. This is the essence of "product-as-hero" advertising. For example, the line drawings of key frames in a television commercial for UPS in Figure 4–3 show the "product-as-hero" technique in action.

FIGURE 4-3 A Product-as-Hero Idea for UPS. Courtesy of UNITED PARCEL SERVICE, INC. Art by Mary Ella.

Notice how the actual product, UPS delivery, is the focal point of the ad. The overnight letter is also connected with an airplane to give the creative idea its newness and originality. But the airplane is not the hero. The UPS service, as exemplified by its overnight letter, is the hero. It gives you speedy, reliable delivery, right on your desk. Here, the product literally *and* figuratively carries the message.

We've discussed this very important concept of connections from three different perspectives. Let's review them quickly. First, creative advertising ideas are themselves examples of connections between realities. Those connections yield new realities. Second, creative advertising ideas connect with the intended target audience. They do this through their relevance to that audience. In turn, the audience becomes involved and is able to connect back to the advertiser more easily and readily. Third, creative advertising ideas connect the matter and manner of the advertising messages. *How* the ideas present the themes or messages mirrors *what* the themes or messages are. Since themes or messages are the advertisers and their features, selling points, and benefits or problem solutions, then *how* the themes or messages are presented should focus on those terms. In addition, neither manner nor matter should upstage each other. Instead, they should be connected and unified as one.

ADNORMS

With the guiding concepts of being first, being right, and connections as a backdrop, the acronym ADNORMS is a means for describing and remembering the essence of what makes for a creative advertising idea. ADNORMS stands for Adaptability, Durability, Newness, Oneness, Relevance, Memorability, and Simplicity. The best advertising ideas contain most, if not all, of these qualities.

Creative Advertising Ideas Have Adaptability

When advertising ideas are *adaptable*, they're able to cross over among and between media. What work as creative advertising ideas in magazines also work as creative advertising ideas in other media such as newspapers, radio, television, billboards, or direct mail. Of course, though a strong creative idea may be peculiar to a specific medium, campaign development doesn't always allow you the luxury of a one-medium message. This is why you must be prepared to cross over to other media.

Go back again to any of the ad ideas discussed in this chapter and imagine their use in other media than were shown. For example, can you imagine the Transamerica idea on television? The *Communication Arts* idea in direct mail? The UPS idea in magazine or newspaper? In fact, what happens if you try to imagine each of those ideas conveyed through several of the major media?

Transamerica? Right away, you may be inclined to think we have some problems with adaptability. This seems like one of those advertising ideas peculiar to a particular medium, magazines. But, isn't it also adaptable to newspaper, outdoor, and especially direct mail? Can you imagine it on television? A flattened city rising to a benefit-oriented narrative from a voice-over announcer. Radio? A strong two-person dialogue about the power of the pyramid rising right before human eyes.

How about *Communication Arts*? The voice of Lee Clow on radio (for the sake of argument, assume media selection would include the broadcast media)? Lee Clow in person on television? Any print or outdoor medium would be no problem.

UPS? Again, no problem in any medium.

This same kind of situation holds especially true for those long-lasting campaign ideas having stood the test of time. Take the Marlboro campaign, for example. For many years now, the idea of the Marlboro man has been restricted to certain media. But, if it weren't, imagine putting him in motion (as he was years ago) on television. Or imagine conveying his image through direct mail. As the conveyor of that well-known term, "brand image," the Marlboro man is adaptable to the major media.

So is the famous M&M's candy campaign. Particularly suitable for television because of its demonstration capabilities, the M&M's campaign of "melts in your mouth, not in your hands" easily crosses over to the other media. All that's needed is to freeze the most telling frame from television and show it. Or use a two-part dialogue on radio.

A man with an eyepatch for Hathaway Shirts? Great for any print and television. Radio? Two women talking about the stunning man they've just seen and how mysterious and intriguing he was.

Think about the many advertising campaigns you grew up with and still remember, Parkay Margarine's "Butter" campaign included, and chances are they had this quality of adaptability.

A for Adaptability. You may not be asked to cover each medium this year or the first time around. Maybe you will in the years that follow, though. Then what? Are you gong to change your creative idea because it won't work in one medium, even though it has worked successfully in another? Probably not.

Creative Advertising Ideas Have Durability

When advertising ideas are *durable*, they're able to last. David Ogilvy, for one, believes their durability should be at least 30 years.[7] Indeed, that's one of his five criteria for recognizing a *Big Idea*. Of course, the ad ideas for Transamerica, *Communication Arts,* and UPS are fairly new and so have not yet stood the test of time. But, if their ideas are tightly coiled around their brand images and are relevant and meaningful to their target audiences, then chances are they will. The key here is the brand image or what Ogilvy termed the "personality" of the product.[8] It's the clear, unmistakable, and appropriate brand image that gives ad ideas their durability.

In Figure 4–4, you see two ads for Maytag. Are these ads very different? Aren't they more or less the same?

In more ways than one, the Maytag creative idea is an example of durability. Sure, it's been revised over time, but the lonely repairman continues to symbolize a key product selling point, that of durability. As an enduring symbol of the product, he personifies the image. It is this kind of clarity and appropriateness in the brand image that has allowed the creative idea to exist for so long. The same kind of situation exists for Marlboro, where a masculine figure has lasted for over three decades as a symbol of the brand's image.

As you generate and ultimately select ideas, the question to ask yourself is whether certain ideas have the potential to last, or are they time-bound, restricted to a specific event or even mood that will change as time passes?

There's another side to this coin that you should understand, however. It's certainly possible that ideas which seem relevant only to a particular time may, in fact, have the potential for shifting into other times. In the Marlboro case, for example, an early tattoo faded as its appropriateness to masculinity faded. But, this didn't prompt the Leo Burnett agency or Marlboro to change the core idea. Slight twists or variations of the idea were added. But fundamentally, the core idea remained the same throughout the decades.

Creative Advertising Ideas Have Newness

When advertising ideas are *new,* they're different. This makes them first, not second and "me-tooish." They have that "quality of the unexpected," a quality evoking surprise from the target audience.

We have spent a considerable amount of time discussing the concept of newness. More than anything else, perhaps, it is what separates creative ideas from noncreative ideas. It's also a vital part of the prescriptions from the most revered advertising creative minds. Think back, for instance, to Chapter Three and the perspectives of such advertising greats as Bernbach, Della Femina, McCabe, Hopkins, Ogilvy, Reeves, and Burnett. Each saw the need for creativity—not unfettered creativity, but strategic and pointed creativity. The kind where the idea mirrors the message, and the kind that also surprises. As Ogilvy notes in his list of the five criteria for the *Big Idea,* it may even make you gasp when you see it.[9]

Naturally, all of this business of newness circles back to the importance of connections and being first. The creative mind connects or associates certain realities and creates a new reality, the creative idea. If that idea is aligned with the target audience, if it is relevant, then the connection completes itself by stimulating the audience's involvement. One of the ways to make all of this happen is by being first with the message or the manner in which the message is presented. Recall that people remember what's first more readily than they remember what's second or third. And to be first invariably means to be new and different.

All of the ad or campaign ideas we've discussed in this chapter are new. Obviously, some are newer than others. The Transamerica ad, for instance, was so new, so unique, that it even managed to get talked about. In effect, it moved out of the media and into the consciousness permeating boardrooms and creative team meetings. Its novelty differentiated the ad from the slew of other magazine ads. This is what happens when ad ideas are new. They elbow their way out from other ad ideas. They gain a foothold in terms of their positioning. As a result, they gain attention and get remembered.

There are, of course, many kinds of new, unique ad ideas. The Transamerica idea was simply one kind, that of reversing expectations pertaining to a particular medium. In the third part of our book, we will look more closely at that technique and others which focus on how the creative mind generates a quantity of ideas in order to allow it the opportunity to select a new and unique idea.

Creative Advertising Ideas Have Oneness

When advertising ideas have *oneness*, they are singleminded, themebound, and continuous. They focus on one governing idea, not many ideas. Again, Ogilvy termed this a part of the *Big Idea*. Reeves termed it the USP. Singular, not plural. As with the quality of newness, oneness is another of those persistent pieces of advice from advertising greats.

Think of a *Big Idea*'s oneness as the sun giving life to all the other elements in an ad or campaign. In fact, like the planets, all the other elements—pictures, words, music, everything—revolve around that sun. They don't drift off on their own. Instead, they are bound to the *Big Idea* for their energy and meaning. For instance, the copywriter selects the words "stand up" as part of the introduction to the pop-up in the Transamerica ad. Or, at the close of the UPS television commercial, the voice-over announcer states that UPS's service is the "Super Saver of overnight deliveries." In both instances, the core *Big Idea* ruled the copy as it did other elements in the ads. This is oneness. Same core idea. Same tone or "feel." Same theme or message. All continuous throughout.

Even when the medium or time changes, the core idea remains fundamentally the same. For example, think of how singular and continuous the

CHAIRMAN OF THE BORED.

Maytag made this man what he is today. We did it through hard work and determination. We did it by building washers that last longer and need fewer repairs. And by making sure every Maytag dryer, dishwasher, range, microwave and disposer meets our rigorous quality standards. Our standards are so high that we make many of our own parts, so you get Maytag quality, inside and out. Every appliance Maytag makes is individually tested to prove it can meet those standards — before it leaves our door.

It's true, not all Maytag repairmen have reached these heights of loneliness. But through hard work and dedication, Maytag is making sure every one of our repairmen will have a chance to find out how lonely it is at the top.

MAYTAG
THE DEPENDABILITY PEOPLE

© 1985 The Maytag Company

FIGURE 4-4 A Durable idea for MAYTAG. Courtesy of MAYTAG CORPORATION.

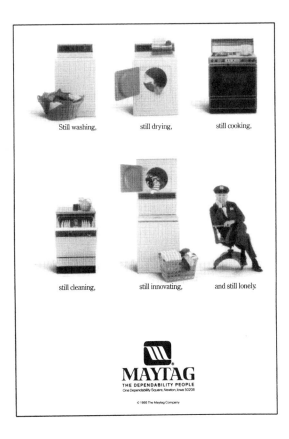

Still washing,   still drying,   still cooking,

still cleaning,   still innovating,   and still lonely.

MAYTAG
THE DEPENDABILITY PEOPLE
One Dependability Square, Newton, Iowa 50208

© 1986 The Maytag Company

image of the Marlboro man has been throughout both the media and time. The same holds true for the most creative of advertising ideas. This is because the audiences for those ideas are not sitting with bated breath waiting to see or hear an ad. In all likelihood, those audiences are apathetic or, worse yet, hostile. When ad ideas are singular, they're easier to understand and more difficult to misunderstand, particularly for audiences lacking a deep-seated interest in connecting with those ad ideas in the first place.

Though the need for oneness is fairly obvious as an ingredient for creative advertising ideas, many beginners (and clients) in advertising have difficulty with it. And, more often than not, the difficulty is a head problem. Unsure, uncertain, and insecure about how advertising works, some beginners insist on packing as many ideas as is humanly (or even superhumanly) possible into their ads or campaigns. The belief may be that it's better to be safe than sorry, and if all possible selling points, benefits, and ideas are brought into an ad, that's safe. It's also very wrong. The reverse is true. The more singleminded an ad is, the better it is.

Remember your target audience and the chances that it's not nearly

as friendly to, or enthralled with, your advertising as you are. You can rea-
sonably expect your audience to give little more than a kind of glazed, half-
hearted approach or focus to your advertising. This is all the more reason
to keep your ad ideas singleminded and continuous throughout. In addition, what you want is for your ad ideas to strike home instantly to the
market. If your ideas are scattered or diffused, they won't be instant. The
audience won't work to understand or remember them. But, if your ideas
are singleminded and continuous, you have made it that much easier for
the audience to understand and remember them.

Creative Advertising Ideas Have Relevance

When advertising ideas have *relevance*, they're linked to the themes of
the advertisers and, more importantly, what those advertisers are, give, and
especially mean for the target audience. You have, of course, been positively
flooded by the importance of relevance since you started reading this book.
Still, there may not be such a thing as being flooded by the concept. It's that
important. It is, along with newness, the soul of creative advertising ideas.

Because creative advertising ideas answer the question "What's in it
for me?" for the target audience, they immediately create involvement on
the part of that audience. The audience can connect with them because
they promise something that is needed or wanted. For example, if you want
innovativeness in your insurance company, Transamerica promises to give
it to you. If you want inexpensive speediness with your overnight mailings,
UPS promises to give that to you as well. If you want your margarine to
taste like butter, Parkay promises that it will. Or, if you want a candy that
won't mess up your hands, M&M's is the answer.

No doubt, creating ideas that are relevant demands a working understanding of all the communication and persuasion variables to be discussed
in the next two chapters. But, when it's all said and done, what it comes
down to is finding those advertiser features or selling points that can be
translated to the relevant benefits or problem solutions the target audience
needs or wants. Often, these benefits or problem solutions are the themes
or messages in an ad. They are then conveyed through unique, attention-
grabbing ad ideas. Remember, they are not replaced by ad ideas. They *are*
the ad ideas.

Creative Advertising Ideas Have Memorability

When advertising ideas have *memorability*, they're able to stick in the
target audience's mind, perhaps for a considerable amount of time, until
they're acted upon. The big question to be answered here is, What kinds of
ideas stick in the mind? To answer that, we can retreat again to all that we
have discussed.

Clearly, if ad ideas are relevant, if what they promise on behalf of the product is wanted or needed by the target audience, they will stick. But that's not all they should do. They should also grab attention, and this means they should be new or different in some way. Again, that newness or difference should be easily connected by the audience to the advertiser, especially what the advertiser is, gives, or means for the audience. The result is that the newness or difference, and what the advertiser is, gives, or means, should be one and the same.

In his often-quoted rules on how people learn, Steuart Henderson Britt lists four criteria.[10] One of those criteria includes uniqueness or difference. We learn things that are different (recall Ries and Trout's view on being first). But two other very important means for learning (and when we have learned, we have remembered) are active involvement and primacy or recency. People learn from active involvement. Of course, if ideas are new and relevant, there will be involvement. Also, however, if people are asked to participate somehow in the formulation or completion of the ideas, they will be even more involved. In this respect, ad ideas eliciting participation are potentially memorable. Incomplete pictures or phrases urge this type of involvement. In Part III of this book, you will play with this as an idea-generation technique called closure.

A third rule for learning, primacy and recency, states that people more easily learn first and last things than they do middle things. Our discussion of positioning and being first is important here. Even within an ad, the same primacy/recency principle applies. Creative advertising ideas present the most important theme right away. As Ogilvy advises, 80 cents of every advertising dollar are in the headline.[11] Immediately, the headline or theme-line, working in tandem with the controlling visual, should say it all because this is what will be remembered above other parts of the ad. Also remembered will be the ad's close. And in referring back to the concept of oneness, the close should coil itself around the *Big Idea* expressed in the headline and visual. Yes, it should urge the action desired, but it should also circle back to the *Big Idea*.

Creative Advertising Ideas Have Simplicity

When advertising ideas have *simplicity*, they are clearly and instantly relevant and meaningful. There is little unwanted work for the audience to do in order to get the message. That's because the ideas aren't cluttered with other ideas or too much busyness. Again, this goes back to the concept of oneness. One idea dominates and controls throughout.

As with oneness, understanding the importance of simplicity is more a head problem than anything else. There is that tendency to want to "get it all in," to crowd the ad and say or show everything that apparently needs to be said or shown. Unfortunately, this is the reverse of what needs to be done. Indeed, this is often the reverse of creativity. Creativity doesn't mean complication. It means simplification. It means boiling everything down to an essence, a sharply, clearly defined essence of the most important idea. The jazz musician Charlie Mingus used these words to describe creativity: "Creativity is more than just being different. Being different isn't necessarily being original. Anybody can play weird; that's easy. What's hard is to be as simple as Bach. . . . Making the simple complicated is commonplace; making the complicated simple, awesomely simple, that's creativity."[12]

The same holds true with the most creative of advertising ideas. They are simple, sometimes awesomely simple, as in the case of the Volkswagen ad in Figure 4–5.

Notice how you can look at this ad for a fleeting instant and still get the message. That's because the headline and visual are inseparable and simple. They complement one another and jointly convey the same meaning. The idea as a whole also happens to be singleminded and relevant to anyone who is interested in owning a car that will save money on fuel. As a tightly unified idea, this Volkswagen ad, now a classic in its own right, exemplifies the creative advertising mind's adherence to the principles of newness, oneness, relevance, memorability by involvement, and simplicity.

Think back to the ads we have looked at or discussed in this chapter, and ask yourself this question; Are they simple or complex? Your answer is sure to be that they're simple. Right away, the messages are conveyed. There's no fuzziness or apparent indecision about what the ads should be saying or showing. Single, controlling ideas lead the way. Because everything else revolves around those ideas, the ads are simple and direct.

ADNORMS

ADNORMS are the characteristic standards of quality found in the most creative of advertising ideas. Of course, not all ad ideas can be expected to satisfy all of the requirements to meet those standards of quality. Some ad ideas may be lacking in one or more areas. Still, ADNORMS is a goal for the creative mind when it comes time for generating and ultimately selecting a creative advertising idea. The more standards that are met, the better the idea.

Adaptability—Can it swing into other media?

Durability—Can it swing throughout time and events?

Newness—Is it different, unique, or first?

Oneness—Does it have singlemindedness? Do all the elements revolve around the single theme and idea?

Relevance—Does it relate the benefit or problem solution, the theme or message of the product, to the target audience?

Memorability—Is it memorable through its newness, singlemindedness, relevance, and involvement potential?

FIGURE 4-5 A New, Relevant, and Simple Idea for VOLKSWAGEN. Ad copyrighted and reproduced with the permission of VOLKSWAGEN UNITED STATES, INC.

Simplicity—Is it simple to the point where the target audience will get the main sellng message clearly and instantly?

CREATIVE ADVERTISING IDEAS

Creative advertising ideas are uniquely and strategically positioned in the target audience's mind. This means they're first and they're right. To be first means the ideas are new. They should present the themes in a way no one has presented them before. To be right means the ideas are relevant and on strategy. It means they are based on themes derived from strategic considerations, not the least of which is their potential relevance to the target audience and advertiser.

Creative advertising ideas exemplify the end result of connecting. They connect separate realities to create new realities. They connect advertiser features, selling points, and benefits or problem solutions to the audience's needs or wants. This stimulates the audience to become involved to the point of connecting back to the advertiser. Creative ideas connect the matter and manner of the ad so that one becomes the other, and they are inseparable.

Creative advertising ideas abide by ADNORMS. They can be adapted to various media. They're durable enough to span time and events. They're new enough to grab attention. They contain the quality of oneness, one idea presented in one way throughout. They contain relevance to the audience and advertiser by way of themes in which the advertiser is central to meeting the needs and wants or solving the problems of the audience. They're memorable because they're relevant, involving, and first. And, finally, they're simple because they rely on only single ideas.

These are the qualities you're looking for with your ad ideas. Be assured, it's much easier to say what these qualities are than it is to generate ideas exemplifying them. There are techniques to help achieve that end, techniques that comprise the entirety of Part III of this book. Before those techniques can be played with and used, however, it's important to understand that creative advertising individuals prepare themselves to generate ideas.

In preparing to generate ideas, creative advertising individuals dwell on vital information providing them with relevant insights to the advertiser, the media, and the target audience. Just like in the preparation and incubation stages of the creative process, the information and insights are gathered and mulled over. During this time they seep into the creative mind. When the mind connects realities to generate ideas, it does so with the information and insights acting as the foundation for those connections.

In this respect, bear in mind that the creative individual is well prepared to be creative about something. Bear in mind, too, that when it comes to advertising, the creative individual is well prepared in the dynamics of communication and persuasion. There can be no mistaking the fact that the best creative advertising ideas are not examples of creativity for creativity's sake. They are examples of creativity for the sake of pointed and purposeful communication and, more often than not, persuasion. Only by being prepared in that respect will the creative individual be able to create ideas that communicate and persuade.

5

COMMUNICATION AND PERSUASION: AN OVERVIEW

Preparation for advertising creativity begins with an understanding of communication and persuasion. Creative ad ideas don't exist in a vacuum. To be relevant, they must exist in the context of communication and persuasion. This means they must exert some form of dynamic influence on those who see or hear them. Always in advertising there is a synergistic relationship (or lack of it) between who is sending the ideas, what the ideas are, the channels through which they are sent, and who is receiving them. To understand this relationship is the focal point of this chapter.

MODELS OF HOW COMMUNICATION AND PERSUASION WORK

There are many communication and persuasion models in existence. And, we could certainly spend the rest of our time wrestling with their complexities. Indeed, many books have. That, however, is not our purpose. Instead, our purpose is to gain an overview of how communication and persuasion work, especially in terms of how they are interrelated. This means we will take a general and somewhat simplistic view of their workings, much like we will do with creative strategy in our next chapter. Remember, our overriding purpose in this book is to provide the techniques for generating ideas. But, prior to that, your mind should be focused on the general purpose of all ads, which is to communicate and persuade.

In Figures 5–1 and 5–2 you will see basic models of communication and persuasion. Figure 5–1 is derived from the Don E. Schultz, Dennis G. Martin, and William P. Brown book, *Strategic Advertising Campaigns*. The model graphically portrays the communicative flow of messages. Figure 5–2 contains a gloss of the steps in persuasion as proposed by William J. McGuire, Robert J. Lavidge and Gary A. Steiner, and the familiar AIDA formula.

Taken together, the models provide you with a general understanding of how communication and persuasion tend to work. You should carry that understanding with you when you begin to generate and ultimately select your creative ideas. Of course, it's one thing to look at any model and supposedly understand how it works, but it's quite another thing to understand it by actually applying it to various situations. What we will do here is apply the models, and we will apply them in a hypothetical situation from real life. That way you can better relate to their terminology and interrelatedness.

A REAL-LIFE EXAMPLE OF HOW COMMUNICATION AND PERSUASION WORK

Let's take an example from real life, one just about all of us can relate to, that of a first date with a special someone. Recall a time when you had your eye on that special someone. Maybe it was yesterday, last week, or years ago. Didn't you do something to let that someone know you were interested? Perhaps you used a go-between, a kind of testimonial or endorsement for you. Or, perhaps you were more direct and simply managed to strike up a conversation with that someone. Either way, you managed to get that someone's attention riveted on yourself and not someone else. And, without that attention, you would have no chance of communicating with, much less persuading, your special someone of your interest.

From Attention to Noise

In respect to attention, notice how it governs the first steps in the persuasion models. In advertising, as in life, this first step of attention is critical to persuasion. The problem is that in advertising, as in life, it's not always so easy to achieve. For example, ads don't exist in vacuums. They exist in the context of other ads, other persuasive messages, and even the contexts of the media in which they appear. Ads are sent through media such as newspaper, television, or radio, all of which contain distractions. News matter, for instance. Or television programming, for another instance. This is what Schultz, Martin, and Brown mean by multiple senders and noise.

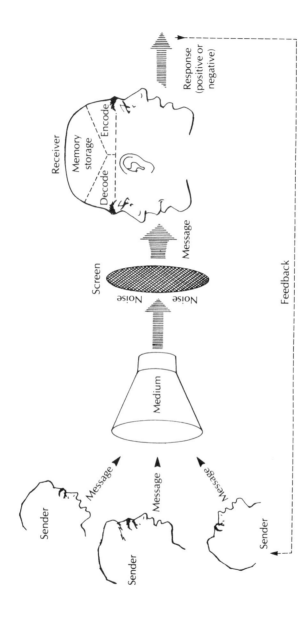

FIGURE 5–1 How Advertising Communicates. Courtesy of the NATIONAL TEXTBOOK COMPANY for Don E. Schultz, Dennis G. Martin, and William P. Brown, *Strategic Advertising Campaigns*, 2nd ed., 1988.

FIGURE 5-2   Steps in Persuasion

—From William J. McGuire, "An Information-Processing Model of Advertising Effectiveness," paper presented at the Symposium of Behavioral and Management Science sponsored by the Center for Continuing Education, The University of Chicago, July, 1969.

PRESENTATION-ATTENTION-COMPREHENSION-YIELDING-RETENTION-BEHAVIOR

—From Robert J. Lavidge and Gary A. Steiner, "A Model for Predictive Measurements of Advertising Effectiveness," *Journal of Marketing*, October (1961), p. 61.

AWARENESS-KNOWLEDGE-LIKING-PREFERENCE-CONVICTION-PURCHASE

—AIDA formula

ATTENTION-INTEREST-DESIRE-ACTION

Rarely does the receiver of a message exist in a kind of a vacuum-sealed, distraction-proof room. Instead, what happens is that the receiver of a message is bombarded by a host of messages, many of which serve to distract that receiver from your message. As Rosser Reeves (Mr. USP) puts it, our receiver is "a beleagured consumer, a confused consumer, battered by television, assailed by print, assaulted by radio, bewildered by posters. It is very difficult to get him to remember, and he is very prone, indeed, to forget." To this, Reeves surely could have added how difficult it is to get the consumer to pay attention in the first place.[1]

The same, of course, holds true in our real life example. For instance, perhaps someone else had an eye on your special someone. Or, perhaps the situation in which you wanted to "make arrangements" was unsuitable because of a variety of obstacles or, as Schultz, Martin, and Brown would say, because of "noise." If such were the case, what would you do? Chances are you would have to go out of your way to gain attention. You may even have to do something unique, something different. In fact, persuasion theorists and researchers know that doing something unique or different is an effective means for gaining attention. Herbert W. Simons, for instance, notes the importance of "novelty" as one of the "external factors" necessary to gain attention: "What is [ɛnsnun may attract attention, and because we expect the the familiar, you may not have noticed that there is an extra 'the' in this sentence."[2] No doubt, our attention is drawn to an otherwise familiar word printed upside down. And, if by chance our eye did notice the repetitive "the," chances are we would pay close and immediate attention to it.

Now, let's say you have only limited time with and exposure to your special someone. Further, let's say others with "eyes" have more time with and exposure to your someone. What are some of the things you might have to do in order to gain your someone's attention? Perhaps you could use your go-between. Perhaps you could create an ad for yourself. And what does that mean, to create an ad for yourself?

Think of yourself as a product that needs to be sold to someone. The problem is that your someone is bombarded by noise, that is by distractions from others. These others have more access to your someone. This is just like advertising in that some advertisers have larger budgets and thus more exposure to their target audiences. So, what you need to do is key into what appeals to that someone. More so, since uniqueness and difference grab attention, you need to do it with flair and originality. In life, as in advertising, this is done all the time. For example, we spritz ourselves with our personal perfume or cologne. This makes our essence larger than our physical size. Our unique scent wafts out from us. And hopefully it carries an alluring image of ourselves with it. Or, we dress in a certain way, a way we believe will appeal to our someone. In fact, we may even talk and behave in certain ways, all meant to make a positive impression on that someone. All meant to grab that someone's attention. All meant to make us appealingly unique and different, especially as we are compared to others.

Perhaps we can take these sage words of advice from William Bernbach to heart when it comes to understanding the importance of grabbing attention: "Unless you were born into advertising with a lot of gold in your budget, you must be aware that not to be different is virtually suicidal."[3] Recalling Bernbach's advice from Chapter 3, it's difficult to believe he wouldn't extend this current piece of advice to gold-filled budgets as well.

Of course, the important point to remember from all of this is that the first task of any form of communication or persuasion is to grab attention. Without attention, all of the other steps in our models will never be reached. Plus, your own message will have to be advertised or shaped in certain impacting ways depending on the degree or amount of senders and noise within the communication flow.

From Comprehension to Remembering

Let's say you did grab the attention of your someone because you were perceived as appealing based on your own ad, your dress, your manner, your overall presence. Is that enough? The answer is no. Communication and persuasion don't stop with attention. On the contrary, attention is merely a beginning point. From there you need to make your way through screens and be comprehended or understood. You also need to be preferred. And you need to be remembered. Only then will your special someone provide you with the positive feedback needed for the two of you to meet again. To reach that point, though, both of you must make your ways through each other's screens.

In the Schultz, Martin, and Brown communication model, screens are the ways in which we ward certain messages off and allow other messages in. As you well know, there are some messages we just don't want. So we ward them off. On the other hand, there are some messages we do want. So we let them in. Those we ward off tend to go against our grain. They don't fit our preconceived notions and beliefs of what we consider important or appealing. Those we let in are more in line with what we are, with what we believe, and with what we consider important or appealing. Heavy smokers, for instance, are inclined to ward off anti-smoking messages more so than nonsmokers. Too much fear and too much negativism alienate the smokers. But, they don't affect nonsmokers in the same way. Thus, we disallow or allow certain messages based on what we are and on what we believe.

In our real life example, we have assumed that the initial screen of your someone has allowed you in since you have grabbed that someone's attention. Now the task is to hold that attention. And the way you do that is by finding a common, appealing, and understandable ground. For example, imagine the two of you go out on your first date. As you did before, you advertise yourself in a certain way, a way in which you feel good about yourself and a way in which you believe your someone will feel equally good about you. This means that you dress a certain way. You have a certain scent. And you talk and behave a certain way.

Let's say you go out to dinner. What do you talk about? And how do you talk about it?

If you were intent on being allowed through your someone's screens, chances are you would begin to talk about things the two of you had in common. The weather. Work. School. Some likes and dislikes. But, would you immediately begin talking about some very personal things? Things like private obsessions or fixations? Would you begin by talking about depressing things? Or would you begin by talking about positive things the two of you had in common? The answer is clear, no doubt. And this is how the two of you begin to build a framework of a relationship. You begin by building a positive knowledge base for one another. You create mutual interest. You seek areas of relevance and meaning. The result is that the two of you begin the relationship by connecting with one another, and connection is always a matter of finding what's relevant and similar.

This is exactly what advertising copywriters do when they write copy for specific target audiences. If I asked you, for instance, to conceptualize and actually flesh out and personalize a target audience for the following copy lines, what would your conceptualizations be?

For Steinway pianos, the first line from the body text of an ad: "Something ineffable exists between an artist and his instrument."

For Zildjian drum accessories: "You've got this polyrhythmic thing happening."

For Technics stereo systems: "Full orchestra fortissimo and piccolo pi-
annisimo."

Think about the Steinway piano copy line. Consider the choices of
words, especially the word "ineffable." Now, based on that word alone, is
this ad targeted to a blue collar receiver? Is it targeted to children? Of course
not. It's obviously targeted to an upscale receiver. Perhaps a receiver who is
a little haughty or sophisticated. And does it even matter what the word
"ineffable" means? If, by some chance, members of the target audience
don't know what it means, it is still impressive. It still conveys a feel and
tone in keeping with the finer things in life.

How about the Zildjian copy line? Is it for the same receiver as the
Steinway line? Clearly not. Instead, it's meant for rockers. A younger set. A
group that would say things like, "Yeah, man. We dig."

Is this the same receiver for the Technics line? No. Here, music afficio-
nados are the target audience. Perhaps an audience a bit sophisticated and
knowledgeable about the subtleties of music listening.

The point is that each of these three lines is tailored toward a specific
target audience. The result of the tailoring is communication between the
sender and the receiver. Moreover, there is an understanding, a kind of
comprehension of what the other is all about. The lines speak the language
of their respective receivers. Just like you and your special someone did on
your first date.

In returning to our example of a first date, it should be clear that
in order for either of you to be allowed through screens and in order for
comprehension and liking to occur, there needs to be this kind of common
interest and involvement. If not, the two of you may never reach the other
steps in communication and persuasion. For instance, what happens if you
discover at dinner that your special someone spends an inordinate amount
of time talking about him or herself? Just suppose that your someone occupies that time with self-consumed "I" monologues. What then? Chances are
you will begin to screen out the messages. And chances are that you will
have difficulty reaching the liking stage of persuasion.

This is the same as advertising. Ads that dwell on the product in a
type of claim and boast format rarely work as forms of communication and
persuasion. This is especially true of ads for new products, just as it would
be true of you and your someone on a first date. What happens, instead, is
that we don't allow the message in. Or, we may react against the message.
Worse yet, we may react against the source of the message.

As far as our communication model is concerned, this means the message and its source will never get to the point of encoding for a positive
response or feedback. And as far as our persuasion models are concerned,
this means the message and its source will never get to the point of liking
and preference.

From Liking to Feedback

When we talk about liking someone or something, we invariably enter the realm of the heart as opposed to the head. For instance, notice how the Lavidge and Steiner persuasion model positions liking as an affective response, meaning it is more emotional than rational. What happens is that we have processed all of the previous information cognitively (rationally), and then we respond emotionally to it. The overriding question, however, is this. What are those things we like and dislike?

We have already identified one key dislike. We dislike braggarts. We dislike others (and products or ads) that spend considerable time boasting about themselves. We dislike those who see fit only to spend their time talking about themselves. What we can assume from this is that we dislike those whose interest is one-sided, usually themselves. What we like, however, is the opposite. We like others who are interested in us. We like others who are genuine or sincere about that interest. In addition, we like others who are similar to us. In fact, sincerity and similarity never stop being important in all the steps of communication and persuasion.[4] Recall, for example, the copy lines from Steinway, Zildjian, and Technics. Though the issue of sincerity may be open to discussion, the issue of similarity seems cut and dry. Those copy lines are similar in feel, tone, and attitude to their respective audiences. The result is that they would be liked by those audiences. Researchers, for instance, have found similarity in both appearances and attitudes to be an important variable in liking.[5]

Beyond sincerity and similarity, what else do we like? Researchers say we like those we can trust.[6] For instance, on your first date, didn't you measure the trustworthiness of your someone along the way? Were you being told things the way they were? Or, were you being told things because of ulterior motives? If you believed in the sincerity and honesty of what you were told, then chances are you began to develop some trust in your someone. The result is that your feelings may have colored the information you were being told. From here, you began to encode your own information. You began, in short, to respond positively in a kind of feedback loop to your someone. And, assuming things were working out for both of you, chances are your someone was doing the same thing.

As your evening progressed and the two of you became convinced of each other's sincerity, similarity, and trustworthiness, your hearts began to rule your heads. This means you entered the affective liking and preference stages of our persuasion models. Gradually, as time went on, you began to prefer one another, perhaps over others. And what initially started out as the medium of voice may have turned to the medium of gesture. You held hands. You kissed. Both are mediums for affection.

Perhaps it's safe to stop here, at the close of an evening and with a kiss. But as you think back through the example, can you see how the communication and persuasion models present themselves over and over again? Can you imagine how noise and screens begin to fade once you like and prefer your someone? Can you understand how inevitable the final step of action will be once the steps of liking and preference are reached? The same holds true with advertising. Take Coke and Pepsi, for instance. Since we already like those products, we tend to prefer them. They match what we are and what we believe. For example, if you're a young teen, then Pepsi's use of Michael Jackson and other rock stars will connect Pepsi with you. If you're more mainstream America, then Coke Classic's use of symbolic appeals to Americana will connect Coke Classic with you.

Of course, we have oversimplified the entire process of communication and persuasion in order to make it generally understandable. And in applying our real-life example, we have been able to better understand how communication and persuasion work, even in an advertising context. But, as you think back on all that we have discussed regarding these two important terms, certain key concepts should step out front and center. The variables in the communication model and the steps in the persuasion process, for instance. Plus, there should be other, more judgmental and qualitative highlights as well. The importance of attention, for example. Or, the need for establishing a common ground in order to be allowed through screens as another example. And, overall, the absolutely vital focus on the message receiver, the intended target audience. It is this message receiver, your someone, who gives meaning to everything in both the communication and persuasion models. In many ways, there are no senders, no messages, no media, noise, or screens, no attention, comprehension, liking, preference, or action without the message receiver. The following lighthearted quip sums up the importance of the receiver as a kind of governor or even umpire over the entire game of communication and persuasion.

> The first umpire said, "Some's balls and some's strikes and I calls 'em as they is." The second umpire said, Some's balls and some's strikes and I calls 'em as I sees 'em." While the third umpire said, "Some's balls and somes's strikes but they ain't nothin' till I calls 'em."[7]

THE RECEIVER OR TARGET AUDIENCE GIVES MEANING TO EVERYTHING ELSE

Most target audiences don't go around reading books on advertising. Consequently, one of the potential dangers for you in reading any book on the subject is that you begin to distance yourself from the receiver's or target audience's point of view. Yet, if there's one maxim that should govern the creation of a promising advertising idea, it's that there is no promising idea unless the target audience believes there is.

With this in mind, I'm asking you to relate to the examples that follow as the different audiences might relate to them. In other words, get out of your head and heart and into someone's else's. This is really the only way to understand how the audience mediates and determines the meaning in the variables and steps of the models we have just discussed.

Audience Involvement

The entire process of communication and persuasion is mediated by the degree of involvement an audience has with the message and its source. Involvement refers to how important the message and source are to the audience. It refers to the degree of audience commitment to that message and source. And that importance or commitment can range from low to high.[8]

To understand the mediating effects of involvement, let's first consider a general view of an audience's perception of advertising messages. For example, do you think most people are anxiously waiting for the next ad to appear on their television screens or in their daily newspapers? Do you think they feel the same kind of anticipation with advertising that you did with your first date? Most likely not. On the contrary, you should expect most people to be one of three things pertaining to advertising—apathetic, skeptical, or hostile. This means advertisers run the risk of trying to deliver messages to people who often could care less or who immediately build screens to ward off those messages. In effect, people are relatively uninvolved with advertising messages, especially considering the number and variety of messages they encounter each day.

Of course, this situation may change if an audience considers a particular product important. For example, if an audience likes pretzels but has been given medical advice to cut back on the intake of salt, then a message for a low salt pretzel may evoke high and not low involvement. Naturally, research will tell the advertiser just what the degree of involvement is. If it's high, as in the case of pretzels and low salt, then the advertiser may not have to work as hard to grab attention and create liking and preference. But, if it's low, then the advertiser may have to work at it.

The first thing to understand, then, is that the relationship of an audience to the message and advertiser is influenced by degrees of involvement. High involvement with a product may help overcome low involvement with advertising. And low involvement with a product may not. To expand this concept of involvement, consider the following situations for toothpaste.

The first thing to realize is that the toothpaste doesn't exist unless you use it. But, you are not you. You're someone else, a target audience. You're a married, working mother, 35 years old, with two children, ages 9 and 12. Your life is hectic, filled with arrangements and the meeting of deadlines. Your husband's life is equally hectic, and the two of you have divided the family responsibilities. Your responsibilities include most of the daily shopping, family health care, and balancing family finances. Now, what's important to you when it comes time to decide which brand of toothpaste to buy?

Since you're responsible for family health care and finances, you would probably give strong consideration to a toothpaste that's good for your children's teeth. And though the cost of a tube of toothpaste is relatively minimal, your degree of involvement with the product is not. The reason is children. Think about it. If you could find a toothpaste to help lower dental bills, lower your anxiety of having to make dental arrangements, and lower your grief in living through the trauma children feel when they visit the dentist, would you buy it? Consider the importance of each of these perspectives and how involving they can make your relationship with toothpaste.

So, for you as this audience, toothpaste is much more than just toothpaste. It can be lower dental bills. Less anxiety. Less trauma. And all for roughly $2.00.

Suppose, however, you were the 9-year old in the family. Then what?

Do you care much about dental bills? Do you care about dental arrangements? How about going to the dentist? Now there's a possible appeal, because there aren't many 9-year olds that any of us know who like going to the dentist. What else might be involving to you about toothpaste? Possible taste. But what about whiteness? Do 9-year olds care much about whiteness? Probably not. How about fresh breath? Again, probably not.

What happens if you change your audience again? Suppose you're a young married or single looking to get married. You're 25 years old. What's important and involving to you now about toothpaste? For instance, is the idea of fresh breath important? Probably so. Ditto for whiteness. Both would probably help make toothpaste a highly involving product for you.

One thing that should be clear from each of these examples is that the degree of involvement changes depending on who the audience is. In other words, the audience provides the meaning for the advertiser. From an advertiser's point of view, this means the creative idea carrying the message must align something important about the advertiser with that audience.

Another thing which should be clear is this: In role playing as the audience in these examples, you never really connected with the product as a tangible item. Instead, you connected with it because it did something for you. Lower dental bills, for instance. Or fresh breath and whiteness. What this means is that a key to advertising messages is how well they promise the right thing to an audience. This promise is what we have termed the benefit.[9] And it can be stretched. For example, perhaps you connected with what lower dental bills could give you. A trip to Hawaii, for instance. Or you connected with what taste could give you. Candy. Or with what fresh breath could give you. Closeness.

In other words, people don't buy things. They buy solutions to their problems or the filling of their needs and wants. And those problems, needs, and wants determine to a great extent the degree of involvement audiences have with specific messages and advertisers.

AUDIENCES NEED AND WANT SOMETHING GREATER THAN WHAT THEY MUST GIVE UP IN RETURN

Pardon this intrusion, but allow me to relate an anecdote to you straight from the classroom.

I once had a student who successfully demonstrated that he understood all of the concepts we've discussed in this chapter. Then he went on to other classes the next semester. As it turned out, this same student asked me if he could make an announcement to my new class. No problem. He showed up as class was beginning and proceeded to ask for a single volunteer to help a student organization call a list of students and remind them to attend a special dinner being held on campus over the weekend. There were no volunteers. What we're now discussing is the answer to why he had no volunteers.

I stepped outside with the student and asked him if he remembered some of the things he had learned the previous semester. He assured me he did. Then I asked him if he remembered that in order to persuade someone of something, you had to offer something greater than what had to be lost or given up in return. He thought about that and stepped back into the classroom. Here's what he said next.

"I'd like volunteers to call students and remind them of the dinner." Now, there weren't any volunteers at this point, but there were some questions. And the reason is that he lowered what had to be lost or given up. No longer, was one volunteer needed. Now it was plural, and for the students that translated into less work, less effort. What he still lacked, however, was a benefit. He included it in what he said next to the class.

"If I have three or four volunteers, then each of you will only have to make ten calls each. If you do, I think I can save you half-price on the dinner ticket. If you're interested, that will save you about seven dollars."

Within a minute he had his volunteers. And the reason, quite simply, is that he increased the positive and decreased the negative. He increased the reward, a benefit, and decreased what had to be lost or given up in order to get it.[10]

Now, if that student were talking to a group of business executives, this same message probably wouldn't work. There would be relatively low involvement, assuming of course that a savings of seven dollars lacked importance. But, if he offered to include company names in a program or to somehow single out the executives for their time and effort, then he might have something.

In all likelihood, this is why headlines such as "Corns gone in 5 days or your money back" are so successful and enduring.[11] The message is tailored to the audience, those with corns. This makes the message relevant. And it makes the benefit needed. Plus, through the money back guarantee, it reduces what has to be lost or given up in order to receive the benefit.

There may well be no more important directive in this book than to create ideas offering benefits that outweigh what has to be given up to get them. Of course, it's not quite as simple to do as it sounds. As the audience changes, so does the relative importance of one benefit over another. Similarly, the involvement of what is to be lost or given up also changes. The point then is to identify which benefits and losses are important and involving to an advertiser's specific target audience.

IN A NUTSHELL

When you generate advertising ideas, there should be a re-creation of a map in your head. This map should direct you to one idea or another. The conceptualization of this map begins with this chapter. When it comes time for being creative, the map should be there reminding you of what it is you're looking for in the way of creative ideas.

With the principles of communication, persuasion, audience involvement, and benefits as a means for charting your way toward those ideas, what remains is for you to construct your map. That is the purpose of our next chapter. It proposes a Creative Prep Sheet and Creative Plan, the guide and map you need to isolate key thematic directions for your ideas. This past chapter, however, is at the core of that prep sheet and plan. As a creative individual, you need to have the concepts and principles we have discussed on call and ready to be used. In a way, these concepts and principles act as rudders for your creativity. And though they may seem to be out of view simply because they're in the back of your mind, you should always be aware of their importance.

6
A GUIDE AND MAP FOR IDEA GENERATION

Your basic understanding of communication and persuasion provides you with direction for your creativity. It also provides you with the information and perspectives needed to formulate a Creative Prep Sheet and Creative Plan. The prep sheet and plan are concise documents acting as a guideline and map when you enter idea generation.

Many times in an advertising agency setting, the core of information for both your prep sheet and plan will be arranged and formalized by others, then given to you as directives. As such, they will acquaint you with the strategic limitations you can expect to encounter during idea generation.

THE CREATIVE PREP SHEET

The Creative Prep Sheet is a six-part description of your target audience. Recall from the last chapter how primary that audience is when you're concerned about creative ideas based on the principles of communication and persuasion. Without that audience there is no sender or advertiser, no message, no medium, no attention, no liking. There is nothing. So, the audience is central when you prime yourself for idea generation. For you to know that audience, really know that audience, is an absolute necessity.

To help sort out your knowledge of the target audience, you need to formalize what research tells you. You need to get it down in black and white for easy reference. With this in mind, let's look at Figure 6–1, the Creative Prep Sheet, with its six-part description of the target audience.

Part 1

The first part of a target audience description contains four general categories—demographics, psychographics, behavioristics, and geographics.

Demographics pertain to commonly known and somewhat linear audience characteristics such as age and sex. Psychographics pertain to the audience's values, attitudes, and lifestyles. Behavioristics pertain to how the audience behaves toward a product class or brand. And geographics pertain to where the audience can be found.

When you consider your target audience, it's not enough to concern

FIGURE 6-1 Creative Prep Sheet

Advertiser: ______________________

Part 1
Demographics: Psychographics:
Behavioristics: Geographics:

Part 2 - Involvement	H	M	L
Media type ______	______	______	______
Media context ______	______	______	______
Comp. Theme/ Idea ______	______	______	______
Your Theme/Idea ______	______	______	______
Features ______	______	______	______
Selling points ______	______	______	______
Benefits/Problem Solutions ______	______	______	______

Part 3 - Persuasion	Att.	Comp.	Like	Pref.	Act
Competition ______	______	______	______	______	______
Your brand ______	______	______	______	______	

Part 4 - Behavioristics

	Buy	Use	Other
How?	______,	______,	______
Where?	______,	______,	______
When?	______,	______,	______
Why?	______,	______,	______

Part 5 - Problems
1. ______________________. 2. ______________________

Part 6 - Consumer Profile
Hello, my name is ______________________

yourself with just one or two of these categories. You need to consider all of them together in order to gain a well-rounded view of that audience. If you consider them independently or alone, you'll find they're limited and insufficient. This can be seen clearly with the limitations inherent to demographics.

In her book on creative strategy, Sandra Moriarty refers to demographic limitations by citing an example from John O'Toole. O'Toole once gave a demographic profile of two women. Demographically, the two women were basically the same: roughly the same age, same backgrounds, and so on. The two women, however, were Tricia Nixon Cox, former Republican President Nixon's daughter, and Grace Slick, rock star of the then Jefferson Airplane.[1] Talk about difference! Yet, a demographic description wasn't enough to point out that difference. More was needed, and that's where psychographics comes into play.

Psychographics refer to the values, attitudes, and lifestyles of the audience. Derived from the VALS system conceptualized at the Stanford Research Institute, psychographics probe beneath the surface layers of demographic patterns and provide us with more of a psychological insight into a target audience.[2]

According to the VALS system, people can be given descriptive titles dividing them into fundamental groups. Recently having undergone a bit of an updating and transformation. VALS uses titles such as belongers or achievers to describe the various groups. On your prep sheet, you are urged to include the VALS terminology but also to include your own descriptions of your audience types. For example, if your audience is comprised of belongers, you may be inclined to include other descriptions such as socializers or partiers. If your audience is comprised of I-am-Me's, then you may include descriptions such as experimenters, individualists, or experientials. Whatever the case, psychographic descriptions are single titles or terms seeking to describe your audience from an attitudinal, psychological, or even emotional point of view.

A third basic way to describe an audience is behavioristics. Behavioristics refer to the ways an audience behaves toward a product class and brand. Generally, these can be organized according to the audience's roles in buying, using, influencing, or decision making. Indeed, the audience's behavior changes according to changes in these behavioral roles.

You can see how these changes influence theme and creative idea decisions by referring back to our discussion of toothpastes in the last chapter. Remember that you were asked to role play as a mother with family health and financial responsiblities. When it came time for you to make a decision in selecting a toothpaste, you made it based on your roles as buyer and decision maker more than on your role as user. And your roles were given meaning and definition according to your children, particularly their dental health. Obviously, then, a message focused on maintaining their dental health would be espcially relevant to you as a mother.

As with most anything else, the further you get into behavioristics, the more complex it can become. For instance, each of the roles can be expanded. You can have heavy buyers, moderate buyers, light buyers, or nonbuyers. In addition, the ways the roles work can also be expanded. For example, you can have impulsive buying, habitual buying, or extended-purchase buying. The key, however, is for you to identify the major roles and to state them briefly and concisely on your prep sheet.

The fourth category for describing an audience is geographics, the most self-explanatory of the categories. Quite simply, a geographic description tells you where the audience can be found. This can be a national, regional, or even local description.

At this point, all of this may seem like a tremendous amount of information to include in what amounts to a relatively small amount of space on your prep sheet. Bear this in mind, however; in working up your prep sheet, you're using key and select terms which are often single words or fragments. In effect, you're discriminating between what's relevant and irrelevant, and you're highlighting the relevance by condensing the information.

Part 2

As with Part 1 of the prep sheet, Part 2 can also be completed in a relatively small amount of space. Using a scale, assessments of the audience's degrees of involvement with assorted variables can be checked off and stored in your mind as you work your way through the incubation and illumination stages of the creative process.

The variables to be assessed in terms of involvement are derived from three main sources—the communication model we discussed in the last chapter, your key theme, and a list of appropriate features, selling points, and benefits. In addition, the variables follow our path of retreat from receiver to media to message to sender. There are seven variables, each of which can be designated as evoking high, medium, or low involvement. The variables are media type, media context, competitor's current theme and idea, your advertiser's current theme and idea, and the key features selling points, and benefits of your advertiser.

Media type refers to where the advertising will be seen or heard. This can include specific magazines, television channels, or even shows.

Media context refers to the environment in which the message will be seen or heard. It relates to what surrounds the message. For example, will the message be seen on the sports page? The fashion page? Late night before going to sleep? Early morning while driving? Here, both a physical and time context may be noted.

Both your competitor's and advertiser's existing themes and ideas refer to those currently being used in their respective advertising. This can be a one-line description for each theme and idea. For example, for Pepsi you might refer to the theme as "being included in a new generation." The idea might be "use rock star associations to symbolize a new generation."

The features, selling points, and benefits depend on what research determines is involving about your advertiser. But again, you can simply check off the degrees of involvement your audience has toward those key terms. Recall, though, that features are the physical characteristics of an advertiser. Selling points are what the features give an audience. And benefits are what those selling points mean to an audience.

More than likely, as a copywriter or artist, you will be given the specific features, selling points, and benefits to include in your creative idea. What you need to do prior to idea generation, however, is make certain you've isolated and highlighted those which are the most important, the most involving. Again, your goal here is to condense and highlight. Then, by referring to your checklist, you can both generate and select appropriate creative ideas.

Part 3

Part 3 of the prep sheet includes placement of the audience on the persuasion steps relevant to your main competition and your advertiser, especially in terms of key themes. After you make assessments along these steps, you will be able to see important relationships at a glance. Of course, you are again dependent on research for providing you with the information needed to make those assessments.

Part 4

Part 4 of the prep sheet is an elaboration of behavioristics as discussed in Part 1. Recall that behavioristics include the ways an audience behaves toward a product, namely buying, using, influencing, and decision making. In Part 4, we're mostly concerned with buying and using.

Unlike Parts 2 and 3 of the prep sheet, Part 4 requires more than just checking off a range of answers. Here, you briefly describe how, where, when, and why your advertiser is bought and used. As always, of course, you're encouraged to use single words, terms, or fragments. This is not an essay you're writing. It's a prep sheet, a work sheet. It's meant to be concise, abbreviated. In fact, use abbreviations when appropriate.

In describing how your product (your advertiser) is bought, refer to impulsive, habitual, or extended buys. These are the three main ways we make purchases.[3] Impulsive and habitual buys are self-explanatory. The extended buy is not. It means we think about our purchase before we make it.

In describing where the product is bought, isolate actual places such as stores or over the telephone. The same holds true for isolating specific times in referring to when the product is bought. Of course, time can be a season, month, week, day, or even an hour.

In describing why the product is bought, you may need to elaborate a bit. And certainly, consideration of a key benefit and perhaps your theme will be important here.

You should repeat all the questions when considering the use of the product. Again, simplicity and conciseness are critical. In essence, though, you're answering how, where, when, and why the product is used.

Part 5

Part 5 of the prep sheet is concise statements of the major problems the audience has toward your product. This part refers back to our previous chapter's discussion regarding what the audience must expect to lose or give up in order to receive something. Remember, it's important to give something more than what will be lost or given up in return.

Part 6

The final part of the prep sheet is also the longest, at least as far as your writing is concerned. Here, you write a consumer profile of your audience. The profile should range from 100 to 200 words. It's a narrative told in the first person from a composite audience member's point of view.

When you ultimately generate and select your creative ideas, it's important to realize that your message must appeal to one individual at a time. This can be a difficult concept to understand since we assume that thousands, perhaps millions, of people are exposed to our ads. This is true, of course. But, it's also a bit misleading. The fact of the matter is that an advertising message is seen or heard by one person at a time. When you create an ad, you should create it for an audience so personalized in your mind that you can actually see and feel an individual. And that individual is your composite audience member.

In creating the consumer profile, you give flesh and blood to an otherwise lifeless entity. In addition, you step into that flesh and blood. You become the person, and the person becomes you. This is why you write the profile from the first person. "I," point of view. Throughout the profile you refer to me, mine, my. But, it's not you as you. It's you as the composite audience member.

It's also important to give yourself a name, a Q-name, a name relevant to your relationship with the theme, benefit, or advertiser. For instance, if you're the mom buying toothpaste for her family, then your name may be Fran Family Health.

You begin your profile with "My name is _____" and proceed to construct a narrative that focuses on the major concerns and insights found in Parts 1 through 5 of your prep sheet.

In their influential book, *Advertising Writing*, W. Keith Hafer and Gordon E. White suggest just this device of a profile as part of creative strategy development. Termed the "Personal Profile," Hafer and White's suggestion is used in the context of strategy development for Weight Watchers dinners. A Clara Wolkoff (no Q-name here) tells her story in a narrative, a closing excerpt for which goes as follows: [4]

> But I can stick with celery, lettuce, and carrots just so long. Then some scrumptious, forbidden dish is put in front of me . . . and I'm sunk. I cheat for a few glorious minutes. Then I feel guilty for hours and days. Like as not, I'll abandon that particular diet completely. Until I take another solemn vow to lose weight. It's rough. And that's been the pattern for several years now. Ladies and gentlemen, I need help. (p. 5)

Clearly, you can see the essence of Clara's problem and what's needed to solve that problem. If only she could have a scrumptious dish that weren't so fattening and loaded with guilt. Hafer and White then show an ad for Weight Watchers Frozen Meals. The headline for the ad is "Lasagna without Guilt.

CREATIVE PREP SHEET OVERVIEW

Your Creative Prep Sheet is a means for you to keep you in touch with your audience. It's a work sheet for increasing the scope of your knowledge in preparation for idea generation. It can be stretched or shrunk to fit your needs. By all means, however, it should be concise and abbreviated.

The key elements to the prep sheet are highlighted in six parts. Part 1 describes your audience's demographics, psychographics, behavioristics, and geographics. Part 2 assesses the degrees of involvement your audience has with a number of variables such as media type and context. Part 3 locates key themes and benefits of your competition and advertiser along the persuasion steps. Part 4 elaborates the buyer and user roles from behavioristics. Part 5 lists the major problems your audience has in relationship to your advertiser. And Part 6 rounds out a view of your audience by means of a first-person narrative.

As a working model, the prep sheet gives you a direction for formalizing a Creative Plan. It also gives you a kind of nutritional energy on which to rely when it comes time for finding creative ideas. As you mull the information and perspectives from your prep sheet over in your mind, they will tend to be absorbed. And though they may recede, they won't disappear. They will always have influence on your creative output.

VARIATIONS OF CREATIVE PLANS

Like your Creative Prep Sheet, your Creative Plan is a concise, formalized series of observations and statements outlining the major considerations guiding your search for a creative idea. Parts of that outline are derived exclusively from the information in your prep sheet. Unlike the prep sheet, however, the Creative Plan frames in the strategy and tactics for your ad. The strategy states what message you will convey in the ad. It deals with the ad's matter, it's theme. The tactics tell you how you should present that theme. They deal with the ad's manner, it's creative idea. Both the strategy and tactics are then synthesized into a brief positioning objective.

You should remember, too, that you're not reading a book here on developing a creative strategy or plan. You can refer to a number of other books for such guidance. This book is more intent on sparking creativity. Still, a large part of being creative is knowing the importance of planning and preparation. If you think creative people are unorganized or unprepared, think again. They're not. Their ideas may stem from flights of imaginative fancy or even chaos. But, creative people also carry solid reference points and organizational maps with them on those flights.

To conceptualize a format for the Creative Plan, let's look at four planning variations in Figure 6–2 with an eye keen in observing their major similarities. Then we will propose our own hybrid variation as your Creative Plan. The variations have been extracted from their contexts in thorough books devoted almost exclusively to creative strategy and planning. In their contexts within these books, the variations are surrounded by all of the considerations leading up to and following the selection of a creative idea. You should look at one or more of these books in order to gain the kind of well-rounded, comprehensive approach to planning that will only be summarized here.

Notice how the variations are strongly similar in the most important respects. In the largest sense, they emphasize the need for a formal document to act as a map for creativity. In addition, they are also dependent on objectives, strategy, and tactics. All four contain objectives. All four suggest the need for outlining a strategy, or what we have termed the theme. In the Hafer and White variation, the strategy focuses on the "principal benefit." In the Jewler variation, it focuses on the "major selling idea." In the Moriarty variation, it focuses on the "selling premise." And in the Roman and Maas variation, it focuses on the "key consumer benefit."

A somewhat similar situation exists for tactics, the answer to how your advertising will present the theme. For example, Roman and Maas's tone statement focuses on the manner of the advertising. It's meant to describe the ad's personality. For Moriarty, the execution statement also refers to the manner of the advertising.

FIGURE 6-2   Variations of a Creative Plan

—From W. Keith Hafer and Gordon E. White, *Advertising Writing: Putting Creative Strategy to Work*, 2nd ed. (St. Paul, Minnesota: West Publishing Co., 1982), pp. 3–4.

SIMPLIFIED CREATIVE STRATEGY: Principal Benefit, Principal Target, Principal Objective, Strategy Statement.

—From A. Jerome Jewler. *Creative Strategy in Advertising.* 2nd ed. (Belmont, California: Wadsworth Publishing Company, 1985), pp. 26–37.

CREATIVE PLATFORM: Objectives, Target Audience, Major Selling Idea, Other Usable Benefits, Creative Strategy.

—From Sandra E. Moriarty, *Creative Advertising: Theory and Practice* (Englewood Cliffs, N.J.: Prentice-Hall, 1986), p. 84.

COPY PLATFORM: Advertising Problem, Advertising Objectives, Product's Distinctive Feature, Target Audience, Competition, Position, Message Strategy (including execution and supporting copy points).

—From Kenneth Roman and Jane Maas, *How to Advertise* (New York: St. Martin's Press, 1976), p. 3.

FIVE STRATEGY CONSIDERATIONS: Objective, Target Audience, Key Consumer Benefit, Support, Tone.

What you have then with these four variations is a composite of creative plans focusing on objective, strategy, and tactics. The objective answers what you seek to accomplish with your advertising. The strategy tells you what you will convey to accomplish it. It's the matter, the theme of your ad. And the tactics tell you how you should present the theme. Tactics are the manner, the creative idea itself.

With these four variations in mind, let's move on to the outline and criteria needed for your creative plan, a large part of which is adapted from the variations. Don't be intimidated, however. The plan is very concise and to the point. In fact, when finished, it takes up all of one page. Simple. Concise. To the point.

THE CREATIVE PLAN

The Creative Plan is divided into four main parts: target audience, strategy/theme, tactics/idea, and positioning objective. You can see how the parts are outlined in Figure 6–3. You can also see how brevity is encouraged since the entire plan fits on one side of a piece of a paper.

FIGURE 6-3 The Creative Plan

TARGET AUDIENCE

Demographics: Psychographics:

Behavioristics: Geographics:

STRATEGY/THEME

1. We should convey _____

2. The theme will appeal to the audience's _____

3. The theme will reduce the audience's _____

TACTICS/IDEA

1. The creative idea should convey to the audience that _____

_____

2. Our creative idea should be _____

3. Our creative idea should present the following copy points: _____

_____

4. Our creative idea is _____

POSITIONING OBJECTIVE

To position _____

Target Audience

The first part of the Creative Plan is designed to keep you focused on your target audience. Here, you simply repeat the key information logged in Part 1 of your prep sheet. This means you use terms and fragments to describe the audience from four perspectives: demographics, psychographics, behavioristics, and geographics.

Strategy/Theme

The second part of the plan is vital since it acts as your guide for what theme or message will be conveyed. This part is also simple, though what it tells you is extremely important. It's simple because you complete three short statements. And it's important because it tells you exactly what the theme is you want conveyed to your audience. Clearly, if the theme is wrong and irrelevant, then the advertising is wrong and irrelevant.

You complete statement 1 by briefly describing the theme. Completion of statements 2 and 3 will help you make certain the theme is right and relevant. Here, you will be matching the theme with the audience's need (statement 2) and problem (statement 3). The three statements are as fol-lows:

1. We should convey _____ (state theme) _____
2. The theme will appeal to the audience's _ (state need) _____
3. The theme will reduce the audience's ___ (state problem) _____

Obviously, all of your answers to the statements will be dependent on what research tells you. This means your research findings need to be accu-rate and perceptive. But once the important points are determined and conclusions are made through research, this 3-part section will act as a map for your creativity.

Think back to some of the creative advertising ideas we've discussed to this point. Recall, for instance, the enduring Maytag campaign with the lonely Maytag repairman. Recall the creative ideas for Parkay, Federal Ex-press, and Charmin. If you analyze each of those creative ideas, you can see how easily the Strategy/Theme statements can be completed. Let's apply the statements to each of those ideas and see how this part of the Creative Plan should work.

For Maytag, the theme is that Maytag machines are durable and reliable (statement 1). This will appeal to the audience's need for reliability when it comes time for doing the washing and drying (statement 2). The theme will also reduce the audience's fear that washers and dryers tend to break down (statement 3).

For Parkay, the theme is that Parkay Margarine tastes like butter. This will appeal to the audience's need for a margarine with a buttery taste. The theme will reduce the audience's dislike of margarine because it doesn't taste like butter.

For Federal Express, the theme is that Federal Express will deliver im-portant packages and mail fast and reliably. This will appeal to the audience's need to have packages and mail delivered fast and on time. The theme will reduce the audience's fear that delivery of important packages and mail is uncertain in terms of time.

For Charmin, the theme is that Charmin bathroom tissue is squeezably soft. This will appeal to the audience's need for gentle caring of her family. The theme will reduce the audience's belief that all bathroom tissues are basically the same.

Regardless of how diverse these advertisers are, notice how the themes for each tend to convey what's important and perhaps different about the products and services, especially as they relate to certain target audiences. For example, washer and dryer durability and reliability are of prime im-portance to a mother or father who is responsible for keeping family clothes clean. Lack of a buttery taste is enough to keep "butter believers" from using margarine. Speed of delivery is of prime importance to a businessman or woman whose job success often depends on the timely receiving or sending of packages. And, if a certain brand of bathroom tissue is softer than others and can help make bathroom duties gentler and more pleasant for a family, then it may be worth a try.

Notice, too, how the Strategy/Theme part of the plan has nothing to say about actual presentation of the theme. It doesn't deal with manner at all. That, of course, is reserved for the third part, Tactics/Idea.

Tactics/Idea

Like the Strategy/Theme part of your plan, this part includes a series of statement completions. You should understand, however, that since the generation of creative ideas follows the development of the plan, the final statement can be completed only after you've generated and then selected your creative idea. Still, the initial statements can be completed, and they will act as guides for your creativity.

1. The creative idea should communicate to the audience that ___ (restate theme) _____
2. Our creative idea should be _____ (state tone or personality) _____
3. Our creative idea should present the following copy points: _____ (state the key features, selling points, and/or benefits and relevant data or perspectives) _____
4. Our creative idea is _____

In order to keep you on track and singleminded with your creative idea, the first statement is completed by simply restating the theme from statement 1 of the Strategy/Theme part of the plan.

Like tone in the Roman and Maas variation of a creative plan, the second statement should be completed with three to six adjectives describing your ad idea's personality. Personality refers to the idea's flavor, feel, or mood. Some ideas are cheery, lighthearted, bright, and outgoing. Other ideas may be serious, straightforward, formal, and dignified. With statement 2 you describe the idea's personality in the same way you would describe an individual's personality.

Statement 3 is completed by listing the key copy points to be used in the ad. There is a wide range of possibilities here, and you should expect to include a quantity of points since they will serve to substantiate or support both the theme and the idea. For example, you may list key features, selling points, and/or benefits. You may also list other known and relevant facts or perspectives such as testimonials, test results, demonstrations, or guarantees.

Completion of the final statement will depend on what you select as a creative idea after you generate a large number of idea possibilities. Part III of this book is devoted exclusively to the techniques you can use to generate ideas. After you generate, you then select, and that idea you select is described in statement 4.

As we did with the Strategy/Tactics part of the plan, let's go back to the four creative ideas for Maytag, Parkay, Federal Express, and Charmin and complete the statements. Once again, you should notice how concise and direct the statement completions should be.

With Maytag, we've said the theme is the durability and reliability of the machines. That's what the creative idea should communicate (statement 1). The tone or personality of the idea is lighthearted, personal, sympathetic, and easy-going (statement 2). The main copy points will center on history of product use and how the durability eases worry and care of the audience (statement 3). The creative idea is to use the personification of a lonely repairman to suggest product durability and reliability (statement 4).

With Parkay, the theme is buttery taste. The tone is humorous, exaggerated, whimsical, and homey. The main copy points might be texture, color, or taste tests. The creative idea is to use an association of the product with butter by having the margarine speak "butter's" name.

For Federal Express, the theme is fast and reliable delivery. The tone is humorous, exaggerated, surreal, and fast-paced. The main copy points might be speed, resolution of the target audience's dilemma, and the means and promise for delivery. The creative idea is to use fast as an opposite of how people and machines speak and move.

For Charmin, the theme is squeezably soft. The tone is lighthearted, whimsical, personal, and social. The main copy points might be squeezability, softness, demonstration, and packaging. The creative idea is to use a slice-of-life situation involving a memorable character to demonstrate the product's squeezability.

Once again, notice how concise the completions are. Notice, too, how they bend to the themes of the various ideas. You should also notice how the descriptions of the ideas are summary statements. They go to the heart of the ideas to describe them. In this way, they capture the essence of the ideas.

Overall, as you rethink the Creative Plan's parts on strategy and tactics, remember to note how the themes and ideas we've discussed tend to boil down to single words or perhaps a few words. Durability and reliability for Maytag, for instance. Or squeezability and softness for Charmin. This is an important consideration before you head into idea generation because what you're after are ideas that adhere to ADNORMS, two important criteria for which are oneness and simplicity. Indeed, as you think about other creative advertising ideas, you may find that you can boil them down to a few simple words.

As final considerations, remember how the creative ideas present the themes in very unique ways and how, for all intents and purposes, they are the themes. And, remember the core of all creative advertising ideas which is to have newness and relevance bound together. What the plan should come down to, then, is a kind of narrowing process, one which focuses closely on the key theme to be presented in a certain manner.

Positioning Objective

Once again, you can go to many books to find a wealth of informative direction on how to write marketing and advertising objectives. A solid advertising plan or proposal contains both kinds. And no doubt, you will be given these before you actually begin to generate ideas. What you're concerned with in this final part of your Creative Plan, however, is the writing of a different type of objective, one we will call a positioning objective. Your goal with this type of objective is to write a single, concise statement summarizing your target audience and theme. In effect, this objective summarizes the conclusions in your statement completions and tells you the two most important considerations to remember as you begin idea generation.

You can begin your positioning objective with the words, "To position," followed by your theme, the main message you want positioned in the mind of your target audience. In the Charmin case, for example, your positioning objective might begin with, "To position Charmin bathroom tissue as squeezably soft. . . . " The next part of the objective specifies your target audience. For Charmin, the complete positioning objective might read as follows: "To position Charmin bathroom tissue as squeezably soft in the mind of a middle class homemaker."

Overall, this positioning objective states what you intend to achieve with your creative idea as it connects with your target audience. In this respect, you want your audience to remember something about your ad. That means you want something to stick in the audience's mind. And what should stick is your theme, your main message.

FROM CHAPTER FOUR TO CHAPTER SIX

For you, this chapter should be a transition between Chapters Four and Five and those that follow.

From Chapter Four you should gain a general understanding of what constitutes creative advertising ideas. They present themes. They possess newness and relevance. They exemplify the act of connection. And they abide by ADNORMS.

From Chapter Five you should gain a general understanding of communication and persuasion. Moreover, you should be aware of the importance of the target audience to both. Without the audience, communication and persuasion don't exist.

From this chapter you should gain an understanding of how your knowledge of the variables in communication and persuasion can be documented and made available for use. The proposed prep sheet and plan are recommended as a guide and map for keeping your creativity on course. They represent the culmination of the preparation stage in the creative process. As such, they give you the information and insights needed to chart your waters during your finding of creative ideas. In a large sense, they become the starting point of your idea generation.

With the prep sheet, you're developing a singleminded focus on your target audience. It should be an intense and clear focus, one that eventually leads you inside the head and heart of that audience.

With the Creative Plan, you're shifting from your audience and moving into the strategy and tactics that will guide your creativity. Notice how the plan asks you to repeat the theme three times. You state it in Strategy/Theme, then again in Tactics/Idea, and finally as part of your Positioning Objective. There can be no mistaking what it should be, and everything - idea, copy, art - should bend to that theme.

With the information from your preparation stage on call, your task from this point is to use that information to play your way through the incubation and illumination stages of the creative process. Unlike these past few chapters, however, those that follow are focused more on creativity and your means for actualizing your creative potential. As a group, the upcoming chapters return us to Part I, with its emphasis on the creative temperament and the means for being creative.

As you move through Part III, you will be exposed to a number of techniques for generating creative ideas. The techniques are toys for your creativity. They're meant to be fun. So have fun playing with them. But as you play, remember to keep part of your mind in touch with something else. Remember to keep in touch with what it is you're going to find. And what you're going to find is inseparable from the chapters we're now leaving.

7

IDEA GENERATION: FINDING THE CREATIVE YOU

Working through your prep sheet and plan will give you direction for your ideas. But what it won't do is help you find the creative you, at least not directly. What you need instead are certain means for doing that, for pushing front and center that part of all of us which is creative. Often, these means are mental and emotional states, such as we discussed in Chapter Two regarding will and belief. Sometimes they're more physical, such as an individualized record-keeping system. And whether they're mental, emotional, or physical, they require conditioning, discipline, and practice.

Finding the creative you is essential during the incubation stage of the creative process. As you recall, since everyone's different, everyone incubates in very different, perhaps even eccentric, ways. Some press. Some let go. Some need the morning. Some need the night. On top of that, the incubation stage overall is an odd mixture of opposite feelings. At times you're up. At other times you're down. At times you're relaxed. At other times you're anxious and nervous.

For us, coping with these opposite feelings is a matter of developing a headstrong belief in balance. That's the prescription here. Balance.

Balance means feel relaxed. Balance also means don't *always* feel relaxed. Balance means feel anxious and nervous. It also means don't *always* feel anxious and nervous. It means expect to experience those feelings, just don't get inescapably caught in one extreme or the other. Don't always feel up. Don't always feel down. Don't always feel involved. Don't always feel detached.

Sounds easy, doesn't it? Of course, it's not. Well, then, how do you do it?

Go with the Flow

Remember when we talked about giving birth and the creative process in Chapter Two? We said there were pain and anxiety involved. They were part of life, part of creativity. We certainly can't hide from pain and anxiety, but we can cope with them better if we believe they're inevitable and necessary. We can even convince ourselves that without pain and anxiety, we couldn't possibly enjoy the birth of a new life or, for that matter, a new idea. Part of their beauty, their creativity, is that both they and we have overcome pain and anxiety.

Think of it like this. We couldn't be creative unless we were able to project ourselves into both positive and negative states of mind. For instance, how can we know what bothers a consumer (the problem we seek to eliminate) if we don't feel the bother? How can we possibly understand the value of dollars to a consumer who doesn't have many if we ourselves have always had plenty? We may pretend that we know and understand. But do we really?

The message in all of us is that feeling rich involves growing from the despair of feeling poor. Or, feeling happy involves growing from the heartbreak of feeling sad. And, feeling creative involves growing from the disappointment of feeling uncreative.

It is a common contention that one of the characteristics peculiar to creative individuals is their ability to unify apparent opposites, to reconcile those things that appear to be irreconcilable with one another.[1] In creativity research, this ability is often referred to as Janusian thinking, named after the Roman god who had the ability to look simultaneously in opposite directions.[2] Curiously, advertising creativity research has also pointed to this ability, particularly in terms of how it is exemplified in award-winning headlines such as "Looks wet when it's dry."[3]

For the creative mind, there can be beauty in ugliness and ugliness in beauty. Richness in poverty. And poverty in richness. Each suggests and gives meaning to the other. They are interdependent, and the creative mind reconciles their harmonious co-existence as part of the balance of life.

This is what is meant by balance. You should believe that all of your feelings during the incubation stage are simply part of the cosmic, creative whole, regardless of how much they seem at odds with one another at the time. And the reason you should believe it is that if you don't, there's a chance you'll get caught in one extreme or the other. Too much of that, by the way, can be detrimental to your creative health.

In many ways, what is being prescribed here is that you go with the flow and make it work for you. In down periods, review. Look over your prep sheet and plan. Or take a break. Do some exercise. Forget your prep sheet and plan. In up periods, go at it. Energize and produce. In other words, where your inner light is guiding you, go. And go while maintaining the faith that what you're experiencing is part of everyone's rite of passage into the creative world.

Much of what we will discuss in this chapter is centered on this kind of acceptance and openness to what the incubation stage has in store for you. Much of that stage is mental and emotional, a kind of ebb and flow to your feelings. Some of it is more physical. And all of it will remind you of our first three chapters, especially in terms of your ability to connect. In finding the creative you, you must connect yourself with the flow, regardless of whether it's smooth and easy or rough and hard.

To help when going with the flow feels threatened, when you begin to have doubts, when connecting opposing forces seems impossible, perhaps you should keep this sage Egyptian piece of wisdom in mind: "The archer hitteth the mark, partly by pulling, partly by letting go."[4]

THE CREATIVE TEMPERAMENT

A vital part of what we have just discussed about going with the flow is the belief that even when you feel down, you're confident you'll eventually feel up. You know the negative state is transient. It will move on and be replaced by something positive. More often than not, that something positive is your creative inspiration.

The problem here is that advertising is a business of deadlines. You don't have the time to wait things out. So, when the creative muse is on vacation, you can't afford to curl up and wait for its return. You need to do something to hasten that return. The idea-generation techniques starting with our next chapter will help you in that regard. Since "being" comes before "doing," however, you must first be and feel positive and creative.[5] You must be confident, bold, independent, and assertive. And, you must feel a certain temperament, a creative temperament. Further, to be and feel positive and creative, you must believe in certain things. More than that, you must believe in them to the point of living them.

It's certainly difficult to talk about a temperament and belief in definitive terms. Often, these are individual matters. This makes them somewhat relative and abstract. Still, here's a quick look at some possibllities you may want to consider. Embrace some. Challenge others. That's up to you. But bear in mind that these possibilities, these foundations for your temperament and beliefs, stem from researchers and theorists devoted to pursuing this whole business of creativity.

Lack of Fear

In his book, *The Creative Mystique*, John Kiel cites "fear—thus impotence" as a major cause of advertising's lack of creativity.[6] Fear, though, is a state of mind that can be dealt with if we condition ourselves to do so. To deal with it, however, we need to identify where it originates. We know it's revealed in us, but what are the sources? Often, those sources are outside of us. Let's identify several.

Others: Authoritative others. Negative others. Restrictive others. Critical others. Those who seem to have it in for us. Those who squelch who and what we are. Those who can't live with difference. But you should. Remember, you're tolerant and flexible.

Connect with something positive about those others. Look for common ground. Try it their way. You might find it's not so bad after all. Empathize with them. Remember, as a creative individual you're empathic. Use it. If you decide there's just no other way, avoid these others. If you can't, nod in agreement and consider doing it your way, anyway.

Finally, you may want to consider this. If you're getting a great deal of flack, maybe you don't belong where you are in the first place. Maybe it's time to find a place among others where you do belong. This is a very big country that in the truest democratic sense allows for differences. Search around. Remember, if you're young, chances are you have relatively little. So you have relatively little to lose.

Evaluations: Usually from those others. Usually in the form of critiques, peer and job reviews, and grades. These are the storms we talked about in our first few chapters. Very real. Sometimes very unavoidable. As we noted in our description of the creative personality, however, creative individuals use their own internal locus of evaluation. This means that when push comes to shove, it's your evaluation, your view, that matters the most.

You may have to compromise along the way. Everyone does. And you do want to keep an open ear and mind to constructive criticisms passed your way. They can help your creative abilities grow. Ultimately, however, you are the most important evaluator.

Perhaps more than anything else, this internal locus of evaluation circles back to our discussion of will and belief in Chapter Two. Recall that having the will goes a long way to fulfilling the creative vision. Further, the will stems from the belief in that vision. All-consuming and singleminded. The belief, too, can grow into a callous or shield to protect your confidence. Take writers, for instance.

All writers worth their salt could probably paper their walls with rejection slips. In spite of that rejection, however, they persist. The same holds true for advertising copywriters and artists. Each has crowded files of rejected ad ideas, many of which they continue to believe in. Yet, in spite of rejection, they continue to create. Yes, they have an ear and mind open to constructive criticism. They want to get better at what they do. Still, however, they listen to that inner voice as well, the one that urges them on to actualize their creative vision.

Institutions: As we know, institutions, whether of specific groups, corporations, ideological movements, or whatever, are very powerful. They exert considerable control over our lives. They pay us. They give us diplomas. They set the patterns for both our beliefs and behaviors. They are, in a word, powerful. As such, we must work within them. We must abide by their rules. But we must remember, too, that institutions can be stultifying to our creativity and our creative beings. Because of this, we once again need to have balance in the degree of commitment we give to those institutions.

In his important article, "Conformity and Creative Thinking," Richard S. Crutchfield notes that the independent thinker is one who strikes a "balance between self-reliance and group identifications."[7] Once again, not too much of one or the other. As it pertains to the creative individual's relationship to institutions, rigid adherence to their norms can lead to convergence or what has been termed a "strain toward uniformity."[8] This strain toward uniformity is the reverse of what creativity is generally considered to be. Creativity is divergence, especially from the norm. The opposite of creativity is convergence toward that norm.[9]

Within a group, there is immediate pressure to conform, to converge. Without a group, that pressure tends to be less. In his book, *Groups: Interaction and Performance*, Joseph McGrath points out that "individuals working separately generate many more and more creative (as rated by judges) ideas than do groups . . . the difference is large, robust and general."[10] In advertising, David Ogilvy agrees when he writes that "in my experience, committees can criticize, but they cannot create."[11]

If McGrath and Ogilvy are right, then it's important for the creative individual to keep a kind of aloofness from the group and a wariness regarding its controlling power. Since institutions are very real, however, the aloofness and wariness need to be balanced with a realization and understanding of the necessity to function within the group's regimen of status quos.

Perhaps another way to state this problem of overcoming fear imposed by institutions is the need to formulate a belief that devotion to an institution (groups, buildings, individuals) is fine to a degree. That degree can be measured to the extent the institution allows you to pursue your own creative vision, assuming that the vision is directed toward positive goals. This means that in order to be creative, you're asked to be your own person first and the institution's person second.

Now, from our discussion of others, evaluations, and institutions, can you see the problem you have? On the one hand, you're asked to disregard them. On the other hand, you're asked to consider them. You're asked to be detached and involved simultaneously. That is a state of mind and something very difficult for which to write a prescription. One thing is certain, though. You can't exist in that state of mind unless you have the confidence to believe you can. Another thing is certain as well. That confidence ultimately comes from within. It doesn't have to be loud or abrasive. It just needs to be.

More than anything else, confidence is your primary weapon against fear. What destroys confidence comes from outside. So be wary of what's outside. If you feel the outside threatening that confidence, you need to do what you must to shield and secure it. You need to go where you find support and encouragement for your creativity. As the old song goes, you need to "accentuate the positive and eliminate the negative." Go to friends. Go to those who appreciate your work. Go to your work, your best work, and revel in it. Pat yourself on the back, Reward yourself. Research shows that positive reinforcement goes a long way toward building self-confidence.[12] Give yourself positive reinforcement for jobs well done and decisions well made. Ultimately, go to yourself. You may be your harshest critic. Chances are you may also be your most avid supporter.

Deferring Judgement

What's wrong with the following two scenarios?

One copywriter is sitting at her desk. She has completed combing through her Creative Prep Sheet and Creative Plan. She's reviewing that plan when all of a sudden an advertising idea emerges. She believes it fits well with her plan and so decides not to generate other ideas.

A second copywriter is sitting at his desk. He, too, has completed combing through the prep sheet and plan. While reviewing, an advertising idea emerges. Immediately, he decides it's wrong and will never work. So he decides to scrap it.

What's wrong with these two scenarios is that both copywriters' actions violate a cardinal principle for creative thinking, that of deferring judgment, particularly at the beginning stages of idea generation.[13] The way to defer judgment is to avoid saying "yes" or "no" to ideas as they emerge.

What tends to happen if we pass judgment too early is that blocks to future ideas spring up immediately. If we say "yes," we deny ourselves the possibility of finding a better idea. If we say "no," we deny ourselves the possibility of reshaping or rethinking initial ideas. What may seem at first glance to be a dull and unworkable idea is never allowed the opportunity to grow into an exciting and workable one.

As with many creative ideas, creative advertising ideas usually don't start out as great ideas. Instead, they may start with an image, fuzzy and incomplete as it may be. Or they may start with a word, term, or phrase that seems promising but is totally underdeveloped. Either way, they're rough and incomplete. Then gradually, over time, the creative mind molds and polishes ideas, ultimately shaping them into completion and greatness. But, they don't start out that way. They're crafted that way. If you say "yes" too quickly, you eliminate any possibility for seeing that potential greatness. If you say "no" too quickly, you eliminate any possibility for finding other ideas which have that greatness.

Quantity Yields Quality

Directly tied to the principle of deferring judgment is that of quantity yielding quality. In relationship to advertising, this means that the more ideas you can generate, the better the probability for finding a good or even great idea. Findings in advertising research tend to support this claim.[14] In this respect, you need to think laterally, not vertically.

Lateral thinking is a principle elaborated by Edward de Bono in his book *Lateral Thinking*. A guiding premise to de Bono's book is that creativity involves digging many different holes over a vast expanse of territory. The opposite of creativity is digging the same hole deeper.[15] It's also curious to note that lateral thinking can be connected to our discussion in Chapter One of being horizontal and thus more in tune with the world. In his book *Lying Down,* Marco Vassi makes just this connection.[16]

In order to produce a quantity of ideas in the hope of finding a quality idea, you need to keep all doors open for as long as your time constraints and deadlines allow. Obviously, this means deferring judgment, but it also means having many techniques available to help you generate as many ideas as possible. This is where our next few chapters will come in handy. Focused on actual idea-generation techniques, those chapters will give you the means for generating a large quantity of ideas.

Negating Yourself

It was the romantic poet, John Keats, who coined the term "negative capability."[17] He used it to describe the creative power of Shakespeare, the essence of which was Shakespeare's unique ability to become so disinterested in himself and the immediacy of his social and cultural pressures that he was able to redirect and project his imagination into his characters. In effect, it was an ability to lose himself in his characters; in other words, an ability to negate himself in favor of others.

We've discussed this concept often. Recall, for instance, the importance of empathy to the creative personality. Or the discussions of communication, persuasion, and your Creative Prep Sheet, the nucleus for which was your target audience. You were asked to role play, to become that audience, and to see all the communication and persuasion variables from the audience's point of view. In effect, you were asked to negate yourself in favor of that audience.

There is perhaps no other lifeblood characteristic so important to the advertising writer and artist than that of negative capability or empathy. Burt Manning, a Vice Chairman for the J. Walter Thompson agency, describes its importance this way: "If I'm writing to an older consumer, concerned with inflation, shrinking savings, the fear of becoming dependent on others, then I try to put myself in that position. . . . Copy should sell by an *understanding* of the people it seeks to reach."[18] Of course, if you cannot identify, truly identify and feel with and for those people, then you obviously cannot create ideas that are relevant and meaningful to them. This is why the ability to negate yourself is so important.

You should understand, too, that negating yourself isn't restricted to a kind of empathic identification with people. It can be an identification with objects or concepts as well. Erich Fromm, for instance, highlights the importance of the creative mind to become one with an object.[19] Also, if you recall our discussion of the world of realities in Chapter One, it was suggested that you be prepared to immerse yourself in that world, to make that world you and you the world. This requires losing your own identity, which, in fact, is central to the creativity technique of personal analogy in the highly successful system of Synectics.[20]

As soon as you're able to negate yourself, the world opens up. You begin to see things from many different perspectives, not just your own. You begin to feel as others feel. In one sense, you're detached. Detached from yourself, that is. In another sense, you're involved, this time with others or even things. As a result, you're more balanced with your world. It no longer revolves around you. You revolve around it, and this allows you to see it more fully and completely.

Being Alert and Ready

In their book *Creativity in Business*, Michael Ray and Rochelle Myers describe the concept of Aikido or what is termed "soft eyes."[21] These are eyes that are open but not focused. Being open, they're aware and alert. The same holds true for all the senses, which are the ways we allow the world to enter us. As the world passes by, it's allowed to enter and isn't closed off because of an arbitrary focus on one thing or another. At the same time, the eyes, or any sense organs, are capable of reacting to stimuli. They can grasp and hold when the time is right. They can exercise a form of penetrating observation. They can connect. This is what is meant by being alert and ready.

To be alert and ready means you are both detached and involved. You're detached in that you allow the world to move by, perhaps slowly, until that moment when you're ready to strike. Before that moment, however, there is no striving, no interference. You're completely open to what is passing in front of you. In his book *The Search for Satori & Creativity*, E. Paul Torrance describes at length the Japanese quest for satori, the quintessential moment, the ultimate insight.[22] It is, in essence, the "soft eyes" allowing the world to move by and then seizing the moment. They can only do so, however, because they are alert and ready.

Once again, in being alert and ready, you're asked to reconcile and connect the apparent opposites of detachment and involvement. You're asked to be passive and receptive at one moment and active and aggressive the next. Not too much of either. Again, a balance of both. If you strive too hard, you end up too focused, and you exclude other possibilities. At the same time, if you don't strive hard enough, you end up floundering helplessly in all the world has to offer. In the words of Pablo Picasso, "I do not seek—I find."[23] To seek is to strive. To find is to discover. To seek is to throw yourself into the world. To discover is to embrace the world into yourself.

As an example of how this concept relates to idea discovery in advertising, consider the case of Ed Biglow, who created a Volkswagen ad with the headline "Mass Transit." The ad showed nuns piling into a station wagon, thus the pun on the word "mass." But, Biglow knew the strategy behind the ad was centered on conveying the roominess of the car. He needed a campaign idea, a creative way of presenting that theme or message. One day he was riding down the freeway and just happened to pass a group of nuns in a car.[24] Wham! There it was. The idea. Importantly, however, he was alert and ready for it. He was open to the world around him. It entered, and he used it for discovery. That discovery was his creative connection with the world.

This important state of alertness or readiness should not, of course, be a surprise to you. Early on we discussed the creative mind's ability to use keen and penetrating observation for its discoveries. We discussed the need for creative individuals to participate and observe simultaneously. We discussed the need to create personae who step in and out as the need arises. This requires openness and flexibility. Openness and flexibility mean being alert or ready enough to use accidents, negative states, or just those everyday realities coming your way.

PREPARING FOR IDEA GENERATION

Beyond these more abstract, conceptual prerequisites for being creative, there are also those which are more concrete and definitive. As with developing mental and emotional states such as self-confidence and alertness, these more definitive prerequisites are sure to be highly customized to you as an individual. They are also easier to manipulate and control. Again, embrace those you wish. Challenge some. Discard others as you see fit. But you should at least consider the following.

Develop Rituals

Recall our discussion in Chapter One regarding the eccentricities of habits and lifestyles of creative individuals. Those eccentricities then became inseparable from the act of creating. In time, they may have even become rituals for creating. As creatures of habit, all of us tend to respond or think in certain ways because of cues which prompt our rituals. Responding and thinking creatively are no different. They, too, can be stimulated by cues leading to the rituals which prod us on to creative achievement. When they're present, they change us in some way. They alter our perspective or mood. The poet Stephen Spender sees it in just this way when he says, "The writer feels the need for a ritual in order to put him or herself into the mood for writing."[25] Naturally, both cues and their resulting rituals vary according to the individual. What's important though, is that you find and use them to enter the creative state of mind, the creative temperament.

The ritual of time and place   In Chapter One we talked about those twilight times, morning and night, when the pressure is off and we can dream and create. You may want to develop a ritual for one or both of those times since they're so conducive to creative thought. If morning and night are difficult, however, then any time will do. Well-known creativity theorist and researcher Eugene Raudsepp suggests just this as a means for becoming "inwardly isolated."[26] Since everyone is different, though, the choice of time varies according to the individual. Perhaps you will have several times within a day. Perhaps just one. Again, you determine the time. The important point is that the time is your time to be creative. It's the time when you feel most in touch with your creative spirit.

Early in the twentieth century, the English author Virginia Woolf wrote a book on the importance of having a room of one's own, particularly if you were a woman trying to succeed in a man's world. Today, regardless of which sex you belong to, her advice should be taken to heart. To have a room of one's own, however, doesn't mean to have a room per se. It can simply mean a place that's for you and you alone. It's your place and you go to it in order to keep in touch with your creative spirit. It's your place for solitude, reflection, and creative production.

Creative individuals throughout history have known the importance of such a place. For instance, consider these words from the French essayist Montaigne in his essay, "On Solitude":

> We must reserve a little back-shop, all our own, entirely free, wherein to establish our true liberty and principal retreat and solitude. In this retreat we should keep up our ordinary converse with ourselves, and so private, that no acquaintance or outside communication may find a place there.[27]

Unlike Montaigne, you may not want to be so reclusive that you shut out others or the world generally. Still, you need a place you can call your own so that when you enter it, it sparks a certain mood, a certain creative feel. This place can be anywhere. You determine that. What's important is that it exists.

The ritual of playfulness   The concept of playfulness is vital to generating creative ideas. The creative individual toys with the world of reality in order to make connections. That toying is a matter of playing, a kind of childlike response and spontaneity to the world's offerings.

Considering this importance of playfulness, it's no wonder that creative problem-solving systems have undergone major transformations when it comes to the concept of play. In Synectics during the late 1950s, for example, the play concept was expanded as a means for the creative individual to "re-enter the child state."[28] To play meant you were open, free, and imaginative. To play also meant there were certain conditions operating at the time, conditions allowing you to be open, free, and imaginative.

We can even look to the animal kingdom to understand how certain conditions can influence playfulness or the lack of it. For instance, confined animals play less than free animals. Animals play more in kind and pleasant weather than they do in unkind and unpleasant weather. Animals that are exceptionally hungry tend also to be exceptionally unplayful. Some animals, such as elephants, play more "flight" games than they do "fight" games.[29] Doesn't all of this tend to be true as well for us humans? We'll play when we feel free to play. We'll play when we're encouraged to play. If we strive too much, we might find it impossible to play. Sometimes we play "fight" games, and sometimes we play "flight" games.

As members of the animal kingdom, for us there are many forms of play. As separate individuals, each of us plays in his or her own way. This makes the entire concept of playfulness somewhat relative. Still, you can be assured of two things. First, it's very difficult to worry yourself into a creative idea. Second, it's much easier to play yourself into one. With this in mind, you should consider the following list of ways to play.

1. *Play the "flight" game.* Go to another world. Make the unreal real, and the real unreal. Go to your special time and place. Take ten minutes and imagine anything entering your consciousness as something else.

   Your dinner fork. What can it be?

   That spatula? Can it be an ice scraper? A fly swatter?

   What about your bed? Can it be a raft on water? A cloud? What happens if you stand it on end? Then what? What happens if you shrink it? Enlarge it? Curl it? Fold it?

   Go ahead. Escape for a bit. Not forever. Just for a bit. Just to play.

2. *Play with your senses.* When you come back from escaping, try playing with your senses. You can even mix and match them.

   What does it sound like to taste something? What does it smell like to see something?

   Play with your senses as a means for increasing your creativity. As John Haefele writes, "To the extent that one can learn to use all his senses on a problem, he can increase his creativity."[30] So, go ahead. Fine tune your sense connections to the world around you.

   Playfully stimulating your senses so that they are sharp and ready to connect with the world can be done in several ways. For instance, based on the findings of several studies in creativity, repetition of sound stimuli can be an effective means for increasing idea production.[31] These sound stimuli can range from the repetition of onomatopoetic words to chants or mantras. Even your favorite music can come in handy here.

The same holds true with senses other than sound. Smells can touch off vivid associations and connections helpful in idea generation. Blind walks can help sharpen your senses of sound, touch, and smell. They can even help sharpen your sense of sight by encouraging you to create crisp, clear images in your mind. To touch someone you care for can help build self-esteem and confidence. To taste certain foods or drink can act as stimulants for actualizing your creativity. The taste and even the smell of coffee, for example. Or the taste of chocolate to indulge yourself, to give yourself a reward, and to feel good.

Surely, all of these examples are individual matters. Because of that, you must determine their appropriateness for yourself. The important point, however, is that your senses can stimulate your creativity or the conditions necessary for your creativity. So play with using them, even before you begin generating ideas.

3. *Play by exercising.* Similar to playing with your senses, playing with your exercise has been found to facilitate creativity.[32] Try it. Run in place for a few minutes. Do some sit-ups or jumping jacks. Or go for a fast walk around the block. Indeed, be even more playful. Dance while you run in place or do your jumping jacks. Twirl, spin, and vary your speed as you go for your fast walk around the block. Get those juices flowing between your body and your mind. But make it pleasurable, playful.

4. *Play by relaxing.* In contrast to exercise, play with relaxation. Breathe deeply from your center. Inhale and exhale with a rhythmic, easy flow. Concentrate on your breathing. See it in slow motion going in and out, in and out. Feel it flowing slowly inside and outside.

    Sit or lie down. Be comfortable. Turn out the lights. Feel yourself detach from the pressured world. Give yourself over to the world of relaxation and rhythm. Ray and Myers call this "surrendering."[33] There are several ways you can do it.

    To "surrender," contemplate and play with water. Give yourself over to water. Ray and Myers suggest you imagine what it's like to live as water. Water is part of our essence, a large part. It's a large part of life, of our earth. It flows. It's rhythmic. It's soothing. In their book, *Understanding Children's Play,* Ruth E. Hartley, Lawrence K. Frank, and Robert M. Goldenson suggest that water gives us a feeling of mastery and liberation. To play with it can even build our egos. Such may be the case when we blow soap bubbles, for instance.[34] Try it. Blow some bubbles. Play with the shapes and sizes. Give yourself over to the world of water.

    You can also give yourself over to someone else. Close your eyes and imagine your prototype of the most creative individual. Give that person flesh and bones. Then, ask that person to guide you to ideas. Offer your hand and be led away. Surrender.[35] Don't run. Flow. Wear something flowing, something loose. Let it hang as you flow away with your creative ideal.

5. *Play by dramatizing.* Another way to play is by acting a role. Get a group together and play roles. Even if you can't get a group together, you play the roles.

    This playing with dramatizing is not uncommon among creative advertising people, who are known to go to improvisation classes where they assume and play various roles.[36] Try it. Play a part, or play several parts. Create your own scene. Act it out. Feel what others feel. Negate yourself. Become the others. All by way of playing and for the sake of sharpening your negative capability.

6. *Play by imaging.* Many creative ideas throughout history began with an image. The pyramids began with an image.
So did cathedrals.
And rockets.[37]
Einstein thought in images, not words.[38] Many creative thinkers do, writers included.

What else is the creative art of writing but a matter of creating striking and appropriate images in the mind of the reader or listener. Indeed, even before the act of writing takes place, the idea of what is to be written can begin with an image. Take the famous British novelist John Fowles, for example. His powerful novel *The French Lieutenant's Woman* began with an image he had of a cloaked woman alone on a jetty near his home in southern England. Or think back to Ed Biglow who saw nuns riding in a car and then created the Volkswagen "Mass Transit" ad mentioned earlier.

There are several ways you can play with imaging, and they begin with observation. You can use a divergent method called "sweep viewing." This is when you observe from a bird's eye view. You can also use a convergent method called "multi-mini-focusing." This is when you observe from a telescopic view. "Sweep viewing" is more general. You don't pick up specific details. You take in a broader, more expansive look. "Multi-mini-focusing" is more specific. Here, you take in the details of a particular object, and you take them in closely.[39]

You can use these methods of observation in two different ways. One is real. One is imaginary. When you're in your special place at your special time (or any place and any time, for that matter), scan your surroundings. Take in a divergent, sweeping view. Observe shapes, sizes, and colors. Observe them in relationship to each other. Then, shift gears and take in a convergent, focused view on one object. Observe its details, its subtle forms and shadings. Then, close your eyes and re-create both observations from that real world. See both views in your mind's eye.

You can do the same thing with an imaginary world. Close your eyes and create your own scene. Observe it with a sweeping view. Then choose an object and converge on it. Observe its details. Describe them to yourself. Use vivid adjectives to color, shape, and size them. Use vivid verbs to move them and bring them to life.

Whether you play with diverging or converging, you can improve your creative potential by imaging. You can even increase the imaging by turning things upside down as you play with the two methods of diverging and converging.

Move those images. Stretch them. Shrink them. Dice them. Slice them. Get under them. Over them. Inside them. Or jumble them together.

Superimpose one image on top of another. Indeed, when you superimpose, you have actually begun to use another means for improving your creative potential through imaging.

Noted creativity theorist and researcher Albert Rothenberg conducted an interesting experiment with writers and artists. He divided them into two groups. One group observed slide images superimposed on each other. Another group observed slide images separated from each other. Rothenberg found that the group of writers and artists exposed to the superimposed images were able to generate more creative metaphors and drawings than the group exposed to separated images.[40]

Try it. Superimpose one or more images on top of others and see what happens. Isn't this what John Fowles and Ed Biglow did? Didn't they superimpose a particular image onto their problem or product? In the case of Fowles, wasn't the image of the cloaked woman superimposed on his problem of writing a novel? Wasn't the image of nuns in a car superimposed by Biglow on his product, a Volkswagen station wagon?

We will focus a considerable amount of attention on imaging in the next few chapters. It can be a very valuable aid for idea generation. It can even be a valuable aid for building your confidence. Take imaging in sports, for example. Basketball players are asked to use imaging in order to improve their foul shooting. They see themselves getting ready for the shot. They see themselves take the shot. They see the ball go into the basket. And they haven't even taken the shot yet.[41]

In our case, imaging can be used as a kind of self-fulfilling confidence builder. Close your eyes and imagine you've created a successful ad idea. What does it look like? How do you feel? See yourself as successful. Then, go backwards from that successful image and re-create the steps you had to take to become successful. In this way, positive imaging can help prophesy your success.

Whether we like it or not, there can be no doubt that we live in a very visual age. Though there has been considerable debate over whether advertising effectiveness owes more allegiance to the visual image or the written word, there is certainly no debate over which of the two has gained more power and influence in recent years. Given such high-intensity images as MTV or television generally, there is a visual orientation to modern-day communication. This is why imaging is so important when it comes to creativity, especially advertising creativity.

Perhaps it's wise for you to take some words from Lewis Carroll's *Alice in Wonderland* to heart when it comes to imaging. Alice says, "How can I know what I think till I see what I say?"[42] When it comes to advertising creativity, there is considerable truth in those words.

The ritual of getting it all down   Creative ideas are slippery devils. They have the uncanny knack for slipping out of the traps in our minds. That's why it's important to get them down somewhere. Very important. Again, we can call on Lewis Carroll for a playful description of that importance. "The Horror of the moment,' the King went on. 'I shall never, never forget it!' 'You will, though,' the Queen said, 'if you don't make a memorandum of it'"[43] Again, there is considerable truth here. That doesn't mean you need to abide by a prescribed system for getting your ideas down, though one will soon be suggested. It simply means you need to get them down. The poet Emily Dickinson put her bits and pieces of poems into a dresser drawer. You can do that, or use a shoebox. Whatever. The problem, though, is that creative ideas don't always occur at your special time and place. Indeed, chances are they won't. Chances are they'll occur when they want to. So what you need is a kind of double-pronged approach to the problem.

First, you need to develop a system of logging your creative ideas as they occur. Napkins are fine. So are notepads. Slips of paper. Your hand. Whatever. But, you need to log them when you think of them. Don't wait. Get them down somewhere. As with many positive habits, over time the inconvenience of logging them will give way to the rewards you feel for having done so. The point is to get them down.

Second, you need to take those ideas you've put down and deposit them into an idea bank. This can be your dresser drawer, you shoebox, your whatever. In all likelihood, this bank will be located in your special place. At the end of the day when your person is stuffed with all sorts of ideas you've logged for that day, empty your pockets or pocketbooks and deposit those ideas into your bank.

One suggestion for an idea bank is the use of a layout pad. There are many available. They're very accommodating for creative ideas. They tend to be unlined so you're not fenced in by some arbitrary decision over how big or small you should write or draw. They're big ($14'' \times 17''$ is probably big enough). You can let yourself go on them. You can be free.

Each night or day, you can add your ideas to the pages of the pad. Gradually, over time, you'll notice the pages filling up. This doesn't mean the pages are necessarily neat and tidy. Our consciousness isn't neat and tidy. Neither is our creativity, and since the pages reflect both your consciousness and creativity as they pertain to the problems you're working on, they're bound to be crowded and filled. If not, they should be. Remember, quantity yields quality.

As an example of a typical idea bank page from a layout pad, Figure 7-1 exemplifies the logging of creative idea possibilities. Though you will see how such a page grows to other pages due to playing with idea-generation techniques, for now observe it as an example of an idea bank, a depository for creative possibilities, both visual and verbal. Call it an idea page.

Notice how filled the page is. What fills it are idea possibilities. Headlines. Images. Connections. In this way, your idea page becomes a bank, a

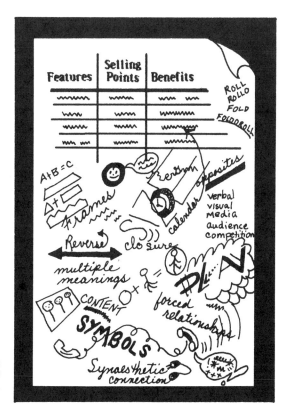

FIGURE 7-1 Your Idea Page with Bits and Pieces of Idea Possibilities. Art by Mary Ella.

place to keep track of your creative consciousness as it pertains to the advertising problems at hand.

CONNECTING FORWARD

No doubt, this chapter should bring you back to Chapter One. With emphasis given to the means for developing a certain mind set, a creative temperament, this chapter should also propel you forward to our next chapters on idea generation. Those chapters are very much connected to what has been expressed here.

The keys to idea generation are found in your being open, alert, confident, playful, and organized. To be open means you defer judgment. To be alert means you observe closely what the world of realities has to offer. To be confident means you lack the fear that blocks your creativity. You're able to co-exist with the origins of that fear, and you're able to balance opposite states of mind and emotions. To be playful means you respond to life with a childlike spontaneity. It also means you're in touch with certain techniques as toys for actualizing your creativity. And, to be organized means you have a grip on those conditions fostering your creativity. You know when and where the creative spirit moves you. Plus, you know how to get the ideas from that spirit down somewhere so they won't be lost.

With these considerations in mind, the remaining chapters introduce a variety of idea-generation techniques. These techniques spark creative ideas. Often, their successful use relies on the kind of creative temperament we've discussed in this chapter.

8
IDEA-GENERATION TECHNIQUES: ASSOCIATIONS

As much as the previous chapter was devoted to helping you find the creative you, the next four chapters are devoted to ways you can put that creative you to work in the actual generation of ideas. These next chapters give you a variety of idea-generation techniques to stimulate and spark your creativity. The techniques can help you overcome blocks. They can help you avoid anxiety. When pressed for time, as copywriters and artists always are, the techniques can help you be creatively productive and fluent. This means they can be used quickly and easily as leads to quantities of ideas. The key term here is "quantities." On the bridge from the incubation stage to the illumination stage, you're not after one idea possibility. You're after many possibilities, many alternative ways of presenting your theme. Remember, quantity yields quality.

To conceptualize what the results should be after using the idea-generation techniques, notice the development over time of a single layout page in Figure 8–1.

You start with a blank page. Looming over it is an advertising problem demanding a creative idea as a solution. To move toward a solution, you begin by logging key advertiser features, selling points, and benefits or problem solutions onto your page. You also log key findings or conclusions from your prep sheet and plan. Initially, these will help stimulate ideas.

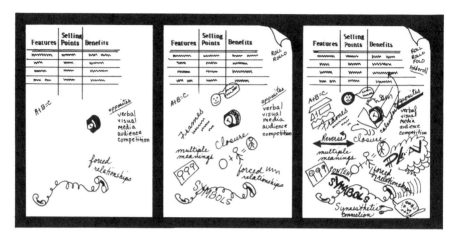

FIGURE 8-1   The Development of a Single Idea Page over Time. Art by Mary Ella.

Later, they can be used as guidelines in the selection of the *Big Idea.* Then, as you play with the techniques, the page gets filled. What fills it are headlines, themelines, sketches, and those idea possibilities gathered over time. Often, the ideas filling it spill over onto other pages as well. That's a goal you should always have in front of you. Put simply, the more idea possibilities, the better.

It's certainly easy to say, "Go find creative ideas, lots of them." It's quite another thing to do it, however. That's where the idea generation techniques come in handy. The techniques are vital to the filling of your pages. They act as toys for stimulating your creativity. You can juggle them. You can alternate them. If one doesn't work, you can move to another. If one does work, you can continue to play with it. If it stops working, you can drop it. Come back to it later if you want. You can also combine the techniques. As we shall see, some of the most creative ideas do just that. They combine more than one technique. So, you can mix and match them together.

More than anything else, perhaps, what you're asked to do with these techniques is to play. Not play in any particular order or for a specified amount of time. Just play. Remember, the techniques are your toys. And, toys are meant to be played with. So, play with them.

All of the techniques are based on connections. To various degrees, all of them rely on A + B = C. Some of the connections from this simple formula are literal and direct. Some are abstract and indirect. Often, these connections and techniques will overlap simply because they are so similar. Not to worry, though, since overlapping is of little concern to us. What we're after are quantities of ideas. The more ways to get ideas, the better. Bear in mind, however, that the goal in playing with the techniques is always to form connections culminating in new realities, those new and relevant ideas.

ASSOCIATIONS

Associations, or the connection of similarities between your advertiser and separate worldly realities, represent the beginning of our idea-generation techniques. In fact, the process and practice of association are a foundation for many of those techniques. There are three important reasons why.

First, the use of associations is one of the most common creative problem-solving techniques in existence. Synectics, for example, uses three types of analogies as part of its system for stimulating creative thinking.

Second, the making of associations is basic to the creative mind. As indirect ways for understanding things, they're like our Chapter One examples of fishing and not looking at the sun.

And third, as an umbrella concept, the process and practice of associations, whether by simile, analogy, or metaphor, are very much a part of everyone's daily living. Daily, all of us talk, think, and feel by associations. We talk about having chips on our shoulders or being chips off the old block. When we perform well in a tough situation, we say we're good when the chips are down. When we feel unsure of how things may turn out, we say we'll let the chips fall where they may. When we feel good, we believe our dispositions are sunny. When we're in a tight spot, we're up the creek without a paddle. When others criticize us, they've rained on our parade.

Daily, both the process and practice of association provide clarity and impact for the meanings in our existence. Quite simply, we're used to associations. And this makes them potentially relevant and involving for target audiences. If the associations are appropriate, then they will occupy two or more tracks in an audience's mind. One track is for the literal words or images such as chips, sunny, paddle, or parade. The other track is for what those words or images suggest in association with something else.

They key to generating ideas by association is to activate the A + B = C formula from Chapter One. You take one reality, A, and associate or connect it with another reality, B, in order to generate C, the creative idea. A, however, should be many things. So should B. That way you will have the opportunity to generate many ideas as you mix and match the associations and connections of A and B.

There are many types of associations you can make, but the following list identifies five main groupings for using associations in advertising idea generation: *feature associations, selling point associations, benefit associations, behavioristic associations,* and *reverse associations.*

Feature associations connect a physical or tangible characteristic of your advertiser with other realities. Selling point associations connect what features give with other realities. And benefit associations connect what selling points mean with other realities. All three of these techniques are critical to the relevance of your creative ideas since their use in idea generation will help keep those ideas on strategy. The same holds true for behavioristic associations which connect your audience's behavior with other realities. The final association technique is reverse associations which turns the tables upside down on each of the previous techniques.

FEATURE ASSOCIATIONS

You generate ideas based on *feature associations* by relying on certain advertiser features and then connecting their similarities to something else. To begin the generation you can complete the statement, A is like _____ B. A is the advertiser feature. The blank is your B. Joined together, they result in C, your creative idea.

Recall from Part II of this book that advertiser features are the physical or tangible characteristics of your advertiser. Every product has features. Every store or service has features. The shape or color of a product, or the large selection of items in a store, for example.

The relative importance of specific advertiser features varies according to the individual advertiser. Obviously, not all advertisers promote the same features in their advertising. Even those individual brands of products that are similar tend to promote different features. Take beers, for instance. One brand of beer might promote the feature of its clear bottle. Another brand might use a special brewing process as its key feature. In generating ideas by feature associations, identify as many features as possible (especially those deemed most relevant through research) and then play with their similarities to a variety of other realities.

When you begin to work on an advertising problem, list all of the features of your advertiser in a single column on your idea page. List as many as you can think of, including those you may at first consider irrelevant.

Let's say you have your column filled with features. Now, check back to your Creative Prep Sheet and Creative Plan to make sure you haven't overlooked something important. Then, stare at your list of features. Jot down anything that pops up by way of connection between the features and something else. When you're done, think creatively by playing with the following.

Form Associations

One possible feature is that of the form or shape of the product. Even if you don't consider it the key feature, however, you can still open the door to some exciting creative ideas by playing with *form associations*. For example, look at the Wheaties ad in Figure 8–2.

FIGURE 8-2 Form Association. Courtesy of GENERAL MILLS, INC.

The Wheaties ad is an example of a form association. The shape of a Wheaties flake connects with the shape of a medal. The connection clearly and uniquely conveys the meaning of Wheaties' enduring themeline, "The Breakfast of Champions."

If you backtrack from the ad idea to the creative thinking behind it, you can hypothesize how the creative mind connects the two separate realities of a flake and a medal. The shape of the flake (A) plus the shape of a medal (B) equals the new idea (C). It's as if the meaning of the shapes of both A and B dissolve in the process of connection and take on a new meaning, C. It's also as if the creative mind has superimposed one image onto the other in order to create a new image.

Close your eyes and imagine the creative mind at play with this ad idea. Can you see that mind staring at the Wheaties flake and transforming it into something else? Can you see that mind connecting the flake's shape to all sorts of similar shapes? Perhaps the mind began by playing with the medal shape and then proceeded from that point to the Wheaties flake. Either way, as an association, the ad idea is the result of separate realities connected by that mind.

What's important to understand here, too, is that if a Wheaties flake were only a Wheaties flake, and if a medal were only a medal, then the creative idea never could have emerged. For the creative mind behind this idea, those two realities weren't rigid enough to disallow the innovative approach of a new idea. That mind wasn't locked into such a preconceived, rigid mode of thinking or perceiving. If it were, we wouldn't be looking at the ad as it now stands. We would be looking at something far less surprising and original.

This element of surprise is one of the results of original, yet relevant associations such as that in the Wheaties ad. The target audience doesn't quite expect to see things the way they are shown in the ad. That in itself is surprising. But on top of that, the audience must make a connection between a winner's medal and a winner's taste. In the process, it connects the positive connotations of winning to the product, Wheaties.

At the same time, who would think that the shape of a Wheaties flake would be a relevant enough feature to include as the spark for a creative idea? In its own right, it's not relevant enough. There's nothing particularly special about the shape of a Wheaties flake in terms of an appeal to the target audience. Once the association is made, however, all the positive connotative connections from medal to flake and from flake to medal take place in the audience's mind. This is why you don't exclude features when you generate. Yes, you would certainly concentrate on certain features above others. Still, to include as many features as possible, regardless of their initial irrelevance or relevance, keeps you open to generating more ideas.

Now, go back to your list of features. Do you have form listed? If not, try it. Play with it. See what happens. If nothing happens or if your particular product just doesn't lend itself to form, then go on to other types of feature associations.

Content Associations

Try playing with *content associations*. As before, use the formula A + B = C. Begin by completing the statement A is like _____ B, only here your A is the advertiser content instead of the advertiser form. For example, in Figure 8–3, notice how there are two associations. One is based on the similarities between the brain and fried eggs, and the other is based on the similarities between drugs and a hot skillet. Both of these associations are then connected together to create the advertising idea. What you have then is a simple variation of the A + B = C formula resulting in (A + B) + (C + D) = E.

With this powerful advertising campaign to stop drug abuse, the creative mind has made at least two associations. One is made between the human brain after drugs and another reality to suggest or symbolize that brain, in this case fried eggs. Another is made between drugs and a hot skillet. These associations are then connected to yield the creative idea. Notice how this idea carries the theme of destroying your brain by using drugs. In fact, the voice-over announcer says quite bluntly that "This is your brain on drugs." And, it is said precisely at the point when the eggs are cracked into the pan and immediately begin to fry.

Now, go backwards again and try to imagine the creative mind at play with this ad idea. Can you see that mind almost compulsively searching for connections and relationships? Can you see the problem simmering in that mind as it watches its owner's hands cracking eggs into a frying pan on a Sunday morning? Can you see it then making the connections?

Of course, this particular ad idea conveys a helpful service or advisory message. It's not based on a tangible product per se. Even so, you can see how considerations of content features can lead to the idea. For you, it means getting inside your advertiser to the point where you're involved with all of its contents. After you list them as features, you then ask what they are like. When you find similarities or likenesses, you connect them and log the possibilities.

Size Associations

Another potential feature of an advertiser is size. Again, you generate your ideas by first completing the statement A is like _____ B. Here, A is the size. For example, the Casio idea in Figure 8–4 makes use of a *size association.*

This is your brain,

this is drugs,

this is your brain on drugs.

Partnership For A Drug-Free America   N.Y., NY 10017

FIGURE 8-3   Content Association. Courtesy of the MEDIA PARTNERSHIP FOR A DRUG-FREE AMERICA.

The photographs you see for the Casio ad are taken from a television commercial in which a hockey player skates down the ice, takes aim at what looks like an ordinary hockey puck, and then proceeds to slap it toward the net. A goalie makes a glove save. Of interest here, however, is that the

Partnership for a Drug Free America
ANY QUESTIONS? :30

Is there anyone out there
who still isn't clear about what
"doing drugs" does?

Okay. Last time

This is your brain.

This is drugs.

This is your brain on drugs

Any questions?
(SILENCE)

Partnership for a Drug-Free America

FIGURE 8-3 Continued.

hockey puck is anything but ordinary. There's a Casio G-Shock watch around it. This means the watch takes the slap shot and is caught by the goalie. All of this action demonstrates the theme of the ruggedness and durability of the product.

If you go backwards again, can you see the creative mind at play with this concept? A hockey puck is not a hockey puck. A Casio watch is not a Casio watch. The creative mind takes the two realities of watch and puck and associates and connects them. Separately, each reality loses its independence and merges with the other. Independently, they dissolve.

FIGURE 8-4 Size Association. Courtesy of CASIO, INC.

Jointly, they bleed into each other. Living with this kind of transformation of realities is a frame of mind needed as a starting point for creativity.

From that starting point, however, the creative mind goes on to make its associations and connections. In this case, size appears to be one association. If you stare at your watch curled up on your nightstand, you'll notice that it's roughly the same size as a hockey puck. At the same time, you'll notice that it's roughly the same shape as a hockey puck. It's possible then that this Casio idea stemmed from a form association. This is how idea-generation techniques can begin to overlap.

Don't be dismayed. So what if they overlap? Let them. The point is to generate as many ideas as possible. These techniques give you alternative ways to do that.

Texture Associations

Still another potential advertiser feature is that of texture. In Figure 8–5, the creative idea for Patcraft carpets illustrates how similarity of texture can be used as a basis for association.

Here, the texture of sand dunes connects with the texture of a Patcraft carpet. As before, however, it's very possible that another feature besides

FIGURE 8-5   Texture Association. Courtesy of PATCRAFT MILLS, INC.

... the sands of time
do not impress this Patcraft carpet!

HARROGATE...elegance personified. This carpet is made with soil hiding, long wearing DuPont Antron® Nylon fibers spun into very fine, slender yarn. The result is a beautiful, finely tailored carpet with a low lustre, velvet look. Treated with DuPont Teflon® for soil retardation and static control, the tight tufting helps maintain its texture and appearance after installation. Its weight/density factor makes it an incomparable plush carpet. Patcraft not only offers 20 fresh, new colorations from inventory, but will supply any custom color for as small an order as 30 feet.

atcraft

MILLS INC.
Box 1087 • Dalton, Ga. 30720

texture led to the creative idea. For example, the use of form may have been the spark. Once again, we have the possible overlap of techniques, which means we have more ways to think openly, laterally. In order to think that way, be ready to use a variety of techniques, either alone or in combination.

Feature Range Associations

We've looked at four ways you can generate ideas based on specific advertiser features. As we've said, though, features span a wide range depending on the advertiser. Those we've looked at represent just part of that range. Not all advertisers are so restricted to the form, content, size, or texture of their products. Many go beyond these features, and that's when *feature range associations* need to be made.

Feature range associations is an all-inclusive term encompassing those features that go beyond form, content, size, or texture. For instance, certain advertisers may require color associations. If such is the case, you simply follow the same method of playing as you did with all of the other features. In order to generate a creative idea (C), you connect the color (A) with something else (B) based on their similarities. Again, this means you can begin by completing the statement A is like _____ B. In this way you can make associations of all features, including color or anything else for that matter.

To play with this technique, consider a hypothetical situation of a store that prides itself on providing its customers with a knowledgeable and friendly staff of salespeople. Store management wants to use those features in its advertising. You, too, believe they should be used. You have determined that they're important to the target audience. And they differentiate your store from others selling similar goods.

Since you intend to use those features as the essence of your theme, you need to find a creative idea easily associated with those features. What you need to do is complete two statements with as many variations as possible. For instance, a knowledgeable salesperson (A) is like _____ B. A friendly salesperson (A) is like _____ B. The range of statement completions supplies you with idea possibilities. Perhaps the core of your creative idea would be an encyclopedia or a smile, both of which are single-word answers to the two comparisons for a knowledgeable and friendly salesperson.

The keys to making feature associations include making certain you have logged as many features as possible. Remember, features are those physical and tangible characteristics of your advertiser. They can be forms, contents, sizes, textures, or any characteristics inherent to specific products, stores, or services. This means you should play with as many A's as possible. The keys also include finding the similarities between those A's and as many B's as possible. You then connect them, almost superimpose them, one on the other, in order to generate your C's, the creative ideas.

SELLING POINT ASSOCIATIONS

Many times in advertising, it is simply not enough to convey features. Often, your creative idea needs to convey more, especially in terms of selling points and benefits. Selling points are those generic, somewhat generalized appeals of what the features give.

In our example of the store with a knowledgeable and friendly staff, the selling points may range anywhere from customer convenience to a congenial atmosphere. These aren't quite benefits yet since they don't fully answer the questions, "What's in it for me?" or "What do the selling points mean to me?" They simply answer, "What do the A's (the features) mean?" Remember, benefits connect with meaning. For instance, the customer doesn't have to spend time gathering information, or the customer can enjoy a relaxed, less pressured, and easygoing shopping experience. Selling points fall short of these more specific and pointed statements.

In a sense, selling points represent translations of the advertiser's features. As with the list of features you have on your idea page, you can create a list of corresponding selling points on the same page. You may want to try doing this in a second column right beside the column of features. In fact, list the appropriate selling points as they correspond to each feature. For instance, in applying our store example, the list of features would include knowledgeable salespeople and friendly salespeople. Beside them you list convenience and congenial atmosphere as selling points. Then, as you did with those features, you complete the two statements of what these selling points are like.

You can see how generating ideas by using *selling point associations* can work by recalling two ad ideas we've looked at, one from Chapter Four under ADNORMS and the other from this chapter under size associations. In Chapter Four we looked at a UPS television commercial in which the next day letter was shown as an airplane landing on a desk (see Figure 4–7 p. 51).

The product feature behind the ad would be the actual scheduling by UPS for its next day mailings. The feature, however, translates into speed as a selling point. The association made is between the speed of the mailing and the similar speed of something else, in this case an airplane. The association is carried all the way through the ad, from on-time, door-to-door delivery to the point when we hear the screeching of brakes as the letter lands on the runway of the desk.

A similar situation exists with the Casio ad we looked at several pages back. If you recall, we termed the ad a size association and considered the possibility of a form association as well. It is also possible that the Casio ad idea may have originated with a selling point association. The feature would be the Casio watch's construction. But, the selling point would be its durability. Here, the creative mind may have completed the statement, durability (A) is like _____ B. One answer for B is a hockey puck or perhaps the sport of hockey itself.

As with feature associations, selling point associations are a matter of logging your selling points in conjunction with their appropriate features. You then find and associate the similarities between them and something else. Finally, you connect them into creative ideas.

BENEFIT ASSOCIATIONS

You may want to create still a third column on your idea page. This would be devoted to a listing of benefits or problem solutions derived from the key selling points and features. Naturally, a reference to your Creative Prep Sheet and Creative Plan can help you here. You can list those related benefits or problem solutions beside the appropriate selling points. As always, they should answer the question, "What's in it for me?" Of course, the "me" is your target audience. Once you list the benefits, you again complete the statement, A is like _____ B. Here, the A is the benefit or problem solution.

In following our store example again, recall that we have identified the benefits of the two selling points, customer convenience and congenial atmosphere, as less time the customer has to spend searching out information and a more enjoyable, less pressured shopping experience. What you do here is apply those benefits to the statement formula. Spending less time (A) is like _____ B. And a more enjoyable, less pressured shopping experience (A) is like _____ B. You then list all the possibilities that emerge.

To see how a *benefit association* controls a creative idea, see the Maxell ad in Figure 8–6.

The promised benefit to the customers who buy Maxell is they will get long-lasting power (selling point) that time and time again will blow them away (benefit). Obviously, this is a benefit that zeros in on a particular audience. It's also a benefit the particular audience can easily connect with and understand. But it's not enough to just say the benefit. What's needed in advertising is to present it in a manner that grabs and holds attention. The manner in this Maxell case is that of a benefit association.

Again, can you see the creative mind at play with this ad idea? Can you see it juggling all sorts of idea possibilities? Perhaps the mind completed the statement, long-lasting power (A) is like _____ B. Perhaps the answer to that was a gusty wind. If so, the creative idea is based more on a selling point association than a benefit association. What seems more likely, however, is that the benefit of getting blown away initiated the association. With this being the case, the mind completed the statement,

AFTER 500 PLAYS OUR HIGH FIDELITY TAPE STILL DELIVERS HIGH FIDELITY.

If your old favorites don't sound as good as they used to, the problem could be your recording tape.

Some tapes show their age more than others. And when a tape ages prematurely, the music on it does too.

What can happen is, the oxide particles that are bound onto tape loosen and fall off, taking some of your music with them.

At Maxell, we've developed a binding process that helps to prevent this. When oxide particles are bound onto our tape, they stay put. And so does your music.

So even after a Maxell recording is 500 plays old, you'll swear it's not a play over five.

maxell

IT'S WORTH IT.

FIGURE 8-6 Benefit Association. Courtesy of MAXELL CORP. OF AMERICA and SCALI, McCABE, SLOVES, INC.

being blown away (A) is like _____ B. Literally and figuratively, it's like getting hit with a gusty wind. And the creative idea is born.

At the same time, the idea may have emerged as a benefit association only after consideration of what Maxell offered as a problem solution. For the target audience, the problem may have been that tapes lose their power, especially after many plays. The benefit or problem solution is offered by

Maxell through the benefit association. Whether by benefit or problem solution, however, a connection was made to something else, and the idea was born.

You can see how benefit associations versus selling point associations also work by looking at the AT&T ad ideas in Figures 8-7 and 8-8. One idea is a benefit association, the other idea a selling point association. By contrasting one with the other, you will be able to see the distinction between benefits and selling points.

In Figure 8-7, the benefit is that your business will increase when you use AT&T's fax system for sending such things as important messages and documents long distances. The creative association is made between increased business and air travel.

As part of a campaign, several ads of this kind were used by AT&T. Figure 8-8 shows another. Notice how this ad idea is not based on a benefit per se. It's based more on a selling point, that of inexpensive speed. Translated, inexpensive speed means increased business or improved business efficiency for the target audience. But on its own, inexpensive speed is a generic, generalized appeal in the advertising. It is a selling point.

What gives these two ads their creativity is the association made between the Fax system and air travel. To make that association, the creative mind had to connect what the fax system does and means compared to something else. The system's speed is like air travel. But air travel is relatively expensive. The fax system is not. To convey how inexpensively speedy the system is led to the selling point association in Figure 8-8. And, the contrast of the price of air travel with the price of the system creates surprise in the target audience's mind.

In Figure 8-7, however, there's an extension of the selling point. That extension includes a specific promise, a benefit to the audience. The ad is suggesting that with the fax system's inexpensive speed, your business will prosper. Now the audience knows what specific relevance the system has for his or her business. But as a creative idea, the use of the headline with its focus on "your business soaring" and the continuous visual connect in a singleminded way with the other ad idea. It's just that this idea conveys the benefit more than the selling point.

With part of your mind focused on your Creative Prep Sheet and Plan, you should be able to generate a quantity of idea possibilities by playing with the various associations. Now, if you go back to your plan, pay particular attention to the theme, the main message you're seeking to convey. Remember that the theme can be boiled down to a few key words or even one word for that matter. Take a look at your theme. Boil it down. Then, generate ideas by associating the theme with a range of similarities from real life. For example, if asked to generate possible ad ideas for Maytag, Parkay, Federal Express, and Charmin, what would happen if you associated their themes of durability, buttery taste, speed, and softness with similarities from

FIGURE 8-7 Benefit Association. Courtesy of AT&T BUSINESS MARKETS GROUP.

Imagine going to Sydney for just $2.17.* Faxed over AT&T
International Long Distance Service, you can make sure your
documents enjoy this low, low fare. With fax, you can send an
exact copy of letters, graphics, charts or signatures to anyone
in the world.**

What's more, sending a fax is a lot more certain than relying
on couriers. And because you don't have to do any retyping, it's
also a lot easier than telex.

AT&T comes through with fax. When you think about it,
is there really any other way to do business?

**From equipment to networking, from computers to
communications, AT&T is the right choice.**

AT&T
The right choice.

*Rate shown is for the first minute of a direct-dialed call from anywhere in the continental U.S. during the Economy Rate Period (3AM-2PM).
Rates vary by country and time of day. Does not include 3% excise tax and applicable state surcharges. ** U.S. export control restrictions
may apply to the transmission of some technical data. For more information on International Facsimile Transmission, call 1-800-222-0400.

FIGURE 8-8 Selling Point Association. Courtesy of AT&T BUSINESS MARKETS GROUP.

real life? Durability (A) is like _____ B. Buttery taste (A) is like _____ B. Speed (A) is like _____ B. And softness (A) is like _____ B.

No doubt, consideration of the theme has already been central to you as you played with the various features, selling points, and benefits. Still, remember how important the theme is to your ad idea. As a result, make certain that it's given priority when you generate. This holds true for associations and many of the other techniques as well.

BEHAVIORISTIC ASSOCIATIONS

If you go back to the features on your idea page, you'll notice that they relate mostly to your advertiser. With selling points and benefits, however, the orientation begins to shift. Both selling points and benefits move more toward your audience and what those selling points and benefits give or mean to that audience. *Behavioristic associations* are similar in that respect.

If you recall from your Creative Prep Sheet, a large part of preparation for creativity is mapping out how your audience behaves toward your advertiser, especially in terms of buying and using. Recall that you were encouraged to answer how, when, where, and why the audience bought and used a product. Some of those answers, particularly to the question of why, carry you over to the area of benefit or problem solution. Your audience will buy or use a product because it promises a benefit or solves a problem. But answers to the other questions don't always identify the benefit or solution. Yet they're important to consider when it comes time for generating ideas. Those answers can now be used to help with that generation.

To play with behavioristic associations, you first create two more columns on your idea page, one for bought and one for used. Then, list answers to the questions of how, when, where, and why the product or service is bought and used. As with features, selling points, and benefits, first focus on your answers and let your mind play. Be patient. If anything clicks, jot it down. Then, if you're blocked, complete the statement, A is like _____ B. Only now, the A identifies the questions of how, when, where, and possibly why the product is bought and used.

You can even expand behavioristic associations to include completions to all the statements as they relate to before, during, and after buying and using. For example, in the statement, A is like _____ B, A can be before the product is purchased. In other words, what is the situation before purchase like? Or A can be what the situation is during or after purchase. In other words, during purchase (A) is like _____ B. In addition, after purchase (A) is like _____ B. You can repeat the statements for use as well. What is the situation like before, during, and after use of the product? Before use (A) is like _____ B. During use (A) is like _____ B. After use (A) is like _____ B.

You can play with behavioristic associations in our store example. How you shop in the store (A) is like _____ B. When you enter the store (A) is like _____ B. Where you shop in the store (A) is like _____ B. Or after shopping in the store (A) is like _____ B. And, so on.

To see how behavioristic associations are used as the nucleus of creative ideas, notice how the Alka-Seltzer ad in Figure 8–9 connects with when the product is used, before the product is used, and after the product is used. You should also notice that the idea could easily have stemmed from a benefit association as well.

As you look at the Alka-Seltzer storyboard, notice how the commercial begins with the problem, stomach discomfort. The association with trains connects with what the situation is like before using the product. The situation is a problem, stomach discomfort, symbolized by the churning, huffing, and puffing action of trains. The problem is then solved by the hero, Alka-Seltzer. After using Alka-Seltzer, the customer is in for a smooth ride, at least as far as the stomach is concerned. This smooth ride can also be seen as the theme, the benefit or problem solution the audience can expect to get from buying and using the product.

Again, can you see the creative mind at play with this idea? Stomach discomfort is like trains churning, huffing, and puffing. The product fine tunes their engines and solves the problem. Now, if trains were just that, trains and nothing else, this creative idea never could have emerged. For the mind behind this ad idea, trains were a reality that could be used in association to suggest something else. They became the toys for the creative mind's play.

REVERSE ASSOCIATIONS

By now, your idea page would be filled with idea possibilities. With columns listing your advertiser features, selling points, benefits or problem solutions, and target audience behaviors, you've included many of your planning considerations. These considerations are then used to spark ideas. In this way, those ideas stand a better chance of connecting back to your Creative Plan. The key, however, is to generate lots of ideas. You already have, but there's still another form of association you can use, that of *reverse associations*.

To play with reverse associations, you need to complete statements in the same way you did with all of the other association types. Only now, the statements take on a twist, that of A is NOT like _____ B. In other words, you're completing your statements with opposite answers. To see how this can work, look at the Crest ad in Figure 8–10.

With the Crest ad, the creative mind may well have asked itself, "What

Consumer Products Division

MILES LABORATORIES, INC.

P.O. Box 340
Elkhart, IN 46515
Phone (219) 264-8988
TWX 810/294-2259

CLIENT: MILES LABORATORIES
PRODUCT: EXTRA STRENGTH ALKA-SELTZER
TITLE: "SHANGHAI EXPRESS"

COMM'L NO.: MIAX 7220
LENGTH: 30 SECONDS

(MUSIC)

ANNCR: That pork chop suey

you got railroaded into

has hit you

like a freight train.

And now you're churning out of control.

(SFX: WHISTLE)

Quick, signal the bubbles

of Extra Strength Alka-Seltzer,

because speed is what you need

to derail that chug-a-luggin' in your stomach and head.

Next time you're on the heartburn express,

flag down the bubbles and get back on track again fast.

CHORUS: Alka-Seltzer to the rescue.
(SFX: TOOT-TOOT)

ANNCR: Try Extra Strength Alka-Seltzer. More of what you take Alka-Seltzer for.

FIGURE 8-9 Behavioristic Association. Courtesy of MILES, INC. Copyright 1987, Miles, Inc.

FIGURE 8-10   Reverse Association. Courtesy of THE PROCTER & GAMBLE COMPANY

is use of Crest not like?" Or use (A) is not like _____ B. The blank would be filled by the word, gambling. To use Crest is not like gambling. It's very possible, of course, that the creative idea for the ad may have emerged from a form association as well. The shape of teeth is like the shape of dice. Either way, the creative idea takes one reality and associates it with another.

To go back to our store example again, you may want to list the opposites for the selling points of customer convenience and a congenial atmosphere by imagining what they are not like. You can do the same for the features and the benefits. For example, a friendly sales staff (A) is not like _____ B. A less pressured shopping experience (A) is not like _____ B.

You can even follow through with behavioristics, including before, during, and after. Going into the store (A) is not like _____ B. Shopping at the store (A) is not like _____ B. After shopping at the store (A) is not like _____ B. And so on. The result is that more alternative ideas surface.

Once again, go back to your plan and make certain you've played with your theme. In the example of Maytag, Parkay, Federal Express, and Charmin, you would need to complete the following statements. Durability (A) is not like _____ B. Buttery taste (A) is not like _____ B. Speed (A) is not like _____ B. And softness (A) is not like _____ B. Of course, in considering the major selling points and benefits, you have probably played with your theme. But since your theme is vital, it never hurts to make absolutely certain it's included.

ASSOCIATIONS IN REVIEW

The use of associations based on listings represents the foundation of our idea-generation techniques. As sparks for creative ideas, these techniques help you overcome blocks, avoid anxiety, and remain creatively productive and fluent while bridging the incubation and illumination stages of the creative process. In beginning with associations, you're keying into important considerations from your Creative Prep Sheet and Creative Plan. You're also keying into various means for grabbing and holding the attention of your target audience. From start to finish, you and your audience are busy connecting.

To create ideas, you must connect separate realities. To understand ideas, your audience must connect as well. Associations, in particular, have that ability to forge their way into the audience's mind and occupy greater amounts of mental space. When they do, your audience has connected with the ideas and has become involved. Obviously, this should be a goal of all creative advertising ideas.

If you follow all or even many of the suggestions presented in this chapter, your idea page should be crowded with possibilities. Ideas. Themes. Headlines. Images. They may be embryonic, to be sure. For some, however, you may see a glimmering of potential. That's what you're after, the glimmer that steps out and says, "This may be a *Big Idea*." If you go back to your prep sheet, plan, and ADNORMS, you will be better able to sort through those ideas that really glimmer and those that don't.

Perhaps at this point you should simply star or asterisk what seem like potentially *Big Ideas*. Don't settle on one yet. It's far too early. You need still more ideas, and they can be found by playing with many other techniques. That's what our remaining chapters provide—many other techniques. Even without those other techniques, however, you should already have many idea possibilities originating from your listings and associations. That's what they're for, to spark idea possibilities. They're a means for helping you find new and relevant ideas to carry your themes. In review, here's a fast look at the techniques of association.

> Listings of features (from one to many) to spark random ideas.
>
> Listings of selling points (from one to many) to spark random ideas.
>
> Listings of benefits (from one to several due to the need for singlemindedness and simplicity in your creative ideas) to spark random ideas.
>
> Feature associations, including form, content, size, texture, and feature range to include whatever features are appropriate to your advertiser.
>
> Selling point associations.
>
> Benefit associations.
>
> Behavioristic associations, including the how, where, when, and why of buying and using. Also including the before, during, and after of buying and using.
>
> Reverse associations, including reversing all of the types of associations by completing the statement A is not like _____ B.

PLAYTIME

The best way to understand the various idea-generation techniques is, of course, to play with them. You will have that opportunity to play at the close of each of these chapters on idea generation. Following each chapter, you can play with the techniques by generating headlines and ideas for one or more advertisers. The advertisers are hypothetical and include specific products or services which you can select from the list that follows. You may want to play with the same product or service after each chapter. Or you may want to play with more than one. The point overall, though, is to play.

What you're after with these techniques are the seeds of ideas, those beginning concepts suggesting how you may present your themes. Of course, you can also go to any of the ads shown to you in these chapters and generate your own new ideas for the advertisers. The problem, however, is that those ad ideas are professionally executed. Recall the Maxell ad idea, for instance. As a result, you may feel intimidated, and justifiably so since it's difficult to compete with the creative quality of professional ads. Plus, as Dick Wasserman suggests in his book, *How to Get Your First Copywriting Job*, to create ads for snazzy products can be a problem for your portfolio since your ads are liable to be compared with their professional counterparts.

To counter the problem of trying to compete with snazzy products or services and professional ads or ideas, what you'll do at the end of each chapter is play with not-so-snazzy products or services. These are the kind for which ads are rarely seen. This is a real challenge for you, because what you're asked to do is create new and relevant ideas for products or services that may seem just plain boring. That can be good, though, because chances are not many others will have them represented in their portfolios. In addition, if you can create exciting and enticing ideas executed well enough to be included in your portfolio, then they will get special notice when they're viewed.

The products or services are listed for you. You will have to draw certain conclusions about them, assuming of course that you don't have research findings at your disposal. These conclusions relate to your Creative Prep Sheet and Creative Plan. For example, you will have to designate a target audience. You will have to project certain market conditions, behavioristic patterns, advertiser goals and objectives, and media placement decisions. You will have to determine key features, selling points, and benefits or problem solutions. And you will have to select key themes to connect with the needs of your target audiences.

Bear in mind that in real life many of these conclusions will be mapped out for you by clients, supervisors, or account executives. Here, though, you must draw conclusions which may be hypothetical. Remember a key goal, however, which is that your ideas should connect with those conclusions.

The first thing to do is to pick one or more of the products or services and draw those conclusions. Fill in your prep sheet and plan. Then list key features, selling points, and benefits. Pay particularly close attention to the theme as it's described in your plan. Once you've finished, begin to play.

ADVERTISERS

Sardines (not a particular kind or brand, just sardines). Wasserman suggests sardines as a good product for inclusion in a portfolio.

Nuts (not a particular kind or brand, just nuts).

Flake fish food.

An all day petsitting service.

A maid service.

A service that will contact its customers to remind them of important dates such as anniversaries or birthdays.

A store that only sells hats.

A store that only sells hubcaps.

A college bookstore.

TECHNIQUES

Have you drawn your conclusions? Do you have your key theme? Do you know your target audience? Have you decided what's different or unique about your advertiser? If so, and if you've mapped out key conclusions on your prep sheet and plan, then play. From this chapter, you can play with associations.

Take your product or service and complete the statements that follow. If one doesn't work, go on to another. If one does work, stick with it and generate some more.

FEATURE ASSOCIATIONS

Form Associations—A is like _____ B.

Content Associations—A is like _____ B.

Size Associations—A is like _____ B.

Texture Associations—A is like _____ B.

Feature Range Associations (pick out your key features)—A is like _____ B.

Take your associations and add A + B. Join them. Let yourself go. Think of possibilities. Are there some possible headlines? Visuals? If so, jot them down.

SELLING POINT ASSOCIATIONS

Turn your features into selling points. For example, if a feature of a store that only sells hats is the many types of hats it has for sale, then play with variety since that is what many types of hats will give to the target audience. Of course, you should have several selling points derived from your product or service features. Repeat the association as many times as you can.

Selling Point Associations—A is like _____ B.

As you did with the features, combine all the A's + B's. Jot down possible headlines or visuals.

BENEFIT ASSOCIATIONS

Turn your selling points into benefits. For example, if the selling point of a store that only sells hats is variety, then the benefit of variety may be that the consumer can choose a hat that will fit his or her personality. Again, you should have several benefits derived from your product or service sell-ing points.

Benefit Associations—A is like _____ B.

Again, combine all the A's + B's and jot down possible headlines or visual ideas.

BEHAVIORISTIC ASSOCIATIONS

Referring back to your prep sheet, begin to play with behavioristics. Here, you're making associations with how, when, where, and perhaps why your target audience will commit to your product or service, especially in terms of buying and using.

Buying

How?—A is like _____ B.

When?—A is like _____ B.

Where?—A is like _____ B.

Why?—A is like _____ B.

Using

How?—A is like _____ B.

When?—A is like _____ B.

Where?—A is like _____ B.

Why?—A is like _____ B.

If you've created a situation where the influencer or decision-maker roles are important to your behavioristic conclusions, then you can complete the statements using the same questions. If so, then change buying and using to influencing and deciding. Again, combine the A's + B's, and if anything clicks, jot it down.

REVERSE ASSOCIATIONS

Take a selection of the associations you've made to this point and reverse them. Try to select a few from each of the association types. Then complete the following statement, eventually joining the A's + B's to help create C's, possible headlines or ideas.

Reverse Association—A is not like _____ B.

Again, combine your A's + B's and jot down the possibilities.

9
IDEA-GENERATION TECHNIQUES: SENSE CONNECTIONS AND CLOSURES

After playing with the association techniques, your idea page should be brimming with idea possibilities. As it fills, the page provides you with a starting point from which to expand your creative consciousness, a kind of branching outward to create ideas from the many realities the world and your advertiser have to offer. But, it should be clear that this branching outward depends on your openness and willingness to follow indirect paths to those ideas. To do that, you need to drop your hard and fast, preconceived notions of what reality can or cannot be. In effect, you must be prepared to create your reality.

At this point, it's also important for you not to be too judgmental in your evaluation of the idea possibilities you've logged on your page. Let them sit and percolate for a while. By all means, don't let them hold you back from generating more. By playing with many of the other techniques to follow, you may find your ideas expanding and spilling over onto other pages. As they do, they should offer you a quantity of possibilities from which to select your *Big Idea*.

The next three chapters continue to outline a variety of idea-generation techniques. Again, use them as toys. Play with them. If one works, play with it more. If one doesn't, set it aside. Don't labor. More often than not in advertising, you simply don't have the luxury of time to dwell on or labor over what may turn out to be an empty pursuit. So, play with these toys quickly. They don't mind. That's precisely their purpose.

SENSE CONNECTION AND CLOSURES

The techniques discussed in this chapter fall under two main headings termed *sense connections* and *closures.*

Sense connections include both association and nonassociation techniques. There are three technique variations, and each relies on the use of senses as the starting point for connection. For example, *sense associations* include associating the features, selling points, benefits, and behavioristic considerations with each of the five senses. *Synaesthetic connections* include the mixing of two or more senses within one creative idea. And, like reverse associations, *reverse sense connections* are a matter of turning the tables or doing the opposite in order to generate ideas. Here, however, the opposite is centered on the senses.

Like sense connections, the *closure* technique also contains variations, with each one providing more alternative means for generating ideas. There are four variations of the closure technique: *visual closures, verbal closures, physical closures,* and *projections.* Overall, the closure technique and its variations make use of the human tendency to complete shapes, lines, pictures, phrases, or even concepts. For example, as you look at Figure 9-1, notice how the shapes and lines are incomplete, but also notice how your mind automatically, almost instinctively completes those shapes and lines. As a result, your mind is much more involved with the images. This is the fundamental purpose of the closure variations, to stimulate the audience to actively participate in the ad's idea or message, thus creating more audience involvement.

Visual closures require the audience to complete shapes, lines, and pictures in order to understand the theme within the idea. Verbal closures require the audience to complete words or phrases in order to complete

FIGURE 9-1   Closure. Art by Mary Ella.

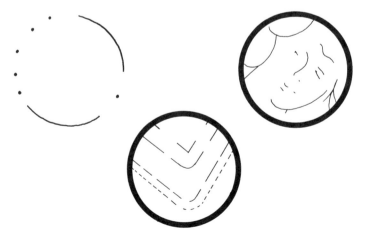

the theme. Physical closures require the audience to physically do something with the ad. And projections require the audience to project the self into the ad.

The value of the sense connections and closure techniques is that they provide you with involving ideas for your audience. They're involving because they gain entrance into the head and heart of your target audience. Normally, though, there's only one way to get to the heart and that's by going through the head. You can accomplish this by going through the entry spots known as eyes, ears, nose, mouth, and skin. Both techniques will help you do that.

SENSE CONNECTIONS

Sense Associations

In order to generate ideas through sense associations, you apply a variation of the statement, A is like _____ B. The variation simply replaces the verb "is" with the sense verbs of smells, sounds, tastes, looks, and feels. As you did with the association techniques, you begin with reference to all of your advertiser's features, selling points, benefits, and behavioristic considerations, and then apply the formula. Once you've made the associations, you connect A with B in order to generate your creative idea, C.

As an example of how a selling point can be used with the sense association technique, look at the Borateem ad in Figure 9–2.

In the Borateem ad, an association is made between the selling point of clean and the sense of smell as symbolically suggested by fresh air. Clean (A) is like the smell of fresh air (B). This association sparks the connection of the two realities and yields the new reality of the creative idea. If you go backwards again from this finished idea, can you imagine how the creative mind played with the selling point of clean? Can you see that mind making all sorts of connections between clean and other realities? Indeed, can you generate new ideas based on connections of clean with other realities, namely other senses? Clean (A) sounds like _____ B. Clean (A) tastes like _____ B. Clean (A) feels like _____ B.

If you also go backwards to many of the ad ideas we've viewed and discussed to this point, you'll find that they, too, lend themselves to sense associations as a technique for generating creative ideas. For example, in the previous chapter, the Maxell ad idea of being "blown away" includes a connection between the product benefit and the sense of touch. Similarly, the Patcraft carpet ad idea comparing the carpet to a sand dune includes a connection between the feel of carpet and the feel of sand.

What you have then in terms of sense associations are a number of techniques embedded into one. Each sense is a workable variation of the one technique. If you form associations and connections between each sense and the various features, selling points, benefits, and behavioristic considerations, you end up with a large number of techniques to generate ideas. Since quantity leading to quality is a key to idea generation, consider using all of those techniques. Again, if one bogs you down, set it aside. If one works, stay with it.

Synaesthetic Connections

Since one of your goals is to get into the audience's head, you should consider playing with synaesthetic connections. Based on synaesthesia, or the mixing of senses in one image, this technique requires a connection of two or more senses within the ad idea. When you appeal to two or more senses, you enter the audience's head through more than one entry point. This is what gives synaesthetic connections such high-impact potential. They have the ability to jar the audience. Plus, they have the ability to stimulate involvement by compounding the audience's sensory commitment to the ad idea.

You can see this high-impact potential of synaesthetic connections at work in the two ads shown in Figures 9–3 and 9–4.

FIGURE 9-2 Sense Association. Courtesy of U.S. BORAX & CHEMICAL CORPORATION for BORA-TEEM BLEACH.

FIGURE 9-3 Synaesthetic Connections. Courtesy of THE PROCTER & GAMBLE COMPANY.

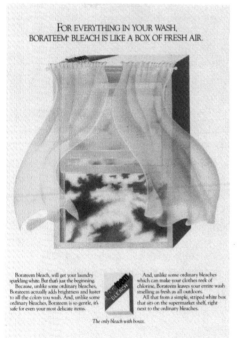

FIGURE 9-4 Synaesthetic Connections. Courtesy of CARILLON IMPORTERS, LTD., for ABSOLUT VODKA.

The Tide ad idea in Figure 9-3 makes use of a familiar advertising technique, that of scratch and sniff, in order to stimulate more than one of the audience's senses into action. Here, you see the ad (sense of sight). Then, you scratch it (sense of touch). And finally, you sniff it (sense of smell). The idea appeals to three senses and thus gains entry into the audience's head three different ways. The result is that it involves the audience.

As you go backwards from this ad to the mental workings of the mind behind it, you may also notice that the statement, A smells like _____ B, appears to be inappropriate here. There's no direct association being made in the ad, except perhaps for the subtle association of the clean smell to the smell of a scentless page. What has been done, quite simply, is to mix the senses together without reliance on a sense association. As this Tide ad illustrates, the use of sense connections, particularly multiple sense connections in the way of synaesthesia, can bypass the more direct associations we've seen being made in some other sensory-based ad ideas.

The ad idea for Absolut in Figure 9-4 also mixes three senses, those of sight, touch, and sound. In order to activate the sense of sound, the reader needs to touch the ad and open it. At this point the Christmas tune "Jingle Bells" can be heard as it plays from a tape embedded behind the glossy black pages of the ad's spread.

As these two ad ideas illustrate, creative ideas based on synaesthetic connections tend to stimulate an audience into action. It's very difficult for that audience to remain passive when two or more of its senses are being stimulated. Once that stimulation occurs, the audience has been absorbed into the ad idea, and the ad idea has been absorbed into the audience, all of which achieves an important advertising goal of involvement.

You should also realize that synaesthetic connections provide you with a new technique to play with when generating ideas. Linked to its parent, sense connections, synaesthetic connections offer a twist on how to use the senses for ideas. One possible tact you can use to generate more synaesthetic ideas is to refer back to those listings of ideas from sense connections and those you made in relationship to the features, selling points, benefits, and behavioristic considerations. Then combine them together to make synaesthetic connections. This will expand your pool of idea possibilities.

Reverse Sense Connections

Still another technique you can play with is that of reverse sense connections. This is similar to reverse associations discussed in the last chapter. With reverse sense connections, you complete the statement, A DOES NOT smell, taste, sound, look, or feel like _____ B.

As a form of contrast, reverse sense connections spark a vividness to the creative idea coming alive in the audience's mind. You can see this vividness exemplified in the reverse sense connection ad idea found in Figure 9-5.

FIGURE 9-5 Reverse Sense Connection. Courtesy of HUNTER FAN COMPANY.

In this Hunter fan ad idea, notice how the product selling point of quietness is conveyed through its opposite, that of noise. The sound image is the reverse of what the product gives. This contrast jars the audience and invigorates the message. To generate the contrast, the creative mind behind the idea had to form a connection between what the product sound was not like, in this case the sound of an old airplane propeller.

As you did with reverse associations in the previous chapter, you can go through all of the features, selling points, benefits, and behavioristic considerations with this reverse orientation in mind. In a sense, it's a bit like changing gears in your head. You stop going forward and proceed to go backward. You reverse. This ultimately provides you with even more idea possibilities.

As always, make certain you've included your theme when you make your sense connections. In this respect, retreat again to the Maytag, Parkay, Federal Express, and Charmin examples. For example, in the case of Maytag, durability (A) smells, tastes, sounds, looks, or feels like _____ B. You can complete the same statements using the individual themes for Parkay, Federal Express, and Charmin. In addition, you can reverse the connections by completing the statement, A does not smell, taste, sound, look, or feel like _____ B.

CLOSURES

Visual Closures

Visual closures is one of the four closure techniques for generating ideas. Remember, if your creative idea enters the audience's head, then attention has been achieved and the chances for involvement are that much greater. With closures the audience's activity in participating with the ad idea means the ad is inside the head. All of the closure techniques seek this as a goal.

With visual closures, audience participation takes on a visual orientation. The audience is visually stimulated to complete the ad idea. For example, the Noxell ad in Figure 9–6 makes use of a visual closure.

With the Noxell ad idea, the headline invites the audience to answer a question through reference to the accompanying visual. A possible scenario to better understand how this can work would include a reader reading the headline and then looking at the two nails in the ad. Just to look at those nails isn't quite enough, however. In addition, the reader must stare at the nails. The reader must give a concentrated focus to their appearance. When this is done, the reader draws the ad closer and closer to the eyes, perhaps literally closer and closer. As the ad is brought up to the eyes, the reader has become absorbed in or involved with the idea.

You should also notice how the closure idea in the Noxell ad carries

FIGURE 9-6   Visual Closure. Courtesy of NOXELL CORPORATION and COVER GIRL NAILSLICKS.

the key message, the theme, in this case a selling point of shininess. The idea doesn't distract from that theme. Further, the idea is extremely single-minded and simple. There can be no mistaking what Noxell will give to the audience. And what it gives is conveyed almost instantly, despite the fact that the audience must be involved to complete the meaning.

With visual closures, the audience relates more to the ad idea's visual than verbal approach. The audience must focus on that visual in order to complete the idea's meaning. As with the Noxell ad, the audience may be stimulated to stare at two pictures and compare them. Or the audience may be stimulated to fill in part or all of a visual. Either way, the end result is a creative idea that accomplishes those two important advertising goals of attention and involvement.

Another variation of how to play with visual closures can be see in the GRAPE-NUTS cereal ad in Figure 9–7.

The visual closure in the GRAPE-NUTS ad is one of mental completion or continuation of the existing visual. In order for the visual to be completed, the audience must span two pages of print. As it does so, it unites the two ad parts found on opposite pages. The parts then come together as one ad. The result is that the ad dominates the double-page spread while actually occupying only one-half of the total space. Once again, this variation of the visual closure technique grabs attention and stimulates audience involvement, this time through the active connection of the ad's two parts.

Verbal Closures

You can use verbal closures to generate ideas by keying yourself into incomplete words or phrases, especially for your headlines. As you continue to go back over the most relevant features, selling points, benefits, and behavioristic considerations logged on your idea page, think of how to get your message across to the audience by not stating it completely. You may, for example, state a part of it. Because only a part of it has been stated, the audience is stimulated to complete the rest of it. You can see how this works in the already classic Volkswagen ad in Figure 9–8.

In this Volkswagen ad, the subordinate clause, "Or buy a Volkswagen" relies on a main clause to complete its meaning. That main clause, however, takes place in the mind of the reader, not on the printed page. In order to complete or close the theme of the ad, the reader is stimulated to create new words, to fill in what is verbally missing. Here, what's verbally missing is the main clause, perhaps something such as, "I can become suicidal over the price of gasoline." This main clause completes the meaning of the subordinate clause at the ad's bottom, "Or buy a Volkswagen." This is an example of the verbal closure technique since the audience has been stimulated to fill in the missing words and thus complete or close the meaning of the message.

As you can tell from this Volkswagen ad, verbal closures can be especially effective since the themes and ideas presenting them are already inside the head of your target audience. For example, can you imagine this ad without that one little word, "Or"? Suppose the headline were simply

"Buy a Volkswagen." Then what? It's that one little word exemplifying the verbal closure technique that's totally responsible for the effect of the ad. Without it, the ad simply isn't the same. With it, the ad enters the head, and the audience is involved. That one little word gives the creative idea its special quality. Indeed, this Volkswagen ad is also something special in other areas pertinent to what we have discussed over the past few chapters.

Recall when we talked about how idea-generation techniques can often bleed into one another and that some creative ideas use combinations of those techniques? In this respect, notice how the Volkswagen ad also contains an association. The association appears to be based on form. The creative mind saw the shape of a gas nozzle as the shape of a gun. In order to do that, the mind couldn't be locked into a rigid perceptual set of what constitutes the two realities of a gas nozzle and gun. For the creative mind, a gas nozzle can be a gun, and a gun can be a gas nozzle.

In addition, notice how the ad exemplifies many of the ADNORMS criteria at work. With a little imagination, the main creative idea of the ad could be adapted to other media. Any other print media are perfectly suitable for the idea. Even the broadcast media aren't out of the picture.

In terms of durability, there may be a problem with the creative idea since the price of gasoline may not always be as significant an issue as it was when the ad appeared. This may pose a problem for the ad's future relevance as well.

The ad is certainly unique, however. It's also most definitely single-minded (oneness) and simple. Right away, the audience gets the message. And the audience gets it quickly because the meaning is so single and simple that it's instantly clear. Due to the tightly coordinated and complementary visual and subordinate clause, the audience is able to create a main clause to complete the meaning. In addition, little time and effort are needed to complete that meaning, mainly because of the idea's strong singlemindedness and simplicity.

If you take all of these factors into account, you can see how this Volkswagen ad serves as an enduring model of what constitutes a creative idea. Based on both closure and association, the ad immediately grabs attention and creates involvement. In addition, both the attention and involvement are centered on, not diverted from, the strategic theme presented by the idea and understood by the audience.

Physical Closures

With physical closures, the audience is physically stimulated to do something with the ad or its medium. Don't think, however, that this technique is restricted to the print media simply because print media are tangible. For instance, an audience can be stimulated to turn off the television set or to turn up the radio. In either case, something physical needs to be

FIGURE 9–7 Visual Closure. Courtesy of GRAPE-NUTS. GRAPE-NUTS is a registered trademark of General Foods Corporation.

FIGURE 9-7 Continued.

FIGURE 9-8   Verbal Closure. Ad copyrighted and reproduced with the permission of VOLKSWAGEN UNITED STATES, INC.

done. And once something physical is done, the audience is involved. You can see how this works by looking at the Honda ad in Figure 9–9.

In the Honda ad, the headline "Quick, turn the page" invites the reader into the medium and consequently into the ad. Immediately, the reader's attention is yoked and involvement follows with the physical action of turning the page. It's almost as if the reader's curiosity is stimulated, similar to anxiously anticipating the opening of a door or a package. The hand turns the page and the surprise headline "Too late" jumps out, carrying with it the idea's theme, that of exciting speed.

Projections

As a technique, projections requires a negation of yourself in favor of someone or something else. You then generate idea possibilities from the perspectives of that someone or something else. In effect, you become someone or something other than yourself. You've already played with this technique when you role played as a mother, developed your Creative Prep Sheet, and were asked to develop your negative capability. Still, you haven't played with it in relationship to the generation of ideas. To do that, you need to project yourself in a way similar to what you see in the Porsche 944 Turbo commercial in Figure 9–10.

Notice how the commercial for Porsche takes place from the point of view of the car. In fact, right at the beginning of the commercial, the voice-over announcer invites the viewer to become the car.

"Imagine you were a car. What would you be?" the announcer asks.

Then, the commercial begins and the viewer is the car, at least as far as the camera angle is concerned. Because of that angle, there's a kind of first-person slant to the commercial. This means the viewer sees things from the car's point of view.

In many respects, projections of this type are closely allied with associations. The difference, however, is that the associations in projections are much deeper. They include being fully involved with and immersed into someone or something else. Recall that when you generated ideas by association you remained somewhat aloof. You were distant, a removed observer seeing things beyond yourself in terms of associations. With projections, though, nothing is beyond yourself since you're inside that someone or something. You're no longer an observer. You're now a participant, actively engaged in being someone or something else.

In playing with projections, you log creative possibilities on your idea page by simply applying a similar statement to the one you've used with associations and sense connections. Only here, you don't always have to be as indirect with your statement. You don't have to use the simile "like." Instead, you might be inclined to use more directness such as A is _____ B. With the Porsche 944 Turbo ad, the viewer or audience (A) is the car (B). Or the car (A) is the viewer or audience (B).

FIGURE 9-9   Physical Closure. Courtesy of AMERICAN HONDA MOTOR CO., INC.

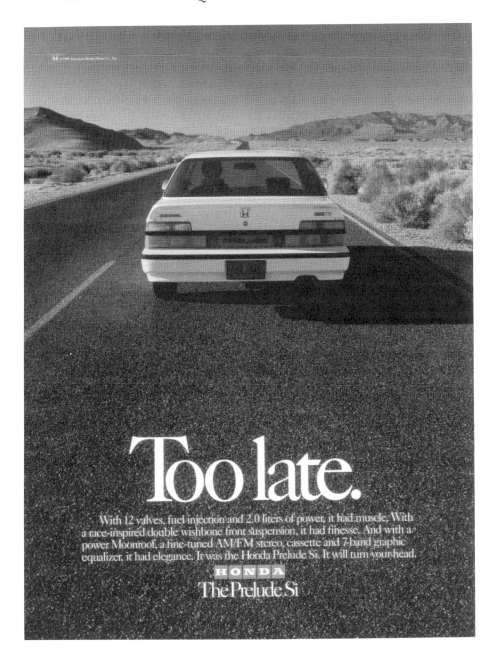

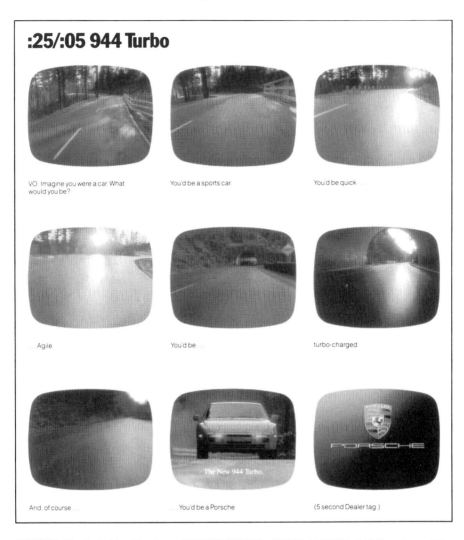

FIGURE 9-10   Projection. Courtesy of PORSCHE CARS—NORTH AMERICA, INC. Porsche and the Porsche Crest are registered trademarks of Dr. Ing h.c.F. Porsche AG.

This doesn't rule out the possibility of actually projecting by being indirect, either. You can still use the basic A is like _____ B statement or even a question evoking a similar answer. With projections, though, you or the audience might be the A, and you would be comparing yourselves to the advertiser or something about the advertiser. The result here would go this way, "What happens if I'm like a car?" or "I'm like a _____ B."

You can also play with projections in other ways as well simply by making the direct associations with any of the features, selling points, benefits, behavioristic considerations, or even senses noted on your idea page. For example, what would happen if you projected yourself into such features as form, content, size, or texture? In other words, what idea possibilities come to mind if you are the form, content, size, or texture of an advertiser, or if those features are you?

As with creative ideas derived from associations and sense connections, creative ideas derived from projections possess high-impact potential, especially in the area of audience involvement. Immediately, the audience is asked to throw itself into a role and to lose itself in favor of that role. As with the Porsche 944 Turbo ad, the viewer is no longer a viewer. Instead, the viewer is inside the television, inside the camera, inside the car, and ultimately inside the ad.

APPLYING THE CLOSURE TECHNIQUES

Since we've been discussing the entire technique of closure as any creative idea requiring some form of audience involvement in order to complete an ad's meaning, you should notice how flexible the concept is in terms of providing you with techniques for generating ideas. For instance, projections range from being another person to being a nonhuman object. Physical closures range from clipping coupons to saving an ad in order to obtain a gift or reward. Verbal closures range from a question in the headline to completing a word or phrase. Visual closures range from completing lines or shapes across pages to filling in parts of specific pictures.

In order to apply this range of closures, you would again refer to your idea page, particularly your list of key features, selling points, benefits, and behavioristic considerations. As you look at each, think of what it would be like to be one. Think of partials. For instance, what would happen if you broke a statement of the benefit in half? Perhaps you could use those three little dots, ellipses, to encourage the audience to read on and become involved in the ad. What would happen if you divided a single ad idea into thirds so that it was expressed in three separate ads? Perhaps you could do this with a before, during, and after buying or use approach. Or what would happen if you created an ad where the audience needs to fill in part of the visual suggesting your key benefit or theme?

You can also generate closures by thinking in terms of questions, invitations, or calls to action in your ideas and headlines. For example, the Noxell ad asks the reader a question. This stimulates the reader to answer and consequently become involved in the ad. The Porsche 944 Turbo ad and the Hunter fan ad, which used the projection and reverse sense connection techniques respectively, serve as examples of invitations and also remind us of how the idea-generation techniques can overlap or bleed together. The Honda ad called for an action on the part of the reader, a call resulting in a physical activity ultimately leading to the meaning of the ad.

To generate many ideas, you should also think beyond what these few examples illustrate. For instance, physical activity isn't restricted to simply turning a page in the print media. As an example, what would happen if you stimulated the audience to use the ad as an object of some kind, perhaps as a placemat or a notepad or a telescope? As a telescope, what would happen if the audience had to look through a hole in one of your ads in order to see a message in another of your ads behind it? Or what would happen if you stimulated the audience to reshape the ad in some way? Maybe it could be reshaped into a paper airplane or a pennant.

Naturally, too, such playing with closure possibilities isn't restricted to the print media exclusively. What would happen, for instance, if you stimulated your audience to turn up the sound? Or what would happen if you offered only parts of messages or pictures in either radio or television?

Finally, you can generate closures by referring back to the many bits and pieces of ideas on your idea pages. Those ideas logged from associations and sense connections to this point, and from other techniques further on in our next two chapters, provide you with the material for adaptation to closure. Can those ideas be broken or framed into questions, invitations, or calls to action? Can they be mixed or matched together within a framework of incomplete sentences or pictures? Indeed, you can generate ideas by combining key statements or message components with those closure techniques already discussed. For instance, what would happen if you combined an elliptical statement with a partial picture stimulating a physical activity on the part of the audience?

SENSE CONNECTIONS AND CLOSURES IN REVIEW

Sense connections and closures are grouped together in this chapter because they have the potential to help you generate involving, creative ideas. When your idea is based on a sense, it stimulates the audience to use that sense. As soon as the sense is activated, the audience is involved. When your idea is based on closure, it stimulates the audience to complete or do something in order to get the meaning of the ad. As soon as that completion or action occurs, the audience is similarly involved.

As with many of the idea-generation techniques, there's considerable overlap between sense connections and closures. Recall, for instance, the Tide ad we classified under sense connections, but which also physically stimulated the audience to do something. As a group, however, sense connections and closures provide you with many more ways to generate creative ideas. As always, these ideas vary in terms of their potential or their completeness and appropriateness. But with them you should have glimmerings of possibilities. Certainly by now you should have ideas that go beyond one page. Embryonic, probably yes. No doubt, some more so than others. But you've expanded your creative consciousness pertaining to the problem at hand. You've also expanded your creative possibilities for solving that problem.

Perhaps it would be wise at this point for you to go back to your initial idea page to make certain you've joined those ideas and key terms with the techniques in this chapter. Again, don't labor. Play. And if you need a quick reference list of what those techniques are, refer to the following:

> *Sense Connections*—All five senses are used as associations and idea generators in multiple relationships with the features, selling points, benefits, and behavioristic considerations. These are termed sense associations. In addition, the mixing of senses inside ideas based on synaesthetic connections have the potential to involve more than one of the audience's senses. Finally, reverse sense connections include ideas based on opposite senses from what might otherwise be presented.
>
> *Closures*—Visual closures, verbal closures, physical closures, and projections are applied as idea generators in multiple relationships with other techniques, ideas, each other, and the key features, selling points, benefits, and behavioristic considerations. Visual closures include using shapes, lines, pictures, or other images requiring completion or a concentrated focus by the audience. Verbal closures include using questions, invitations, or incomplete words or phrases requiring answers or completions by the audience. Physical closures include physical activity on the part of the audience in relationship to the media in which the ad ideas appear. Projections include a negating of the self in order to project that self into someone or something else.

PLAYTIME

Think back to the close of Chapter Eight. You selected a product or service (maybe more than one), mapped out key conclusions, and generated headlines or ideas using the association techniques. Now with sense connections and closures you have new techniques to help spark more possibilities.

First review the key conclusions for your product or service. Pay close attention to your key features, selling points, and benefits, and especially your theme. Then play with some sense connections. Begin with sense associations by completing the statements below. The only change from the associations in Chapter Eight is the use of sense verbs. Apply the sense verbs to the most important features, selling points, and benefits. If your theme isn't represented in one of these three categories, then make certain you apply the verbs to it as well. The chart below can be used for brief quick notations.

SENSE ASSOCIATIONS

	A smells like	sounds like	tastes like	looks like	feels like
Feature	_____ B.	_____ B.	_____ B.	_____ B.	_____ B.
Selling Point	___ B.	_____ B.	_____ B.	_____ B.	_____ B.
Benefit	_____ B.	_____ B.	_____ B.	_____ B.	_____ B.
Theme	_____ B.	_____ B.	_____ B.	_____ B.	_____ B.

As you did in Chapter Eight, combine your A's + B's, and if something clicks, jot it down.

Behavioristics

You can repeat the associations for behavioristics as well. Simply associate how, when, where, and why the product or service is used and bought with each of the five senses. For instance, how it's used smells like _____ B. How it's used sounds like _____ B. Or, when it's bought tastes like _____ B. Where it's bought feels like _____ B. Again, repeat as many of the associations as possible. Don't labor over any one.

For convenience, you can use the chart below to fill in your associations for using. Repeat the chart separately for buying. And remember that you can repeat it again for influencing and decision-making.

	A smells like	sounds like	tastes like	looks like	feels like
How?	_____ B.	_____ B.	_____ B.	_____ B.	_____ B.
When?	_____ B.	_____ B.	_____ B.	_____ B.	_____ B.
Where?	_____ B.	_____ B.	_____ B.	_____ B.	_____ B.
Why?	_____ B.	_____ B.	_____ B.	_____ B.	_____ B.

After you repeat the chart for buying, combine your A's + B's and jot down the possibilities.

SYNAESTHETIC CONNECTIONS

With *synaesthetic connections* you're seeking to create headlines or ideas which merge senses together. In order to do that, you can begin by merging some of your statement completions for sense associations. Go back to those completions and scan your answers. If anything connects, jot it down.

After playing with your statement completions, play with the media in which your idea will appear. For example, if you plan to create a print ad (newspaper or magazine), then play with ways you can merge a sense with the senses of touch and sight. Can you, for instance, include the sense of smell as in scratch and sniff or the sense of sound as in the sound the page will make when turned or crumpled?

REVERSE SENSE CONNECTIONS

To play with *reverse sense connections,* you can re-create your statement charts as they apply to features, selling points, benefits, and behavioristics. The only difference will be in reversing the sense associations. Here, you're generating headline and idea possibilities based on what your key conclusions are not like in respect to the senses. For instance, the smell, sound, taste, look, and feel of sardines, nuts, a college bookstore, or whoever your advertiser happens to be, are not like _____ B. You can continue to play by inserting appropriate features, selling points, benefits, and behavioristic conclusions at the beginning of each statement.

As you've done with sense associations and synaesthetic connections, join your A's + B's, and if something clicks, jot it down.

CLOSURES

With *closures,* you'll be moving away from the more direct associations of the previous techniques. But, you'll still have to connect. You'll have to connect your key conclusions with the four variations of the technique: *visual closures, verbal closures, physical closures,* and *projections.* An effective way of playing with *closures* is to use a question format. Here, you're pushing yourself to give answers that relate to the technique and its variations. To get started, consider the following ways to use the four *closure* technique variations. For each, make certain you've reviewed the key conclusions pertaining to features, selling points, benefits, and behavioristics.

VISUAL CLOSURES

How can I suggest the audience find something in the visual?
How can I suggest the audience complete something in the visual?
How can I suggest the audience insert something in the visual?
How can I suggest the audience create something in the visual?
How can I divide my idea or visual so that it needs another place or time for completion?
How can I only show a part of something in the visual?

VERBAL CLOSURES

How can I match what I say with ideas from my *visual closure* technique?
How can I suggest the audience give an answer?
How can I suggest the audience find a statement?
How can I suggest the audience complete a statement?
How can I suggest the audience insert a statement?
How can I suggest the audience create a statement?
How can I divide my headline so that it needs another place or time for completion?
How can I only say a part of something in my headline?

PHYSICAL CLOSURES

How can I suggest the audience do something with my ad?
How can I suggest the audience do something with the medium?

PROJECTIONS

With *projections,* you're required to change your point of view entirely. This means you or your audience need to be someone or something else. To play with projections, try using the following format.

Imagine you're the audience. Talk about the product or service. Talk about what you like and don't like about it. Talk about what you expect to get from it. Talk about how it can help you. Talk about how, when, where, and why you behave toward it the way you do. Jot down phrases or terms that seem promising.

Role playing as your audience, imagine yourself as the product or service. Talk about it. What is it like? What's good? What's not so good?

Again as your audience, imagine yourself as a specific feature, selling point, or benefit. What is it like? How does it feel? Do you like what you are? Why? Why not?

Now go back to being yourself. Imagine you're the product or service. Talk about yourself. What is it like being a sardine, a nut, a college bookstore, or whoever your advertiser happens to be? What do you like about yourself? What don't you like about yourself? What might your audience like or not like about you? Again, jot down phrases or terms that seem promising.

Imagine you're a specific feature, selling point, or benefit. What is it like to be what you are? How does it feel? Will your audience like you? Why? Why not?

If you've been jotting possibilities down right along, you may have some glimmers of ideas. Don't stop here, though. Continue to generate by asking yourself the following questions.

How can I put the audience into the idea?
How can I suggest the product or service (or its features, selling points, or benefits) be the audience?
How can I suggest the audience be the product or service?
How can I present my theme from the audience's point of view?
How can I present my theme from the product's or service's point of view?

10

IDEA-GENERATION TECHNIQUES: FROM OPPOSITES TO CLOCKS AND CALENDARS

After using your techniques to generate and log idea possibilities, you may feel a little tilted. A little bit out of whack. By now, you may feel the gears grinding in your mind. You may believe that doing your work also means your mind isn't supposed to think in such ways. With idea-generation, however, it is.

Though we often apply associative and closure thinking to our daily routines, thoughts, and conversations, when it comes time for work, we tend to believe that an orderly, straight-and-narrow approach to our thinking is the path to success. When we're asked to think differently, then those gears in our minds will grind. Remember, though, that a large part of creativity is just that, thinking differently. This includes thinking differently in a variety of ways as well. In advertising creativity, this is the path to discovering successful creative ideas.

Since your gears may be grinding, however, at this point it's important to reinforce in your mind several key points developed in our earlier chapters. First, the advertising professional community wants new, innovative, different, and ultimately creative ideas. Second, your success may well depend on your taking chances with those creative ideas. Third, creative ideas aren't irrelevant, misleading, or distracting. And fourth, the way to discover creative ideas is to keep yourself open, think laterally, and have many means available for your discoveries.

With all of these important points in mind, you can continue to generate creative idea possibilities by playing with the techniques introduced in this chapter. Once again, not all of the techniques will work all of the time or under all conditions. If some don't, then don't labor over them. Set them aside. Perhaps come back to them later. But if some work, play with them until they stop working. Then go on to others, perhaps back to associations, sense connections, and closures. Remember, the idea-generation techniques don't have to be played with in any particular order. What's important is that they're played with. That's all.

As with the previous techniques, the new techniques in this chapter are a means for generating ideas that grab attention and involve the audience. Unlike the techniques based on associations and the senses, however, those in this chapter extend beyond direct or indirect forms of association. One technique, *opposites*, includes alternatives for breaking media, audience, or competitive expectations. Another technique, *verbal plays*, includes alternatives for playing with letters, syllables, words, or phrases. A third technique, *personalizations and personifications*, includes alternatives for selecting audiences and personifying messages. A fourth technique, *clocks and calendars*, includes alternatives for linking messages with specific times and events relevant to those times. As a group, these techniques keep you branching outward and upward with your ideas. No doubt, after you play with them, your idea pages should be overflowing with creative idea possibilities.

OPPOSITES

To an extent, you've already played with opposites when you generated ideas by playing with reverse associations and reverse sense connections. What you did was to turn things around in your mind and generate idea possibilities as opposites of other idea possibilities. You can now expand this means of generating when you think of opposites in other respects as well. The key is to generate ideas through techniques aimed at breaking expectations in a variety of ways. We'll look at three techniques grouped under the heading of verbal and visual opposites.

Verbal and Visual Opposites

As a rule of thumb, *verbal* and *visual opposites* are a broadbased means of thinking in reverse about idea possibilities. Since they stem from a more general approach, they will govern the more specific techniques of media, expectation and competition opposites. This means you should expect over-laps. Still, verbal and visual opposites get you started thinking exclusively in reverse. However, play with the techniques in your own way, bearing in mind right along that the more varieties of techniques you have, the better your chances for discovering quantities of idea possibilities.

As you can see in the Volkswagen ad in Figure 10–1, a verbal opposite is used to convey a product selling point, that of smallness.

This classic Volkswagen ad exemplifies how the creative mind recon-ciles and balances opposites, in this case verbal opposites. The common-place expression at the root of the ad is that of "Think big." All of us have heard it. Many of us have grown up with it. For the creative mind, however, it's possible to turn that expression around to suit whatever the creative goals happen to be. Here, the goals are to grab attention and create involve-ment through a creative idea carrying the theme of smallness. Thinking of a verbal opposite is one way to reach those goals. By referring to a key product selling point, smallness, and then noting expressions based on that selling point's opposite, bigness, the creative mind generates an idea break-ing expectations.

With visual opposites you follow the same pattern of thinking you used with verbal opposites. Obviously, the difference is that the opposite is a visual, not a verbal, approach. For example, if smallness is the selling point to be conveyed, then a visual using bigness would be a consideration. A big ad containing a small picture of the product may be another alternative. In this respect, the Volkswagen ad connects the verbal and visual techniques. Notice, for example, how the small car is placed in the context of a great deal of ad space.

Naturally, your choice of what expressions or visuals to use as oppo-sites depends on what you're advertising. Once you decide on the theme to be conveyed, boil it down to a key word or two, and then think of familiar expressions or visuals with the potential for reversal. For instance, suppose you were creating a print ad for preventing child abuse. You want your idea to grab attention and create involvement. Plus, you know how important it is to be different in order to achieve those goals. Surely, one way to be different is to do the opposite of what's expected. The expression "Spare the rod and spoil the child" is commonplace and expected. But what hap-pens if you turn it around to say, "Spoil the rod and spare the child"?

To begin playing with opposites, log those verbal and visual opposites that come to mind during or after your review of features, selling points, benefits, and behavioristic considerations. Use key words to suggest expres-sions or visuals. In our Volkswagen and child abuse examples, those key words would be small, big, and child. Jot those expressions and visuals down. Then play with turning them around.

FIGURE 10-1 Verbal Opposite. Ad copyrighted and reproduced with permission of VOLKSWAGEN UNITED STATES, INC.

Media Opposites

You can also generate idea possibilities through *media opposites* by logging the characteristics of your media on your idea page. Then ask yourself what would happen if your idea did the opposite of one or more of those characteristics. For example, the Transamerica ad we looked at in Chapter Four is an example of a media opposite (See page 49).

As you've done several times before, re-create how the creative mind played itself into an ad idea. Realizing magazine was a medium of choice, and understanding the ever-present need for advertising to grab attention, the mind connected advertiser features, selling points, and benefits with that medium. One of the key features is the unique Transamerica building. One of the key selling points is the innovativeness of Transamerica's insurance policies and business practices. So, the creative problem is how to present that uniqueness and innovativeness. Clearly, one way is to be unique and innovative with the advertising idea since this means the idea would mirror the message or theme. Still, the question is, How do you do that?

Since the creative mind needs to convey uniqueness and innovativeness through the creative idea, then by their very nature, media opposites would be one alternative means for achieving that goal. Media opposites are different. They do the opposite of what the characteristics of particular media suggest they should do. In doing the opposite, and thus being different, they're also new. Consequently, if the mind is able to connect certain opposites with the feature of the building and with the selling point of innovativeness, then a creative idea that is both new and relevant should emerge.

By considering the characteristics of a particular medium, in this case magazines, the creative mind can then proceed to turn each characteristic around to its opposite. Ultimately, this is what sparks creative idea possibilities. For instance, characteristics of magazines include all of those features we discussed in Chapter Eight under feature associations. Included here would be features such as form, content, size, or texture. To these you can add others such as pages, color, and flatness.

Clearly, the Transamerica pop-up ad exemplifies the opposite of flatness. Most, if not all, pages in magazines are flat. All ads are flat as well. Not so, however, for the creative minds at Della Femina McNamee, WCRS, Inc. There, an ad can stand up. It can rise from the page. This is an example of an idea containing a media opposite, in this case the opposite of flatness.

Ideas originating from media opposites aren't restricted to magazines or to innovativeness as a selling point. Since your goal is to generate as many ideas as possible within your time constraints, you may be wise to avoid constricting yourself with too much reliance on selling points or benefits, at least at the outset. This means initially giving more focus to ideas sparked by opposites of the media characteristics and then returning to those ideas to see how they connect with your Creative Plan.

In using the Transamerica ad as an example, you can apply the same type of creative thinking to generate your ideas, regardless of the media in which those ideas will appear. For instance, if your creative idea is to be used on television, log the characteristics of television and then consider idea possibilities by doing the opposite of those characteristics. Since most televisions are color, what would happen if you created a black and white commercial? Since television commercials use sound, what would happen if you didn't? Indeed, what would happen if you thought beyond the television screen per se? As an example, consider what happens in a Greyhound television commercial, the key frames of which are line drawn in Figure 10–2.

This Greyhound spot, titled "'Knock Knock /Ann," features the spokeswoman actually knocking on the viewer's screen and saying, "Excuse me. Why are you sitting there? It's time to take advantage of Greyhound's low, low summer fares." This is the way she introduces the commercial in the first frame, by knocking on the screen and speaking those lines. The point is that the strength of the creative idea hinges on doing the opposite of what's typically done on television. In effect, Ann is looking at you as much as you're looking at her. This is a kind of role reversal or projection conveyed through a reversal of the medium's characteristics.

As the last two frames of the spot suggest, the ad's conclusion revolves around Ann actually turning the television off. She clicks a knob, and the screen darkens (frame 3). In this way, Ann has complete control of the television. Here, the reversal of roles jars the audience and creates instant attention and involvement. By knocking on the screen and then turning the set off, Ann has broken the veneer of the television and has addressed her audience directly, one-on-one.

Regardless of the medium and how idiosyncratic or autonomous you believe each to be, you can still generate idea possibilities by doing the opposite of what the medium's characteristics suggest should be done. Simply note the media's characteristics or features and proceed to turn them around into idea possibilities.

FIGURE 10-2 Media Opposite, Courtesy of GREYHOUND LINES, INC. Art by Mary Ella.

Expectation Opposites

Closely allied with media opposites is the technique of *expectation oppo-sites*. Only here, you generate ideas based on the opposites of what the audi-ence expects to see or hear from you or the media. Obviously, the two tech-niques of media and expectation opposites often result in overlap. If you play with both, however, you'll tend to guard against the possibility of over-looking or exluding a potentially exciting creative idea.

To generate ideas based on expectation opposites, note what expecta-tions the audience has regarding your advertiser and the media in which your idea will appear. Then ask yourself what happens if you turn those expectations around. For example, the Cosmopolitan ad in Figure 10–3 ex-emplifies an expectation opposite. Also, as you look at the ad, notice how it serves as an example of a media opposite as well.

Typically, a reader of a magazine is accustomed to seeing ads with vi-sual elements facing out from the page, not into it. In the Cosmopolitan ad, both the woman and the Cosmopolitan name face into the page. Their appearance is the opposite of what the audience has been predisposed to expect. Because of this jarring of expectations, the attention of the audience is yoked and riveted to the ad.

In Figure 10–4, you see another example of an expectation opposite. In this case, the opposite is personalized by none other than Joe Isuzu. Here, the exaggeration of Joe Isuzu's "lies" goes against the grain of what an audi-ence is expecting when it encounters an ad. Of course, an audience will expect that an ad idea and copy will present the vested theme of the adver-tiser. But will the audience expect such outrageous lies as those given by Joe Isuzu? It's doubtful. What we end up with as a result is a creative cam-paign idea that has grabbed the attention and interest of a large part of society, particularly its young people.

One way to increase idea possibilities from this technique of expecta-tion opposites is to log two sets of expectations on your idea page. Devote one set to what the audience is likely to expect from the particular media in which your idea will appear. Devote the other set to what the audience is likely to expect from you as an advertiser. Perhaps the audience will ex-pect you to be serious and formal. If so, at least think about ideas that are the opposite of serious and formal. Similarly, if the audience expects you to be lighthearted and informal, think about serious and formal ideas. For instance, when confronted with the topic of life insurance, most people are inclined to be serious. They expect the advertising for life insurance plans or companies to be equally serious. In generating idea possibilities for such an advertiser, however, consider a more whimsical, lighthearted approach.

Again, bear in mind that your goal is to generate quantities of idea possibilities. Though you may not necessarily use the ideas stemming from opposites, they should be logged so that they may be used later on. Don't rule anything out. This means you need to keep yourself open to those ideas

FIGURE 10-3   Expectation Opposite. Courtesy of COSMOPOLITAN.

in line with the media characteristics and audience expectations. You also need to keep yourself open to those ideas not in line with what those characteristics and expectations are as well. Generating by media and expectation opposites is a means for finding those ideas not in line.

"To demonstrate how the Lotus suspension improved the Impulse's handling, I took it for a spin on my test track."

He's a little off track.

You don't have to go to an amusement park to try the Impulse's new handling. Just take it around your block. But hold on tight because Lotus, the renowned leader in sports car handling, spent five months giving the Impulse what *Motor Trend* calls, "a dose of handling magic."*

They experimented with 250 different shocks. Tested over 300 tires. Travelled over 30,000 miles. Until they found the perfect combination of shocks, stabilizer bars and wide Bridgestone Potenza tires. So you can fly around corners without flying out of your seat.

And if it's more speed you're after, try the fuel-injected, intercooled Impulse Turbo. You'd have to wait in line for a faster ride.

But the biggest thrill of all is getting the Impulse for as little as $14,109.** Now that's something to scream about.

For free Isuzu brochures call: (800) 245-4549. In California: (714) 770-3490.

*Motor Trend, February 1988 **M.S.R.P. P.O.E. excluding tax, license and transportation fee. Prices subject to change.

ISUZU

Proud sponsor of the 1988 Summer Olympics on NBC.

FIGURE 10-4   Expectation Opposite. Courtesy of DELLAFEMINA, MCNAMEE WCRS, INC. Actor: David Leisure.

Competition Opposites

Generating ideas from *competition opposites* initially requires that you have a good hold on competitive advertising. A good hold means you understand both the matter and manner of that advertising. You understand what the competitive themes are and how they're being presented. Of course, all of this relates directly back to research and to your Creative Prep Sheet and Creative Plan. When you review them, summarize your competition's advertising on your idea page. Then generate idea possibilities by doing the opposite of what your competition is doing. For example, the AT&T "Superman" ads in Figure 10–5 make use of competition opposites.

One AT&T ad is a magazine ad. The other is a television spot shown here via a storyboard. Generally, companies such as AT&T and products such as a special AT&T Card for business use tend to be serious in their advertising. They tend to take a formal, perhaps sophisticated or high technology approach. Not so with this ad idea. It uses a cartoon format to convey the serious theme.

Here, we're assuming the opposite is that of the competition. It should also be clear, however, that the opposite may be either the media or the audience. For instance, as a media opposite, the cartoon format reverses what magazines and television typically show as advertising. As an audience opposite, the idea breaks the expectations we have regarding AT&T advertising and the more typical and expected executions we're likely to find in a magazine such as Industry Week or on television. Either way, the idea is unique, surprising, and continuous from one medium to the next.

In keeping with your goal of finding quantities of ideas, opposites stimulate you to think beyond the typical and ordinary, especially in terms of typical and ordinary expectations. Once again, however, to think that way places demands on your own preconceived notions of what reality can and cannot be. To play with opposites, you must be open and willing to let those gears in your mind grind against those preconceived notions. You must be open and willing to see reality stood upside down on its head and a full one-hundred and eighty degrees from what it ordinarily suggests.

VERBAL PLAYS

Typically, verbal plays make use of poetic devices such as onomatopoeia. Be warned, however. When creating headline or copy ideas, you're not creating poetry for the sake of poetry. You're creating ideas that strategically and innovatively present themes derived from your Creative Plan. This means the ideas can't get in the way of your themes. They can't be poetic for the sake of poetry any more than they can be creative for the sake of creativity. Instead, they actually must be, or at least mirror, your themes.

Despite this warning, be assured of this as well: Advertising copywrit-

AT&T Communications–Business

Title: "Superman"

Comm. No.: AXBL 6334
Length: 30 Seconds

LOIS: Gosh Clark, we've got to get back to the office and call London . . .

. . . before the meeting's over.

TAXI !!!

(MUSIC)

(MUSIC)

VO: With the AT&T Card . . .

your people have the power . . .

to handle business better.

LOIS: TAXI TAXI !!!

VO: From anywhere, to anywhere.

LOIS: Come on, Clark . . .

CLARK: It's OK, Lo. everything's taken care of.

LOIS: You always disappear in an emergency?!?

VO: Order the AT&T Card.

VO: It gives your people enormous abilities.

FIGURE 10-5   Competition Opposites. Courtesy of AT&T BUSINESS MARKETS GROUP.

FIGURE 10-5 Continued.

ers love and respect words. And they love and respect them because of what words can do. This means copywriters aren't as far removed from poets as some are inclined to believe. Both copywriters and poets have a similar view of words and their power. It's just that the goals of each are different in terms of the motivations for playing with words. This also means they can learn from each other. In respect to creative advertising ideas expressed through words, copywriters can learn an important lesson known to poets throughout the centuries. Appropriate use of poetic devices energizes words, gives them power, and makes them meaningful and memorable, helping them stick in the heads and hearts of the audience.

To generate idea possibilities through verbal plays, take key words or terms from your features, selling points, benefits, and behavioristic considerations, and apply poetic devices to expressing those words or terms. You've already seen one such device at work with the Volkswagen headline "Think small." The device was contrast, or what we called a verbal opposite. There the familiar expression "Think big" was turned upside down. What emerged was "Think small," with smallness being a selling point for Volkswagen. Beyond this kind of contrast of opposites, however, there are many other poetic devices you can play with to give your ideas an attention-grabbing, memorable quality.

Alliteration, Rhyme, Onomatopoeia, and Multiple Meanings

While referring back to your key words and terms, play with poetic devices such as alliteration, rhyme, onomatopoeia, and multiple meanings. You can start at the very beginning with the name of your advertiser. No doubt, one goal of all advertising messages is that the name of the advertiser stick in the audience's mind. You can help make that happen by applying the poetic devices. Take the first letter, syllable, or complete name of your advertiser and play with it. What happens if you draw it out, meaning you stammer through the letter, syllable, or name? That's what HERSHEY'S did in its campaign idea of "H-H-H-HERSHEY'S. One of the All-Time Greats." You'll probably recognize that campaign idea from the radio script shown in Figure 10-6.

With the single, controlling, and simple idea continuous through both television and radio, the stammered "H" gives the HERSHEY campaign a special touch, adding to its memorability. Unexpected and surprising, the sound of "Heh-Heh-Heh-HERSHEY'S" in the mind helps make the product name stick.

Another technique, that of associations, is used in this HERSHEY'S campaign. For instance, "All-time Greats" is repeated throughout the campaign and is given visual meaning in television through the associations the viewer makes with other all-time greats. These include greats from the art and entertainment worlds. Overall, governing the television idea are associ-

```
                                                    AS  PRODUCED
                                                    8/28/87


                     HERSHEY'S MILK ALMOND

                  ALL TIME GREATS (RADIO :30)


Music
Female Singer                       H-H-H-Hershey's.

Female VO                           Got to have a--

Female Singer                       One of the all time--
                                    One of the all time greats.

Female VO                           Know what I mean girls?

Female Singer                       One of the all time greats.

Female VO                           When ya' gotta have a--

Female Singer                       Pure milk chocolate

Female VO                           Smooth

Female Singer                       Almonds

Female VO                           Delicious

Female Singer                       Nothin' but a Hershey will do.

Female VO                           Am I right?

Female Singer                       H-H-Hershey's
                                    Hershey Bar.
                                    One of the all time--
                                    One of the all time greats.
                                    H-H-H-Hershey's.
                                    One of the all time--

Male VO                             Pure milk chocolate,
                                    With or without almonds.
                                    Hershey Bar.
                                    One of the all time greats.

Female Singer                       Ooohhh yeah--
                                    (Fade out)
```

FIGURE 10-6 Verbal Play (Alliteration). The ONE OF THE ALL-TIME GREATS advertisements are reprinted by permission of the copyright owner, Hershey Foods Corporation, Hershey, Pennsylvania, U.S.A. HERSHEY'S and ONE OF THE ALL-TIME GREATS are registered trademarks of Hershey's Foods Corporation.

ations between HERSHEY'S as one of the all-time greats and other all-time greats. In effect, the creative mind completed the statement, as an all-time great, HERSHEY'S (A) is like _____ B.

Combined, the stammered "H" and association make the HERSHEY'S campaign unique and therefore memorable. As such, the campaign should suggest to you the openness needed when you play with the idea-generation techniques. Be open to combinations. Be open to playing with more than one technique in order to merge unique approaches into one creative idea.

Keeping yourself open and returning to product name considerations, try generating idea possibilities based on the first letter, syllable, or complete name of your advertiser. For instance, Price Pfister, a manufacturer of bath fixtures, uses words such as fabulous, fancy, and faucet in its advertising. The words, however, are spelled creatively as Pfabulous, Pfancy, and Pfaucet and can be seen in Figure 10–7.

Notice how the words in the Price Pfister commercial are actually shown on the screen. Their alliterative spelling aids the attention-grabbing potential of the campaign while simultaneously helping product name memorability. Obviously, it's no mistake that the name, Pfister, contains an identical beginning to words such as pfabulous or pfancy. Obviously, too, it's no mistake that those words beginning with "pf" are also key selling points for the product.

Beyond alliteration for the product name matched with features, selling points, benefits, or behavioristic considerations, also consider playing

FIGURE 10-7   Verbal Play (Alliteration). Courtesy of PRICE PFISTER COMPANY and EISAMAN, JOHNS, & LAWS, INC. ADVERTISING. Art by Mary Ella.

with other poetic devices such as rhyme or onomatopoeia. Ask yourself what rhymes with the advertiser's name or what rhymes with key features, selling points, or benefits. Even ask yourself what those features, selling points, or benefits suggest in the way of meanings derived from the sounds of other words. For instance, the Jello ad in Figure 10–8 uses an off-rhyme of jiggle for jingle. In fact, the word "jiggle" is also onomatopoetic, in that its sound suggests the actual meaning, in this case the product feature of Jello's behavior as a food.

We'll see this Jello ad again when we talk about another idea-generation technique, once again demonstrating the potential interplay of technique combinations. In reference to the ad idea as shown here, though, the idea exemplifies playing with words in order to surprise, grab attention, and still convey a product selling point. "Jiggle" is an off-rhyme with "jingle." As readers, immediately we pay attention to the off-rhyme since it's not quite right. It's a bit different, a bit off-center, and thus it's more memorable. Since the very sound of "Jiggle" (onomatopoeia) suggests the meaning, we also understand the message conveyed by the creative idea.

Using onomatopoeia to convey your advertiser's important features, selling points, and benefits or problem solutions helps the audience consolidate and unify theme and idea together. When connected with the theme, the sounds of the words themselves tighten and harden the impact of the ad idea. For example, the Alka-Seltzer ad idea "Plop. Plop. Fizz. Fizz. The Sound of Fast Relief" in Figure 10–9 connects theme with idea in a tight, unified structure.

Notice how the Alka-Seltzer idea uses a sensory connection, in this case the sound of the product in use, and unifies it with the benefit to the consumer. The sound of the product, the plopping and fizzing, is really a product feature, a characteristic of the product. But the feaure leads straight through to the benefit, that of relief. Also notice how the rhythmic quality of "plop" and "fizz" and the musical cadence of the entire theme line join together to make the idea attention-grabbing, memorable, and, of course, relevant. The consumer will feel a kind of harmony in the digestive tract, a kind of rhythmic, easy feeling, which is really the benefit from using the product.

Another verbal play technique to use for idea generation is that of multiple meanings. As with alliteration, rhyme, and onomatopoeia, multiple meanings can be very effective for grabbing attention. They have additional power and impact, too, since they occupy extra space in the heads and hearts of your audience. In this respect, they produce effects similar to those produced by associations and sense connections. The audience must think on two or more tracks and even respond in more than one way. This means ideas relying on multiple meanings have considerable involvement potential, stimulating the audience to connect meanings. When the audience does connect, it becomes involved with the idea that now occupies

Jiggle bells,

Jiggle bells,

Jiggle all the way...

FIGURE 10-8   Verbal Play (Off-Rhyme and Alliteration). Courtesy of GENERAL FOODS CORPORA-
TION/DESSERT DIVISION.

Oh, what fun for fruit to have a Jell-O®holiday.

Nothing makes fruit more jolly than Jell-O® Brand Gelatin. Berries get merry, cherries cheer up, and nuts come out of their shells when paired up with that jolly old favorite. And if fruit jumps for joy, just imagine how your family will react. You better watch out.

Cranberry Tarts A-Glow

1 package (4-serving size) JELL-O® Brand Strawberry Flavor Gelatin or Sugar Free JELL-O® Gelatin
1 cup boiling water
¼ cup Ocean Spray® Cranberry Juice Cocktail
½ cup Ocean Spray® Whole Berry Cranberry Sauce
8 baked 3" tart shells
1 to 1½ cups fruit (banana slices, halved seedless grapes, drained canned mandarin orange sections and additional whole berry cranberry sauce, drained)

Dissolve gelatin in boiling water. Measure ⅓ cup; add juice and set aside. Add cranberry sauce to remaining gelatin and chill until very thick. Chill clear gelatin until thickened. Spoon cranberry mixture into shells. Arrange fruit on top; add drained cranberry sauce. Carefully spoon clear gelatin over fruits to glaze. Chill 1 hour. Makes 8 tarts.

Cheers to Cherries Parfait

1 can (8 oz.) pitted dark sweet cherries
1 package (4-serving size) JELL-O® Brand Strawberry or Cherry Flavor Gelatin or Sugar Free JELL-O® Gelatin
¾ cup boiling water   Ice cubes
1 cup thawed COOL WHIP® Whipped Topping
¼ cup slivered toasted almonds

Drain cherries, reserving ½ cup syrup. Quarter the cherries. Completely dissolve gelatin in boiling water. Combine measured syrup and ice to make 1¼ cups. Add to gelatin, stirring until slightly thickened. Remove any unmelted ice. Let chill until thickened. Measure 1¼ cups, add half of the cherries and the chopped nuts; set aside. Fold whipped topping into remaining gelatin; add remaining cherries and nuts and spoon into glasses. Chill until set but not firm, about 15 minutes. Top with clear gelatin mixture. Chill about 1 hour. Garnish with whipped topping. Makes about 5 cups or 4 to 6 servings.

Banana Nut Wreath

1 can (8 oz.) crushed pineapple in juice
2 packages (4-serving size) JELL-O® Brand Lime Flavor Gelatin or Sugar Free JELL-O® Gelatin
2 cups boiling water
½ cup sour cream
1 large banana, sliced
Pecan halves

Drain pineapple, reserving juice; add water to juice to make 1½ cups. Dissolve gelatin in boiling water; add measured liquid. Measure 2 cups and chill until slightly thickened. Blend remaining gelatin into sour cream; add the pineapple and chill until thickened. Arrange banana slices and pecans in about ⅓ cup of the clear gelatin in 5- or 6-cup ring mold. Add remaining clear gelatin and chill until set but not firm. Add creamy mixture. Chill until firm, at least 3 hours. Unmold. Garnish as desired. Makes about 5 cups or 10 servings.

JELL-O & SUGAR FREE JELL-O GELATIN
WE'VE GOT FRUIT APPEAL

FIGURE 10–8 Continued.

FIGURE 10-9 Verbal Play (Onomatopoeia and Rhyme). Courtesy of MILES INC. Copyright 1979 Miles Inc.

at least double the mental and emotional space of a more straightforward idea.

When the U.S. Marines say they're "looking for a few good men with the mettle it takes to be Marines," the power and impact of that copy line relies to a great extent on the multiple meanings of the word "mettle." Each meaning is central to the Marines and the appeal they make in their advertising. Literally, mettle means inner strength and courage. Beyond that, meanings exist for medal and metal as well. Both words conjure up images or symbols of what being a Marine is all about. These images or symbols are then translated into meanings by the audience. What results is a kind of expanding reverberation of these meanings in the audience's mind so that the entire creative idea, complete with drum roll, medals, and sabers, occupies greater space in the mind. This is the kind of effect to be realized when creative ideas use multiple meanings to convey key messages.

Not only do multiple meanings require your audience to think expansively about your idea and theme, they also require the same of you in order to generate them. You're required to think beyond the literal meanings and realities of words. In a sense, you elasticize the words, stretching them out to include layers of meaning relevant to the matter and manner of your message. For example, the Ten Huntington Restaurant & Bar ad in Figure 10–10 exemplifies how the creative mind thinks in this way.

Clearly, the tone of the Ten Huntington Restaurant & Bar ad is light-hearted and humorous. But the tone also stems from the double meaning of the word "consommé." Without that double meaning, the tone is lost. Quite possibly, the power and impact of the ad are lost as well. The total effect of the ad is just not the same as it is with the play on the word "consommé."

If you re-create how the creative mind arrived at that play on the word, you would have to include that mind's openness to expand beyond the word's literal meaning as it's known in the world of gourmet food. Perhaps the mind noted the various features of the bar and restaurant, one of which was consommé. From there, the mind thought laterally, elasticizing what that literal word, or another word close to it could mean. The result was the headline. "For Those Who Think Consomme Is Something The French Do On Their Wedding Night." Not only is that headline dependent on the double meaning for its power and impact, it's also dependent on it for the tone or feel of the ad idea.

Similar effects can be felt from the self-promotion billboard for Carlisle Advertising in Figure 10–11.

On the Carlisle billboard, the word "Board" has been stretched to include a play on the word "Bud" as in a well-known beer slogan and theme line. But the use of the word "Board" in this context also suggests the tone behind the message. What you have is a kind of tongue-in-cheek, light-hearted feel to the ad idea. Plus, the double meaning urges the viewer to give a double-take to the message, almost like two yanks on the viewer's mind.

Many words, such as board or consommé, lend themselves nicely to multiple meanings as an idea-generation technique. As you refer back to the key words in your features, selling points, benefits, and behavioristic considerations, keep an eye open for such potential with those key words, and think expansively beyond their literal meanings. You may even consider stretching them somewhat, such as what was done with the word "Board" in order to connect it with the word "Bud."

Regardless of which verbal play technique proves to be most successful for you as you generate headlines and ideas, play with each of them, if only

A RESTAURANT FOR PEOPLE WHO UNDERSTAND THAT CONSOMMÉ ISN'T SOMETHING THE FRENCH DO ON THEIR WEDDING NIGHT.

Complimentary parking with dinner.

Dinner served Monday-Saturday, 6-10 pm

10 Huntington Avenue at The Westin Hotel, Copley Place, Boston 262-9600

FIGURE 10-10   Verbal Play (Multiple Meaning). Courtesy of THE WESTIN HOTEL, COPLEY PLACE, BOSTON/TEN HUNTINGTON RESTAURANT & BAR.

FIGURE 10-11   Verbal Play (Multiple Meaning). Courtesy of CARLISLE OUTDOOR, INC.

for a limited time. Juggle them, and juggle with them. Don't labor over those that don't work. Move on. Use another. Generate some more.

To see how productive and even enjoyable verbal plays can be, glance through the headlines that follow. They were generated by students asked to use verbal plays as a source for their headlines and ideas. Don't just identify the specific techniques involved, though. Look into the headlines and you'll see the possibilities of easily coordinated visuals. Look into the headlines and you'll see some fun behind them, too. You'll see young minds playing, but playing with intent.

The first two headlines refer to print ad ideas for a Nissan competition. The target audience for both ads was the college student. The first headline was for the Nissan Pulsar NX, and the second was for the Nissan Sentra.

GIVING RUSH A NEW MEANING. THE NISSAN PULSAR NX.
NISSAN SENTRA HELPS YOU CUT CORNERS.

The third headline refers to a campaign idea for an American Academy of Advertising competition. The target audience was parents. The objective of the campaign was to provide parents with helpful advice in how to communicate with their children about the dangers of drug abuse.

NO TO DRUGS IS TO KNOW YOUR CHILD

The last three headlines are campaign ideas for Philadelphia. Students selected their own target audiences, but their objective was to sell Philadelphia as a mini-vacation alternative for those in the mid-Atlantic states.

PHILLY, PFAMILY, AND PFUN.
THRILLADELPHIA
GET YOUR PHIL IN PHILADELPHIA

PERSONALIZATIONS AND PERSONIFICATIONS

When you generate ideas through *personalizations* and *personifications,* you're transforming your key features, selling points, benefits, and behavioristic considerations into something human. You're personalizing and personifying them for your target audience. When you do that, you're really creating a common ground for communicating with that audience. As individuals, your audience can connect with the personalized, human element in an ad idea, assuming of course that the human element is in keeping with what the audience likes or respects. Plus, the human element has that uncanny knack for warming up your message and for breaking down the walls of aloofness and insincerity.

As always, you begin to generate ideas using personalizations and personifications by first referring back to those initial lists of features, selling points, benefits, and behavioristics noted on your idea page. Then, tap into your creativity by playing with the two techniques.

To play with personalizations, imagine yourself in one of two scenarios. First, imagine you're with your target audience. The two of you are friends, and you're leisurely walking side by side. You happen to believe something. In this case, you believe something about your advertiser. It may be one of those important features, selling points, and benefits or problem solutions, and you believe your friend should believe it, too. With those beliefs in mind, imagine you turn to your friend. What do you say? How do you say it? Jot the answers to those questions down on your idea page. Do they spark idea possibilities?

In the second scenario, imagine you want to grab the attention and involvement of your audience, only this time the audience isn't necessarily your friend. And you're in a crowded room to boot. Once again, what do you say? How do you say it? Jot down the answers and see if they spark idea possibilities.

The ideas stemming from the first scenerio should feel highly personalized and warm. Perhaps they include testimonials. In actuality, when you spoke to your friend, you were giving a testimonial. Perhaps your ideas include words or images your friend can connect with. They may even call your friend by name. This kind of idea, commonly referred to as selective headlining, borders on the ideas originating from the second scenario.

From the second scenario, you may have generated idea possibilities intent on selecting your audience. For instance, we've already discussed the headline, "Corns gone in five days or your money back." We discussed it in terms of offering a benefit to the audience. Here, think about that headline in terms of selecting the audience. Only those with corns or those fearful of getting them will pay attention to the headline. As you generate ideas through *personalizations,* think about ways you, too, can select your audience. Call the audience by name, for instance.

Once you've planted the seeds of idea possibilities from personalizations onto your idea page, turn your attention to personifications. This technique is a bit more concrete than personalizations in that it requires you to construct an individual or trade character symbolizing one or more of the key items from your lists.

Consider creating a real person as the core of your creative idea. Of course, that person should personify something important (the benefit, for instance) about your advertiser. As an example, notice again the ad idea for Maytag which appeared in Chapter Four (See page 56).

As discussed in Chapter Four, for years Maytag has used the lonely repairman as the core of its enduring creative campaign idea. The lonely repairman personifies Maytag's dependability. You can count on Maytag machines not to break down. As the core of the idea, it's the repairman who personifies this theme. As a result, the idea is personalized with the human element.

Because of the warmth of the human element, advertising is brimming with individuals personifying specific advertiser features, selling points, and benefits or problem solutions. One of the most captivating in recent history was Clara in the popular Wendy's "Where's the Beef?" campaign. She can be seen in Figure 10–12.

With her endearing and easily remembered voice, face, and manner, Clara personified the unique selling proposition for Wendy's, that of more beef. There's also something to recognize about Clara, though, and it should be taken into account when you generate ideas through personifcations.

As you construct an individual to personify something important about your advertiser, make certain that individual is unique in some way. Make the individual an individual, not a clone. A little eccentricity if need be. Give a little twitch here. One eyebrow raised higher than the other there. Make the voice slightly off key. Elongate the nose. Shorten the legs. In other words, above all else, make the individual human. Breathe life into that individual. Remember, perfection is an illusion. Imperfection is real. To make the individual supposedly perfect is to make the individual nonhuman and unreal. And, that's difficult for anyone to connect with.

THE WENDY'S NATIONAL ADVERTISING PROGRAM, INC.

TITLE: "FLUFFY BUN"

LENGTH: 30 SECONDS
COMM'L NO.: WOFH-3386

CUST. #1: It certainly is a big bun.
CUST. #2: It's a very big bun.

CUST. #1: A big fluffy bun.

CUST. #2: It's a very...big...fluffy... bun.

CUST. #3: Where's the beef?
ANNCR: Some hamburger places give you a lot less beef on a lot of bun.

CUST. #3: Where's the beef?

ANNCR: At Wendy's, we serve a hamburger we modestly call a "Single"— and Wendy's Single has more beef than the Whopper or Big Mac. At Wendy's, you get more beef and less bun.

CUST. #3: Hey, where's the beef? I don't think there's anybody back there!

ANNCR: You want something better, you're Wendy's Kind of People.

FIGURE 10-12   Personalization and Personification (Real People). Courtesy of WENDY'S INTERNATIONAL, INC.

Talk about imperfect. In Figure 10–13 you see the prototype of the imperfect and yet memorable individual, Joe Isuzu. His exaggerated behavior, complete with lies, sarcasm, and wit, takes him out of the ordinary and makes him all the more memorable as a result. This is the important point about using personalizations in your ideas. Yes, they need to be real so we can connect with them. But they also need to have a twist about them, something eccentric and different that makes them memorable. Such is the case with Joe Isuzu.

Still another slant to playing with personifications is to create a trade character as the center of your creative idea, and one who once again personifies something important about your advertiser. For example, for years Alka-Seltzer used the character of Speedy Alka-Seltzer in its advertising. He's seen in Figure 10–14. Cute and endearing, he personified an important product benefit, that of speedy relief.

As you looked at Speedy Alka-Seltzer, did you notice how spry he appears? Imagine him running and how quick, how speedy, he would be. The point is that your character should be what the product is, gives, or means. In the case of Speedy Alka-Seltzer, he is what the product means to the consumer.

To create an individual or trade character isn't necessarily to create an advertising idea per se. But such personifications can help launch an idea. Plus, they're often the center of a governing idea, especially if they strongly suggest the theme presented by that idea. An example of how central such characters can be to creative ideas can be seen in an ad for Met Life shown in Figure 10–15.

In the Met Life ad, the theme line "A Flight to Quality" clearly exemplifies another technique, that of clocks and calendars, to be explained shortly. The ad also exemplifies the use of recognizable and endearing characters to help present the theme. These Peanuts characters grab audience attention to the ad, not away from it. Plus, the context in which they're shown is one representing the theme.

In playing with personalizations and personifications, you're beginning with a human element that has the potential to bring your creative idea to life. As you generate specific individuals or characters, you'll find they begin to move and speak. When they do, they suggest other possibilities in your mind. They expand your own creative consciousness toward the problem at hand. Ultimately, they may reach a point where they become inseparable from the creative idea. It's a point where you cannot have one without the other. It's also a point where you know you've achieved the communicative strength of the human element, even with imaginary characters who are, after all, more human than nonhuman in many respects.

CLOCKS AND CALENDARS

To generate ideas using *clocks and calendars,* connect the key items from your lists with those events relevant to certain times. Time can include an hour, part of a day, a season, a year, an era, or even those events occurring at certain points in time. This means you should think laterally in respect to time. You need to think in the present. You also need to think forward into

"Isuzu Trooper II.
The 4x4 that conquered Everest."

What a snowjob.

The truth is, if you want to reach the top of Mt. Everest, you'd be better off driving a yak. On the other hand, you don't have to beat a Trooper II with a stick to get it moving.

Shift into 4-wheel drive and its fuel-injected 2.6 liter engine will eagerly take you just about anywhere. Barren deserts. Snow covered streets. Muddy riverbeds. And *some* mountains.

Shift back into 2-wheel drive, and it'll eagerly take you through long stretches of highway or cramped supermarket parking lots. Or fold up the rear seat, making sure all rear seat passengers are gone, and you've got 71 cubic feet of storage space.

And unlike a yak, a Trooper II can be ordered with automatic transmission, captain's chairs, and 2-door or 4-door body styles.

The result is something that handles like a station wagon. Hauls like a Sherpa. And looks like nothing else on or off the road. All for thousands of dollars less than other comparable vehicles.

Looks like our rivals have slipped.

ISUZU II

FIGURE 10–13 Personalization and Personification (Real People). Courtesy of DELLAFEMINA, MC-NAMEE WCRS, INC. Actor: David Leisure.

He's not lying, he's just optimistic.

But then again, he's got a reason to be. Because Isuzu has already won the grueling Baja 1000 twice* and this is our most advanced 4x4 ever.

Under all that mud (and great options) is a bigger new body that's aerodynamically shaped to cheat the wind. With more ground clearance to cheat the ground.

While under the hood is a new 2.6 liter electronically fuel-injected powerplant that churns out 120 horsepower, more than any other base-priced import in its class.

And to make all that power easy to handle, it also comes with standard power steering and the only standard 4-wheel disc brakes in its class.

Of course, the nicest part of our new Isuzu 4x4 is that it's not just our newest. It happens to be the newest 4x4 on the market.

Which means this Isuzu has the most up-to-date engineering you can buy. And that's not just optimism.

ISUZU

*Class 7S, 1984; Class 14, 1986.

Proud Sponsor of the 1988 Summer Olympics on NBC.

FIGURE 10-13   Continued.

FIGURE 10-14 Personalization and Personification (Characters). Courtesy of MILES INC. Copyright 1953 Miles Inc.

the future and backwards into the past. Again you're expanding, thinking laterally beyond your current position, in this case your position in time.

Hours and Days

Try using the question method when you play with clocks and calendars. Ask yourself questions, such as When is the advertiser used (behavioristics)? or When will the ad appear (media)? For example, Löwenbräu used the headline "Tonight, Let it be Löwenbräu" in its advertising. Michelob used the headline "Weekends were made for Michelob." Each of these headlines controlled the creative ideas and exemplify the consideration of time.

As you ask yourself these questions, jot down your answers. Then jot down headlines using those answers. For instance, consider the question. When will the ad appear? Answer it with specifics, even down to the hour or day. If the answer is morning, then generate ideas using the morning as a starting point. Think of all things pertaining to morning and connect them with the key items from your lists. Consider the rising sun, a rooster, breakfast, alarm clocks, traffic, or cups of coffee. Then do the same thing

FIGURE 10–15 Personalization and Personification (Characters). Courtesy of METROPOLITAN LIFE INSURANCE CO., and UNITED MEDIA LICENSING. PEANUTS Characters c 1965 United Features Syndicate, Inc.

as you answer other questions, such as When is the product puchased or used?

Seasons

As you ask yourself these questions, try to expand the answers as they relate to time. In other words, go beyond the hour or day to a season. For example, suppose one of your answers is Christmas time. What can you do with that answer? The two ads for Tanqueray Gin in Figure 10–16 suggest some possibilities.

Notice how Tanqueray Gin inventively uses the Christmas motif to present the messages in the ad idea. There are, of course, any one of a number of physical manifestations of Christmas that can be used to generate creative ideas. That's one of the advantages of using clocks and calendars as a technique. Once you've keyed into a specific time, Christmas, for instance, you can think of a number of relevant words or images to help present your theme. For Tanqueray, the Christmas tree and Christmas wreath become the creative ideas but the creative ideas could just as easily have originated by thinking of a sleigh, stockings by a fireplace, or a snowman on the porch.

To generate ideas, then, jot down the physical manifestations of whatever time is relevant to your ad and when it will appear. Or jot down the manifestations of when your advertiser is purchased or used. Then, as is evident in the Tanqueray ads, imagine how you can put your advertiser in that manifestation of time.

Before we leave the Tanqueray ads, though, bear in mind still other important points about their creativity. The creative mind behind these ad ideas wasn't locked into a preconceived notion of what constitutes reality. For the creative mind, a Christmas tree is not just a Christmas tree. A wreath is not just a wreath. They can be more. In order to think of them as more, however, you need to dissolve and transform their ordinary frames of reference in reality.

As with the Tanqueray ad ideas, the connection made by the creative mind was one of a seasonal shape and the product. This should remind you of the form association. The difference, however, is that the form association connects the shape of the product with the shape of something else. With the Tanqueray idea, the shape of something else is connected with the advertiser, regardless of its shape. This allows you to include many things into the seasonal shape. Typography in the shape of a Christmas tree, for example (or anything else for that matter).

At the same time, don't be misled by the reliance here on the visual approach. You can also connect a verbal approach to a particular season in much the same way the verbal approaches (headlines) for Löwenbräu and Michelob connected with specific times of day. Recall, for instance, the Jello ad you looked at in conjunction with verbal plays. The headline for the ad was, "Jiggle bells, Jiggle bells, Jiggle all the way . . ." There, the connection to the Christmas season was achieved through a verbal approach. In this respect, consider jotting down words, phrases, or even songs that are relevant to the particular season, and then connecting them with the key items from your lists.

Happenings

Think about introducing new questions to stimulate answers and ultimately ideas, For instance, ask yourself, What's happened recently? What's happened not so recently? or What's liable to happen? Jot down answers. Then, connect those answers with the items from your lists. Does anything emerge?

You can see how this technique works as you look at the ad for Chemical Bank in Figure 10–17.

In the fall of 1987, the stock market took its worst plunge since the beginning of the Great Depression in 1929. Many investors were stunned. Many lost confidence in the stock market as a viable alternative for reaching financial goals. With this as a backdrop, the Chemical Bank ad idea exemplifies how the creative mind uses news events (things that are happening) as a foundation for a creative idea. Here the familiar bull, symbolizing the positive spirit and vigor of an upward-bound stock market, is seen shedding a tear. The headline, "Maybe it's time to put your money in Chemical Bank," summarizes the meaning of the strong visual. In addition, this same kind of connection to the newsworthy stock market crash was at the core of the Met Life ad you viewed a short while ago.

It should be clear that to use happenings, you need to be up on your news. For instance, if you didn't know the stock market had crashed when it did in 1987, then you wouldn't have been able to generate the Met Life and Chemical Bank ad ideas. Or, if you weren't up on the news pertaining to the health benefits of aspirin, it wouldn't have been possible to generate the idea you see for Bayer Aspirin in Figure 10–18.

In the mid-1980s, scientific research results pointed out that aspirin was helpful in reducing the risk of heart attack. During 1988, this topic received wide news coverage across the country. Ads for aspirins began to appear more frequently, obviously promoting these newly found benefits of using aspirin. Even before 1988, however, the news was out, and Bayer Aspirin was one of the first to advertise it.

Of course, the point overall is that you can connect the items on your list with any one of a variety of timely and relevant news events in order to stimulate ideas. You can, in fact, expand beyond news events to include songs, movies, or contemporary expressions and sayings. Jot them down. Use them to generate and connect.

FIGURE 10-16   Clocks and Calendars (Season). Courtesy of SCHIEFFELIN & SOMERSET CO., for TANQUERAY GIN.

FIGURE 10–16 Continued.

FIGURE 10–17   Clocks and Calendars (Happenings). Courtesy of CHEMICAL BANK.

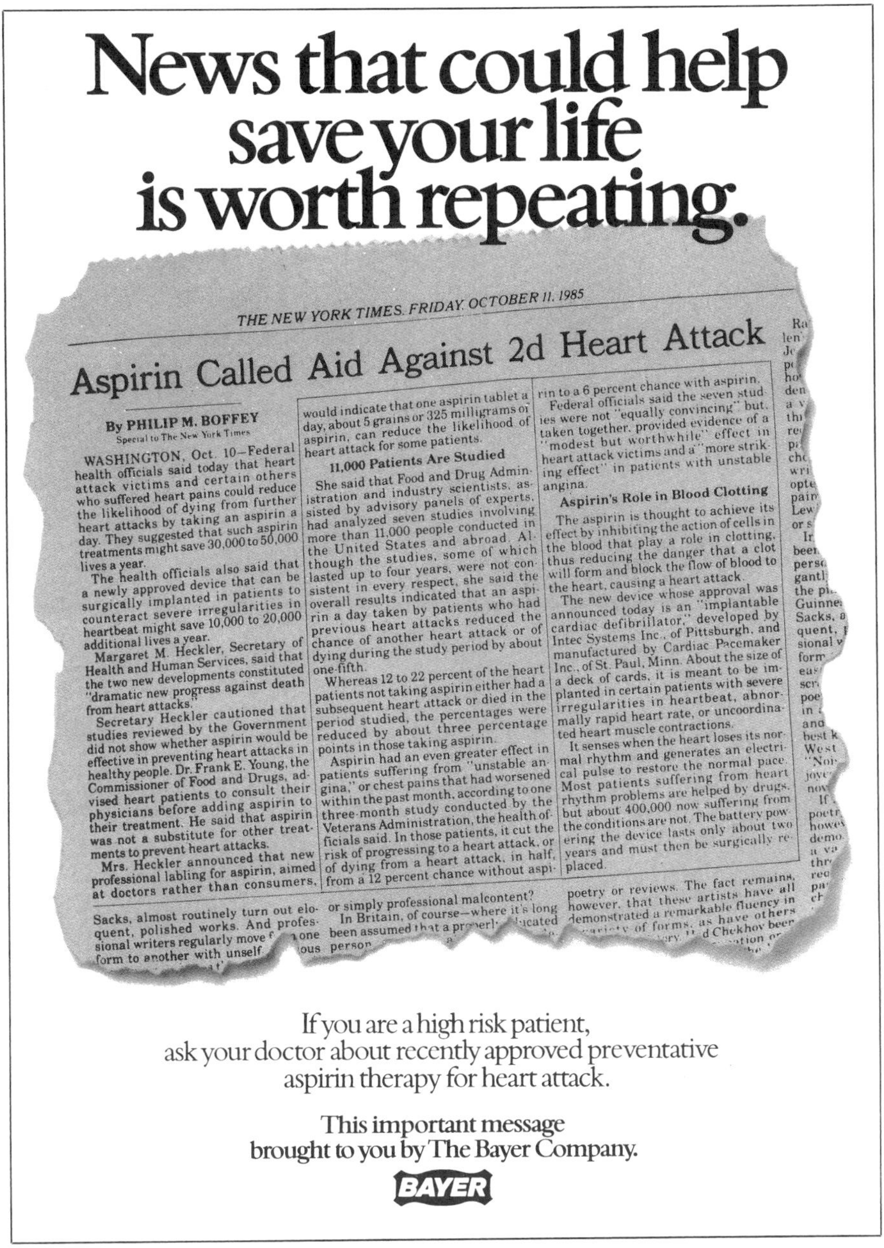

THE NEW YORK TIMES, FRIDAY, OCTOBER 11, 1985

Aspirin Called Aid Against 2d Heart Attack

By PHILIP M. BOFFEY
Special to The New York Times

WASHINGTON, Oct. 10—Federal health officials said today that heart attack victims and certain others who suffered heart pains could reduce the likelihood of dying from further heart attacks by taking an aspirin a day. They suggested that such aspirin treatments might save 30,000 to 50,000 lives a year.

The health officials also said that a newly approved device that can be surgically implanted in patients to counteract severe irregularities in heartbeat might save 10,000 to 20,000 additional lives a year.

Margaret M. Heckler, Secretary of Health and Human Services, said that the two new developments constituted "dramatic new progress against death from heart attacks."

Secretary Heckler cautioned that studies reviewed by the Government did not show whether aspirin would be effective in preventing heart attacks in healthy people. Dr. Frank E. Young, the Commissioner of Food and Drugs, advised heart patients to consult their physicians before adding aspirin to their treatment. He said that aspirin was not a substitute for other treatments to prevent heart attacks.

Mrs. Heckler announced that new professional labling for aspirin, aimed at doctors rather than consumers, would indicate that one aspirin tablet a day, about 5 grains or 325 milligrams of aspirin, can reduce the likelihood of heart attack for some patients.

11,000 Patients Are Studied

She said that Food and Drug Administration and industry scientists, assisted by advisory panels of experts, had analyzed seven studies involving more than 11,000 people conducted in the United States and abroad. Although the studies, some of which lasted up to four years, were not consistent in every respect, she said the overall results indicated that an aspirin a day taken by patients who had previous heart attacks reduced the chance of another heart attack or of dying during the study period by about one-fifth.

Whereas 12 to 22 percent of the heart patients not taking aspirin either had a subsequent heart attack or died in the period studied, the percentages were reduced by about three percentage points in those taking aspirin.

Aspirin had an even greater effect in patients suffering from "unstable angina," or chest pains that had worsened within the past month, according to one three-month study conducted by the Veterans Administration, the health officials said. In those patients, it cut the risk of progressing to a heart attack, or of dying from a heart attack, in half, from a 12 percent chance without aspirin to a 6 percent chance with aspirin.

Federal officials said the seven studies were not "equally convincing" but, taken together, provided evidence of a "modest but worthwhile" effect in heart attack victims and a "more striking effect" in patients with unstable angina.

Aspirin's Role in Blood Clotting

The aspirin is thought to achieve its effect by inhibiting the action of cells in the blood that play a role in clotting, thus reducing the danger that a clot will form and block the flow of blood to the heart, causing a heart attack.

The new device whose approval was announced today is an "implantable cardiac defibrillator," developed by Intec Systems Inc., of Pittsburgh, and manufactured by Cardiac Pacemaker Inc., of St. Paul, Minn. About the size of a deck of cards, it is meant to be implanted in certain patients with severe irregularities in heartbeat, abnormally rapid heart rate, or uncoordinated heart muscle contractions.

It senses when the heart loses its normal rhythm and generates an electrical pulse to restore the normal pace. Most patients suffering from heart rhythm problems are helped by drugs, but about 400,000 now suffering from the conditions are not. The battery powering the device lasts only about two years and must then be surgically replaced.

FIGURE 10–18 Clocks and Calendars (Happenings). Courtesy of GLENBROOK LABORATORIES, DIVISION OF STERLING DRUG, INC.

Bear in mind, however, that you're not restricted to the relative present when you generate ideas by playing with happenings. It's possible to expand beyond the present and consider the past or future as well. Certainly, nostalgia-based ideas fit in here. Recall, for instance, the H-H-H-HERSHEY'S campaign idea discussed earlier. Futuristic ideas fit in as well. Again, you're thinking laterally, beyond the somewhat restrictive reality of the here and now.

OPPOSITES, VERBAL PLAYS, PERSONALIZATIONS AND PERSONIFICATIONS, AND CLOCKS AND CALENDARS IN REVIEW

Once again, using your prep sheet and plan as starting points, you can apply the techniques in this chapter to generate a quantity of ideas. By switching from one technique to the other and going back to the techniques in your previous chapters, your ideas should be spilling over onto other idea pages. Again, many of those ideas are sure to be embryonic. They're beginnings, not completions. That's the point of the techniques, however. They get you started and moving, and they get you started and moving in many different directions.

From this chapter you have clusters of four main techniques to generate ideas. Those four main techniques are divided into technique variations. With opposites, for instance, you begin with a generalized verbal and visual approach. Then you play with media, expectation and competition opposites. With verbal plays, you use a number of poetic devices such as alliteration, rhyme, onomatopoeia, and multiple meanings. With personalizations and personifications, you play with real people or imaginary characters as personified suggestions for key advertiser features, selling points, and benefits or problem solutions. And with clocks and calendars, you play with time and events in time in order to generate ideas.

As you generate ideas using these techniques, remember to keep part of your mind focused on your prep sheet and plan. Don't lose sight of the fact that you're a communicator and persuader. This means you need to keep in touch with your audience and advertiser. Not only do you need to keep in touch with them, you need to connect them. Many of the idea possibilities you've generated should be viewed from that perspective.

Though you may be inclined to apply judgment at this point in the creative process, don't. Not yet. Don't select your *Big Idea* or what appears as the beginning of your *Big Idea*. There are still other techniques you can play with to generate even more ideas. We'll run through them quickly in our next chapter. As with those you've come in contact with already, though, these new techniques are "unblockers." They're meant to keep you fluent with your ideas, to keep you generating quantities of idea possibilities. Again, use those that work, and avoid laboring over those that don't. And, of course, play.

PLAYTIME

Once again, go back to your selected product or service. Review your key conclusions. Make certain they're firmly in place in your mind. Then you can begin playing with the techniques from this chapter.

VERBAL OPPOSITES

As you scan your key conclusions, try turning the words or images around in your mind. For example, recall our discussions of Maytag, Parkay, Federal Express, and Charmin. Recall that we isolated several key terms which could summarize the themes for each of the advertisers. In playing with *verbal opposites,* you turn these key terms around. In so doing, the opposites suggest possible headlines or ideas. Instead of durable for Maytag, what happens if you play wth flimsy? Instead of buttery taste for Parkay, what happens if you play with artificial? Or slow for Federal Express? And hard for Charmin?

The first thing to do then is to turn those key words or phrases around. Log their opposites. Then think of common, everyday sayings or clichés that may apply to your product or service such as what Volkswagen did with its headline, "Think Small." Turn those around as well. Again, if anything clicks, jot it down.

VISUAL OPPOSITES

To play with *visual opposites,* take a few of your most promising ideas from the previous techniques and chapters and think of ways to turn them around. Do the opposite.

Then, expand beyond those promising ideas and think visually by imagining your product or service as the opposite of what it seems. Do the same for key features, selling points, and benefits. For example, a sardine can is small. What happens if you make it big? Can a college bookstore be a gameroom? Can an all day petsitting service be shown as a spa or fitness club? Can you use feet, socks, or shoes in an ad for a hat store? Log the possibilities.

MEDIA, EXPECTATIONS, AND COMPETITION OPPOSITES

Once you've logged some idea possibilities, begin to use the technique variations for opposites. To do this, list the characteristics of your medium, the expectations of your audience, and the characteristics of your competition's advertising. Then generate ideas by thinking opposite of what those characteristics and expectations suggest. You can use the format below to organize your thoughts. When you're finished filling in the sections, you can play with combinations. Remember to keep yourself open to possibilities.

Media Character-istics	Opposite	Audience Expecta-tions	Opposite	Competi-tion Character-istics	Opposite

VERBAL PLAYS

In playing with the technique of *verbal plays,* you're looking for verbal twists, the kind that will give your theme memorability. You can begin by playing with the product or service name. Use alliteration, rhyme, onomatopoeia, and multiple meanings as you play. Again, you can refer to the chart below to make quick notations of possibilities.

Name _____

Alliteration	Onomatopoeia	Rhyme	Multiple Meaning

Once you've jotted down possibilities from your chart, use the same poetic devices to generate ideas for key features, selling points, benefits, and behavioristic conclusions. Remember to include your theme. In fact, you may want to think of your theme separately and generate ideas solely based on that theme. Again, you would use alliteration, onomatopoeia, rhyme, and multiple meanings. To keep yourself organized, you can repeat the use of the chart as many times as you need.

PERSONALIZATIONS AND PERSONIFICATIONS

With *personalizations,* you create headlines and ideas which pay particular attention to your target audience. As you did earlier in this chapter, imagine you're walking side by side with your audience. You speak to your audience about your product or service. What do you say? Jot down the bits and pieces of what you would say. Look for headline or idea possibilities. Then answer this question, What would I call my audience if I wanted to grab attention? Jot down the possibilities and consider using a selective headline, one that actually addresses the audience by a name or descriptive title such as mothers, teens, or achievers.

With *personifications,* you generate ideas by bringing your advertiser to life. You give your product or service flesh and bones. You give it a personality. You make it human, if even as a caricature or trade character. To do that, you can begin by fleshing out a person to represent your advertiser or some salient feature, selling point, or benefit. Again, consider your theme as well. You can flesh out your person by answering the following questions.

If my advertiser (or feature, selling point, benefit, or theme) were a person what would he or she look like?

What sex?

How tall?

What color hair? Eyes?

What kind of body frame?

What quality of voice?

What is my person's occupation?

How does my person dress for his or her occupation?

What eccentricity is unique to my person?

What's memorable about my person?

If my person were placed in a situation to demonstrate or exemplify the benefit or theme, what would the situation be?

When would the situation take place?

Where would the situation take place?

Of course, you may consider other questions as you think of them. But these should get you started. In addition, remember to mix the techniques as you go along. For instance, consider creating a person who would be the opposite of your prototype individual. And, as always, remember to log the possibilities as they occur to you.

CLOCKS AND CALENDARS

With *clocks and calendars* you will need to focus on time and those events or happenings that take place in time. You will also need to focus on behavioristics. In this respect, you will need to answer how, when, where, and why the product or service is bought and used. Is it morning? Night? On the weekend? During a particular season? In addition to behavioristic connections, you should play with media connections. This means you will need to determine when your ad will appear.

Once you identify the purchase and use of the product and the audience's exposure to your ad in reference to time, you should play with realities central to that time. As mentioned earlier in this chapter, the morning may suggest a rising sun, a rooster, breakfast, alarm clocks, traffic, or cups of coffee. What happens, then, if you connect these realities to your advertiser?

In reference to your list of advertisers and time, is it possible that you can have Salty Sunday with Sardines? How about Go Nuts Tonight? Or Hats Off to Saturday? Or special Hubcap Hours?

In the same way you've made connections between time and purchase, use and media exposure, you should play with events or happenings that take place in time. This can include new or old. New songs. Old songs. New movies. Old movies. Current events. Old news stories. Make a list of happenings and connect the items on your list with your product or service. Does anything click? Jot it down.

11
IDEA-GENERATION TECHNIQUES: FROM SYMBOLS TO STRAIGHT SHOW AND TELL

By now your idea pages should be brimming with ideas. No doubt as you logged those ideas, you also stopped along the way, thinking that certain ones glimmered. That's fine. Note those that glimmer. But don't let that stop you from generating more. Go back and play with a few of your favorite, more productive techniques again. Or go ahead to the new techniques introduced in this chapter. They're especially appropriate for overcoming creative blocks. When you feel walled in, try playing with them. They will help you break down your predisposed patterns of perceiving and thinking.

As a group, the techniques in this chapter will be covered quickly. This doesn't mean they're less important than the techniques from other chapters. On the contrary, you may find them very important to your idea-generating capabilities. Because they lack a group identity, however, they are not classified under any particular heading. They're more random, more diverse. Individually, though, they are still toys. So, play with them.

SYMBOLS

As an extension to associations, *symbols* are used to convey the meaning of one thing by connecting it with another. As opposed to associations, however, with symbols you're not always asking yourself what something else is like. Many times, you're simply listing all concrete or physical realities symbolizing something important and relevant about your advertiser.

To generate ideas through symbols, again focus on the key terms from your first idea page. Then, list concrete realities that connect with and symbolize those terms. For example, assume that a key selling point is the saving of time. To generate idea possibilities, list all time symbols. Your list might include wall clocks, grandfather clocks, wristwatches, stopwatches, pocket watches, calendars, hourglasses, or sundials. From there you would visualize and verbalize creative approaches.

Or assume a key selling point is solidity, such as you might find with a financial institution or investment firm. What you would do is list all concrete realities connecting with and symbolizing solidity. Certainly, that's what Prudential-Bache Securities accomplished with its "Rock Hard, Market Wise" campaign idea. Other symbols might include pyramids or steel.

One of the areas to concentrate on with symbols is Mother Nature herself. She offers you a full range of possibilities. If you recall, the Maxell ad in Chapter Eight used wind as the basis for its association. Wind can be used as a symbol from nature. So can anything else derived from nature, including animals. Here, you may want to list those animals symbolizing your key terms. For instance, if strength is an important selling point, then list those animals known for their strength. List those trees known for their strength as well. List anything else from nature symbolizing the key term. In fact, look at the list of potential selling points that follows. Can you name or identify one bird, one fish, one mammal, and one other concrete reality from nature for each of those terms on the list?

Graceful
Intelligent
Speedy
Efficient
Cute
Pretty
Exciting
Adventurous
Lovable

Obviously, the list could go on indefinitely. And no doubt you've been able to think of many symbolic references to Mother Nature. What happens if you use them in your headline? In your visual? Jot down the possibilities.

FRAMES

In generating through *frames,* you're looking for ideas based on symbolic casings. This means you need to list all possible enclosures for the main copy and visuals. In effect, your ideas either originate from, or actually are these symbolic enclosures. For example, if you were advertising for a travel agency, you might list those symbols relevant to travel and then imagine them as enclosures. A suitcase frame, for instance, may enclose or house all the copy and visuals. A hotel door could do the same thing. So could a lounge chair or a swimming pool.

As another example, if a key selling point is the saving of time, then consider using those symbols of time talked about earlier as frames. For instance, instead of simply using a clock as a symbolic part of the visual or as a spark for a headline, consider framing everything inside it so that your creative idea is driven and controlled by the clock enclosure.

With frames, what you're looking for are visual approaches to suggest additional ideas. The act of framing in your mind allows you to see the main points of your message together as a unified whole. When those main points are encased in a relevant symbol, the idea begins to take shape. Indeed, the frame itself can act as a spark for generating headlines, especially if you note the words describing the physical characteristics of the frame. Using these words as a starting point, you can then generate headlines to coordinate with the frame visual.

FROM THIS TO THAT

One of the important goals of every creative idea is to make your audience aware of some change resulting from use of your product or service. Somehow, life just isn't quite the same when your audience chooses you instead of someone else. You can recall your first date as an example. If you were liked by your special someone, then chances are that someone would perceive the realistic possibility of your adding something important to his or her life. That someone would perceive you changing that life somehow, no doubt in a positive way. In other words, your special someone could perceive a benefit. This is exactly what you should consider when you use *from this to that* to generate ideas.

On your idea page, list the conditions of your audience prior to purchasing and using your product. Then list how the conditions change after buying and using the product. Of course, conditions can be many things, but what you're really after are physical, mental, or emotional states. By purchasing and using the product, your audience should go from one state to another. What is that state? Is it from warm to cold, or cold to warm? Is it from less knowledge to more knowledge? From boredom to excitement? Again, jot down the possibilities.

It should be clear that using from this to that as a technique is still another way of getting at benefits. Recall from the previous three chapters that benefits were vital as foundations for generating ideas. This new technique offers you another way to play with benefits.

FORCED RELATIONSHIPS

Like associations, *forced relationships* are a common idea-generation technique suggested for use by leading researchers in the field of creativity. For
instance, Sidney J. Parnes of The Creative Problem-Solving Institute is one
of the foremost advocates of forced relationships. As a technique for overcoming creative blocks, it has also been advocated by Edward de Bono. He
referred to it as random stimulation. Here's how it works.

When you're blocked or when you feel as though you're shut off from
new approaches and ideas, force your problem or a key item from your first
idea page together with anything entering your consciousness. To do this
obviously demands openness on your part. Keep your mind open. Let it
wander. Jot down those random images or words that enter. It doesn't matter what they are. It doesn't matter whether you believe they're appropriate
or not. Remember, defer judgment. Don't rule anything out at this point.

In recalling our beginning chapters, you should remember how important it is to be a keen observer of the world around you. Do you remember
how the workings of the creative mind are a matter of connecting realities
observed and experienced in real life in order to create new realities, creative ideas? This is what you're doing when you play with forced relationships.

Look at your surroundings. What are the physical realities of those
surroundings? Jot them down. Close your eyes and open a book to any page.
Place your finger on a spot on the page. Open your eyes and look at what
your finger is pointing to. Jot it down. You can even try doing this with a
dictionary.

As you're jotting down these random images or words, try forcing your
problem or key item together with them. What happens? Does anything
click? Does the seed for an idea emerge?

To better understand the technique and how it can be helpful in the
generation of ideas, consider these examples from two creative students.
Both were working on a national competition for Nissan Corporation. The
first student noted several idea possibilities on an idea page. The page also
contained a number of random images and words he was asked to note as
part of his playing with forced relationships. One of those images was a
boxing ring. When I asked the student if he could "feel" a creative idea
from his page, he said "no". He was firm in his answer. Here's how the rest
of the conversation went.

Me: Okay, you have a sporty, high-performance car. It has a lot of zip and punch.
      It's also smooth riding and easy to handle. Have you tried to connect those
      selling points and benefits with some of those images and words on your
      page?
Him: Yeah, sure. But nothing works.
Me: What about the boxing ring? Have you tried that?

Him: (laughing) Come on! You can't connect a boxing ring and a sports car.
 Me: Why not?
Him: Because they don't go together, that's why not.
 Me: Do me a favor. Go take a walk and don't come back here until you've con-
       nected something about the boxing ring and your car. Make the connection
       a headline.

Disgruntled and put off, the student stomped out of the room. Within ten minutes he was back, standing in the doorway with that wild "Eureka!" look in his eyes.

"How about this," he shouted. "Floats like a butterfly. Stings like a Z."

He executed the idea by putting the car in a boxing ring and using those exact words as his headline. The judges at the competition thought enough of the ad idea to grant him an award.

A second student was working on a similar problem, only this time for a different car model. When I asked her what the target audience could derive as a benefit from the car, she answered with one word, "Fun." But, she followed that up with an explanation of how frustrated she had become in her search for a creative idea. I asked her if she had tried playing with forced relationships. She hadn't. So, I asked her to tell me the first thing that came to her mind. "Clocks," she said. I then urged her to force clocks or time together with her car and fun. She did and created the headline, "Time flies when you're driving fun."

Obviously, this student's headline suggests a number of coordinating visuals. The same holds true for the other student's headline. And it's certainly safe to say that both headlines have a kind of creative "feel" to them. They have originality and promise, assuming that they're strategically right and appropriate, of course.

As you think back to these student examples, there are two important points to remember, First, forced relationships sparked the creative ideas and headlines. They provided a springboard for the students' creativity. They helped them get over preconceived realities. They helped them overcome the blocks put in their way by those realities. Second, to play with forced relationships demands an openness to idea possibilities grinding against the gears of those realities. That's why when you play with forced relationships, you must begin from the premise that nothing is and everything can be.

Now, let's take that premise of nothing is and everything can be and play with forced relationships. That way, you will get a fuller idea of how the technique can help you generate ideas. In fact, let's not make the playing too particularly easy. Instead, let's make it challenging. Let's use sardines from Chapter Eight as the product to be advertised.

First, make lists. Include product features, selling points, benefits, and behavioristic and target audience considerations in that list. Assume you're trying to increase awareness of sardines as an appealing additive for salads, side dishes, casseroles, and the like. Stare at the list. If anything comes to mind, jot it down. Then, play with forced relationships.

To help you get started, I'll note some things that happen to flip their way into my consciousness. These things may appear to be unrelated to sardines. But remember how to play with the technique, which is to take anything in your consciousness and then force it together with your problem, all the while being alert to possible solutions or ideas. In this way, you're trying to force connections, to force creativity. With this in mind, try and cram or force the following objects, terms or concepts together with your sardine problem. Be on the lookout for seeds of headlines or visuals. And jot down any possibilities.

As I look around my room I see a clock, a radio, a door, a fishtank, a cup, a window, a book. What happens if you force your problem together with any of those objects?

Now I hear a horn, a drum, a whisper, a knock on a door, a laugh. What happens if you force your problem together with any of those sounds?

Now I'm thinking about a gift (it's close to the holidays), snow, a sunset, dinner, a roaring fire, an unfinished piece of writing, maybe an unfinished piece of anything. Try forcing your problem together with those thoughts or images.

I'm yawning, I'm blinking, I'm sitting, I'm hunched over, I'm puzzled, I'm sleepy. Try forcing your problem together with those actions or images.

This is how you should play with forced relationships. You take anything in your consciousness, jot it down, and force it together with your problem. Of course, you don't need me, or anyone else for that matter, telling you what you need to log as part of your consciousness. You can do the logging on your own. Still, if you were thinking of the sardine problem while you were reading the log of my consciousness, chances are you came across some seeds for ideas. Maybe they took the form of headlines or fuzzy, incomplete visuals. Regardless, they were there, weren't they? Maybe you plan on taking the yawn out of your audience's salad. Or you'll let the audience know about a surprise gift for dinner tonight. How about an unfinished salad symphony?

Regardless of your product or the complexity or difficulty of the problem to be solved, the technique of forced relationships has a unique way of sparking your creativity. It helps you overcome blocks and barriers. It helps you overcome predisposed ways of viewing reality. As a result, it helps you keep fluent and original with your ideas.

GRIDS

Another technique advocated by leading theorists and proponents of creative problem solving is that of *grids*. Like forced relationships, they'll help you overcome blocks because they'll stimulate you to make somewhat unexpected and unordinary connections. In fact, grids are extremely flexible in that they can be expanded to include any one of a number of criteria used for connections.

To play with grids, construct a crosshatched set of lines on your idea page similar to the one you see in Figure 11-1. Across the tops of all the vertical rows of boxes, insert your choices of criteria. These can range from visual or verbal elements to media. For example, if you're striving for a visual approach, you may want to list criteria such as setting, color, size, frame, typography, action, and form. You would note these criteria across the top as they pertain to each vertical row of boxes. You then list a number of various settings, colors, sizes, frames, typographical choices, actions, and forms in their specific rows. Then mix and match possibilities for a visual approach governing your creative idea.

You can do the same thing with a verbal approach using criteria such as action verbs, nouns, adjectives, questions, features, selling points, and benefits. Then you mix and match each in all sorts of different ways in order to generate idea possibilities. In Figure 11-2, you see two grids. Notice how the bold line intersects, crisscrosses, and swerves through the various alternatives for the criteria. Imagine those lines picking up the alternatives. Then set your creativity to work by mixing and matching those alternatives.

Grids can also be used from the perspective of media. For example, assume you're trying to think of a creative way to use media. You want to generate ideas based on the creative use of the media. One way to approach this task is to list different kinds of media across the top above the vertical

FIGURE 11-1 Grid Structure for Generating Ideas. Art by Mary Ella.

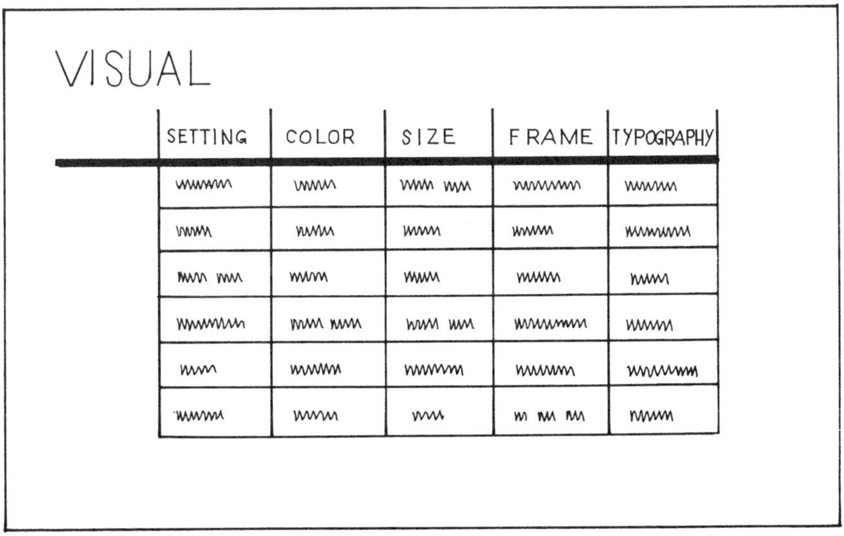

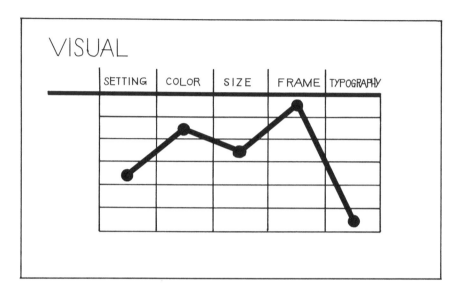

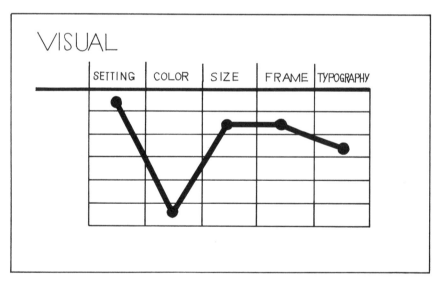

FIGURE 11-2   Two Routes for Generating Ideas. Art by Mary Ella.

MEDIA GRID

MEDIA	TV	NEWSPAPER	BILLBOARD	DIRECT MAIL	RADIO
CHARACTERISTICS	MOVEMENT	PAPER	PICTURES	OPENING	SOUND EFFECTS
	SEQUENCE	COLOR	TYPOGRAPHY	ENVELOPE	MUSIC
	COLOR	FOLDS	RECTANGULAR	FOLDS	VOICE
	DEMONSTRATION	FLATNESS	COLOR	TRIAL PACKAGE	VOLUME
	SCREEN	TYPOGRAPHY	SCALE	TYPOGRAPHY	DISC JOCKEY
	KNOBS	PICTURES	EXTENSIONS	LETTERS	KNOBS

FIGURE 11-3 Media Grid for Generating Ideas. Art by Mary Ella.

rows. Then list the characteristics of each medium in their respective rows. Figure 11-3 is a reproduction of this type of listing.

As you look at Figure 11-3, mix and match the various characteristics of the different media. For instance, under the heading of television you'll see the characteristic of moving, sequential pictures. What happens if you force that together with outdoor billboards? Is there something that can be done to make billboards more motion-oriented and more sequential? The billboard campaigns for Carlisle Outdoor in Figure 11-4 reflect just this type of approach, reminiscent of the classic Burma Shave road sign campaign from many years ago. One Carlisle campaign idea is represented over a distant span of roadway. The other is represented over a span of time.

Try mixing and matching some other possibilities. For example, what happens if you try mixing the moving, sequential pictures of television with the characteristic of radio sound in order to generate a creative approach to a newspaper advertising campaign? In other words, is it possible to create a television storyboard, complete with quoted conversation, all together as a newspaper ad? How about separating the storyboard into several ads found in the newspaper?

As an idea-generation technique, grids keeps you open, flexible, and fluent with your ideas. You can choose any number or kind of criteria to list across the vertical rows. You're not restricted in this regard. All you have to do is add more rows or more boxes. Plus, you can play with grids in much

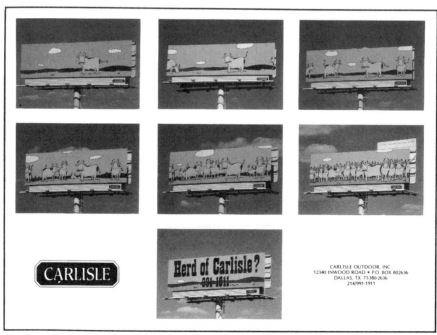

FIGURE 11-4 Grids Leading to Ideas. Courtesy of CARLISLE OUTDOOR, INC.

the same way you played with forced relationships. They stimulate you to make unexpected connections. In this respect, they're particularly valuable in helping you overcome creative blocks.

ACCIDENTS AND NEGATIVES

In Chapter Seven we discussed the need for you to keep alert to and ready for what the world has to offer. This means remaining open to stimuli as sources for ideas. This includes all stimuli, both positive and negative stimuli. Even in creative problem-solving systems such as Synectics, participants are encouraged to pay attention to apparent negatives as sources for ideas. Most of us, for instance, would consider tipping over garbage as a negative. But in Synectics, tipping over garbage is seen as an opportunity to look for problem solutions and increase your creativity.

We can expand this opportunity to include accidents as well. Recall, for example, Ed Biglow's inspiration for the "Mass Transit" Volkswagen idea. Seeing nuns riding by in a station wagon was unplanned. It was one of those serendipitous, accidental occurrences, one of those many experiences we encounter daily but usually disregard as inappropriate for generating ideas. Not so for the creative mind. Generating ideas to solve problems means paying attention to everything. It means sweeping both positive and negative stimuli to the problem center, then stepping back to see what you have in the way of an idea or solution.

To generate ideas using *accidents* and *negatives*, begin by referring to your Creative Plan and the problems your audience has with your advertiser. Can those problems be turned around into idea opportunities? Take the case of Blue Nun wine, for instance. When Della Femina, Travisano & Partners started work for Blue Nun, they were confronted with the problem of the name. Who, after all, would want to indulge in a wine with the name of Blue Nun? What the agency did was to turn that negative around into a positive. The agency created a series of commercials featuring the comedy team of Stiller and Meara. The comic copy lines were centered on the name, Blue Nun. From something negative, the agency created an advertising idea that was positive.

As you go about your daily routine, you'll undoubtedly encounter problems along the way. A flat tire here. A missed appointment there. Many such occurrences during the day. What happens if you force those together with your advertising problems? Do they spark ideas?

Playing with accidents and negatives requires a mind so open and so flexible that it's willing to use just about anything the world can toss its way in order to be creative. Often, the inclination is to look the other way when accidents or negatives occur. But, in playing with accidents and negatives, you can't look the other way. They demand that you look their way. When you do, you connect them with your problem to generate even more idea possibilities as potential solutions.

STRAIGHT SHOW AND TELL

As a final technique, *straight show and tell* does the opposite of all we've been discussing in Part III. It just shows and tells the theme. No bells. No whistles. Just straight, sort of like "Less salt than Brand X" or "Corns gone in 5 days or your money back." Don't think, however, that straight show and tell is uncreative. It can be very creative, especially if everyone else isn't doing it. In this sense, as you observe your competition and the media in which your creative idea will appear, notice if most ads are trying to outdo the bold creativity of each other by using even bolder creativity. If so, try to show and tell it like it is, almost as a re-creation of a flat, unadorned benefit statement. If no one else is doing that, and it's relevant, you're creative.

MANY TECHNIQUES IN REVIEW

As a diverse group of techniques, those in this chapter represent a kind of rounded finish to all of the techniques presented in Part III. As generators, each of the techniques can be played with at random and in no particular order. Again, just play. As always, however, the play should be purposeful. It should be intentional and goal-oriented.

Your ultimate goal throughout all of the chapters is to create advertising ideas that are new and relevant. To do that, you need to be open enough to expand your idea possibilities. Often, you need to see things not as they are but as they can be. In this respect, you can't be limited by what reality is. In reality, margarine doesn't talk. Magazine pages don't stand up or play Christmas songs. Overnight letters don't behave like airplanes. Commercial actresses don't switch off our television sets (we're supposed to do that). And watches don't belong on hockey pucks.

Of course, the list could go on beyond our pages indefinitely, no doubt. In advertising creativity, reality is often something else entirely. It's a new reality formed from connections of old realities. All of your techniques can help you make those connections. If you've been connecting right along, then your idea pages should be loaded. Maybe from a distance they even look like Figure 11–5.

From this chapter you should take with you the techniques of symbols, frames, from this to that, forced relationships, grids, accidents and negatives, and straight show and tell. Combine these with the variety and number of techniques from other chapters, and you have the toys you'll need to play yourself into creative ideas. Naturally, you'll need to feel playful first.

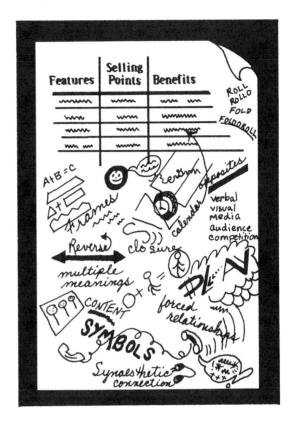

FIGURE 11-5 Quantities of Idea
Possibilities. Art by
Mary Ella.

This means you'll need to believe it's okay to play. Of course it is. You've seen many ad ideas exemplifying just that, the playful, creative temperament. To lift a cross-section of those ideas out of hypothetical situations, however, our next chapter will take an inside look at how the minds behind those ideas played.

In the next chapter, six creative ideas you've seen throughout Parts II and III of this book are discussed in terms of their actual development. Often you'll notice that the seeds for those ideas connect with strategic planning. Often, too, you'll notice that the ideas themselves reflect the playing of the creative mind. Invariably that playing is a matter of making connections, the kinds of connections we've discussed and looked at throughout this book.

PLAYTIME

In playing with several of the techniques from this chapter, you will need to keep yourself open to possibilities. You will need to think beyond direct or even indirect associations. This means you will have to draw upon a range of the world's realities in order to make your connections. As usual, you can begin by reviewing the key conclusions for your advertiser. Then play with the following.

SYMBOLS

Go to Mother Nature. Think of all the realities from Mother Nature that could symbolize your product or service. Consider the animal and plant kingdoms, for instance. Or, consider the worlds of water, air, land, and sky. Make a list. You may want to include lions, tigers, bears, birds, trees, flowers, rivers, seas, winds, mountains, plateaus, and stars. Do they suggest possibilities? If so, jot them down.

Make another list, this time devoted to concrete objects not necessarily from Mother Nature. Things like buildings, machines, desks, or cars. Clearly, this list could go on interminably. But create one and see what happens. Can you make some connections to your advertiser or its features, selling points, and benefits? Can you make connections to your theme?

FRAMES

Consider all possible frames in which you could place your headline, copy, or visual. Here are some to get you started. You may want to think of more.

Doors. Suitcases. Windows. Outlines. Silhouettes. Profiles. Geometric shapes. Tubes. Containers. Packages. Furniture. Houses. Keyholes. Binoculars. Telephone receivers. Typewriters. Computer screens. Television screens. Fireplaces. Stairs.

FROM THIS TO THAT

As suggested earlier in the chapter, make a list of your audience's needs or problems before buying or using your product or service. Then make a list of how things change after buying or using. Can words or phrases from those lists be connected into possible headlines or ideas?

FORCED RELATIONSHIPS

In playing with *forced relationships,* you need to be open, wide open to possibilities. You can't rule anything out. And for the time being, everything has potential. This includes everything in your consciousness at a particular point in time, regardless of how irrelevant certain things may seem for the moment.

Take five minutes and list all things entering your consciousness. Look around you to get started. Jot the names of items down. Then force your advertiser and its features, selling points, and benefits together with those items. Does anything click? Jot it down.

Pick up a magazine or newspaper. Turn to any page. What do you see? Force it together with your advertiser.

Turn on the television. Turn to any channel. What do you see? Force it together with your advertiser.

To show you how far you can go with forced relationships, you can even force together items from your original list of potential advertisers. For example, what happens if you connect sardines and hats, or sardines and pets? What happens if you connect flake fish food and a telephone service, or fish food and hubcaps? Jot down the possibilities.

GRIDS

Using the grid charts you saw earlier in the chapter, fill in the blanks for visuals, words, and media. Then zigzag through your answers, making connections as you go. Try alternative routes. Log the possibilities.

ACCIDENTS AND NEGATIVES

As we've mentioned, we experience accidents and negative occurrences during our daily routines. Because we perceive them as negative, we tend to discard them as useless annoyances. With idea generation, however, these accidents and occurrences can be used to spark ideas.

Log those accidents and negatives you've encountered recently. Force your advertiser with them and see what happens. If you need a starting point, what happens if you force your advertiser together with the following?

A flat tire. A broken watch. An unexpected bill. Tipped garbage. A dead battery. Burned toast. Traffic. Waiting in line. Spelling errors. A dull razor. Spilled milk. A stolen book. A leaky pen. No hot water. Oversleeping. A missed appointment.

STRAIGHT SHOW AND TELL

As a final idea-generation technique, think about just showing or telling it like it is. Take your theme and state it in a sentence or question. Use it as the headline. Show the product or service doing or being the theme.

12
CASES OF CONNECTIVE THINKING AT THE ADVERTISING AGENCY

We've seen over forty ad ideas. We've referred to many others. We've discussed all of them in reference to how they exemplify connective thinking and idea-generation techniques. As such, these ad ideas serve as models for you. By viewing them and then thinking about them, you should be able to see the connective thinking process leading to their inception and completion. In this respect, what follows shouldn't surprise you. More than anything else, much of what follows is a reaffirmation of what we've discussed. There is a twist, however, and it's this. What follows are perspectives from those advertising professionals integral to the generation and selection of the ideas we've seen. Straight from the horses' mouths, so to speak. As a kind of wrap-up for all we've discussed, these perspectives should help you connect the steps in the creative process as they are realized in the generation of creative advertising ideas.

TRANSAMERICA

We've identified the Transamerica pop-up ad idea as an example of a *media opposite* (see Figure 4–1). We've also identified it as an example of a solid creative idea with strong underpinnings to ADNORMS and connective creative thinking. In the largest sense, it exemplifies the kinds of connections to be made if one is to generate new and relevant creative ideas. As you'll see, those connections were rooted in strategy and openness, two terms important to all you've read.

It was Intervisual Communications, Inc., a firm that produces pop-up books for children, who went to Della Femina McNamee, WCRS, Inc. with an idea for a pop-up ad. There had been pop-up ads before, but somehow they didn't have the quality and staying power that became a hallmark of the Transamerica pop-up ad. What they were lacking was a unified idea, one where the pop-up concept was tightly bound to the advertiser and what the advertiser could give to the target audience.

The agency was aware that postal deregulations had opened the door for such creative techniques as pop-up ads. The agency also knew it had a courageous, perceptive client in Transamerica, a client viewing itself as a major financial institution and insurance company. It was also a client in an arena with major competition and, consequently, major competitive advertising spending. Because of this, Transamerica had to be innovative. It had to do things more innovatively than those others whose advertising exposure to the public was vast and impressive (remember your special someone and the many others who had their eyes on that someone).

Strategically, the agency knew that Transamerica prided itself on its innovative programs and policies. Plus, the Transamerica headquarters building was innovative in its own right, a downtown pyramid praised and known for its architectural uniqueness. We have called attributes such as programs and buildings advertiser features. For Transamerica, both of these features were considered important, especially since they differentiated Transamerica from other companies in the public mind and could be used to build awareness of or attention to the company.

Now, can you see the connective thinking taking place at the agency? In comes a company with expertise in pop-ups. Postal deregulations allow them. Here's a cherished client who is innovative in two important respects, programs and headquarters. Here also is a client in among heavy advertising spenders. Thus, innovation (pop-up as an opposite to the media) + innovation (company programs and building) = creative idea.

With media, creative, and a business connection taking place, the agency set out to literally build its pop-up ad. The ad took one year. As a hand-assembled insert, there were 5.5 million pieces produced. The day the ad was to break, the agency unveiled a 12-foot scale model of the ad in front of the Transamerica Building. Cameras clicked. Reporters took notes. And to date, over 500 articles pertaining to the ad have been published worldwide.

Following the ad's appearance, recall tests produced astonishing numbers, upwards of 95% recall. Starch readership scores produced equally astonishing numbers. Over 90% noted the ad, over 60% associated the ad with Transamerica, and over 40% read the ad. Independent research scores indicated that close to 70% of those who read the ad held favorable attitudes toward Transamerica.

The big question, of course, is, Why these terrific results from one little ad?

The big answer has several main parts. First, it's not a little ad in the most important respects. It's much more. It's an ad in coordination with public relations activity. In other words, the ad expands to the point of becoming a media event.

Second, it's an ad controlled by a solid creative idea. This means the idea is rooted in planning and strategy. Key advertiser features evolve as the theme. But, the theme is the idea, and the idea is the theme. As a media opposite, the idea is innovative. This blends with the strategic theme of innovativeness. As a tightly constructed concept, the entire idea revolves around this singleminded approach.

Third, the idea also revolves around the advertiser as the hero. Transamerica is innovative, just like the ad idea is innovative. For the target audience, the innovativeness of Transamerica, mirrored through the ad idea, separates the company from other companies. If insurance and financial innovativeness are what the audience is looking for, they can expect to find them with Transamerica.

Finally, the idea recognizes the importance of the first step in persuasion, that of attention. Existing in a crowded environment, the Transamerica ad idea stands out and up, literally and figuratively. Because of its uniqueness, it grabs attention. Because of its tightness and quality, it becomes a first. And because of its relevance to the advertiser and the audience, it's also right or on strategy.

As we leave the Transamerica ad idea, it's important to remember this. The idea never could have existed if the minds at Della Femina, McNamee, WCRS, Inc. and Transamerica had been closed. Instead, they were open. Creative individuals were willing to take what the world of reality had to offer and connect it with an advertising problem. In so doing, they fused realities to create a new reality, the creative idea. This meant they were willing to see things not as they are, but as they might be. No doubt, such openness involves the risk inherent in being different. So does creativity.

CASIO

The Casio G-Shock watch idea (see Figure 8–4) uses the slapshot of a hockey puck to convey the theme of durability. We've identified the creative idea behind the television commercial as a size association. We've also identified it as one of those ideas crossing over to other techniques as well. A form association, for instance. As with the Transamerica ad, our point here with Casio is to trace the connective thinking at the core of the idea.

Initial meetings between the advertising agency personnel from Doremus & Company, New York, and the client produced a classic advertising situation. None of the television storyboards presented to the client were considered satisfactory. Something more powerful was needed, and, of course, it had to be based on sound strategic thinking.

Both agency and client were intent on positioning the watch as durable. That position of durability was a key theme underlying the creative stragegy. But durable to whom? In this respect, the target audience for the watch was identified as sports-minded males. Their lifestyles (psychographics) were active. They were tough-minded, young individuals, 18 to 34 years old. They would be exposed to the ad idea during the winter season, a media-planning decision to be connected with the creative idea (recall our discussion of clocks and calendars).

Using "odd associations," the creative director at Doremus, John Garre, spearheaded the generation of the creative idea. He knew the watch was tough. Just how tough was it? He thought of a slap in the face. The word, slap, was then connected with slapshot. He went where the associations led him. Connecting slap and slapshot with the target audience, he then connected that connection with the winter season. This led him to a hockey motif. He had a puck. He had a watch. One looked like the other. He saw the watch on the puck. He saw the watch around the puck. He saw the watch and puck as one. He saw it being hit. He saw the hitting as a means for demonstrating the key selling point and theme of durability. In other words, he saw the creative idea. Eventually, the truthfulness of the claim behind the idea was tested, and the idea became a reality.

In this reliving of the creative mind, notice how vital the target audience, the media, and the advertiser were to the generation of the creative idea. The audience was sports-minded and tough. The watch was tough. The media exposure lent itself to demonstration and the winter season. From there, the mind connected by associations. Sports + tough + winter = hockey. Puck + watch = demonstration of a key advertiser selling point or theme. Threaded together, these assorted connections became the generative seed for the creative idea.

Again, as with much creative thinking, the creative mind behind the Casio ad idea wasn't resricted to certain realities. Indeed, realities for that mind were something to be associated with something else. Realities were elastic and flexible. By using associations based on product features, selling points, target audience characteristics, and media timeliness decisions, the creative mind was able to connect realities in order to generate a new reality, the creative idea.

MAXELL

We've identified the Maxell ad idea (see Figure 8–6) as a benefit association. The ad shows a young man being "blown away" by the overpowering, wind-like sound from a Maxell audio tape.

Historically, Maxell had been more interested in advertising to the trade than to consumers. The nature of the trade audience directed the advertising focus onto technical information. But in the late 1970s and early 1980s, the growing consumer demand for audio tapes helped to change the situation. Maxell management decided it was in their best interest to advertise to consumers, particularly a younger skew of males whose music listening was a vital part of their entertainment. The problem was that Maxell didn't have an identifiable image among that audience. Since the bulk of Maxell's advertising had been geared toward the trade, the new consumer audience posed both a problem and an opportunity.

The problem confronting Maxell and its agency, Scali, McCabe, Sloves, was one of having no image on which to build an appeal for a young consumer audience. The opportunity was there, however, for starting from the gound up and creating an image. Given the nature of the audience, it was clear that highly technical information, conveyed in a dry manner, skirted the audience's interests and lifestyle. Such a creative approach would be inappropriate because the image would be wrong, at least in terms of what that audience expects from its audio tapes. From here, the creative wheels at Scali, McCabe, Sloves began to turn. One of those wheels belonged to associate creative director, Lars Anderson.

When Lars Anderson was faced with the Maxell problem, he saw it as a matter of connecting with this particular audience. That connection would be based on creating an idea where the image of Maxell was aligned with the interests and lifestyle of the audience. This meant the image had to be unique, expressive, and active. It couldn't be staid, reserved, or withdrawn. At the same time, the ad idea had to convey the theme of the Maxell tape's strength and durability.

Applying what he terms "logical illogic," Anderson sought a dramatic visual to convey the image and theme. While listening to his own Maxell tape, he projected himself into an image of a young man sitting in a chair facing the stereo system. He turned the sound up. Way up. He felt himself being fused with his imagery. He could feel the results of using the product just as the target audience would feel the results of using the product. And, he saw the sound from the product move. That's right. The sound moved.

Now, we've discussed several of these experiences throughout your book. For instance, when Lars Anderson projected himself into the target audience, he exemplified the creative personality traits of empathy and negative capability. He also exemplified the act of closure, and specifically, the idea-generation technique of projections. In feeling the results of product use, he was thinking behavioristically, again from the point of view of the all-important target audience. And in seeing the sound move, he was engaged in synaesthetic imaging.

As you picture that Maxell ad idea in your mind, notice how it uses a synaesthetic connection as well as a benefit or selling point association. Again, it took a creative mind to see the sound, to experience the synaesthetic image. In order to do that, the mind had to overcome a preconceived notion of what constitutes the reality of sound. In other words, the mind had to be open enough to allow realities to connect, regardless of how opposed to connection they seemed to be. Then, the mind had to see the result of that connection in a dramatic visual, one that tied the theme of durability and long-lasting power together with the audience and its hero, the Maxell audio tape.

HONDA

We've identified the Honda ad idea (a winner of several prestigious advertising awards) (see Figure 9–9) as a physical closure. The first page of the spread ad asks the reader to "Quick, turn the page." The reader does, and is immediately confronted by the headline "too late," and a rear shot of the Honda Prelude presumably dashing off into the distance.

The problem confronting the agency of Rubin Postaer and Associates was one of how to breathe some flair and excitement into the image of a car that had been around for some time. Though not suffering from an image of stodginess, the Honda Prelude still needed an aura of sportiness and thrill about it. Creative director Larry Postaer saw the need for a creative idea to "put an exclamation mark on the car," an idea that could take off in the reader's mind. That reader was a young to middle-aged male. Successful. Active. Energetic. And an appreciator of humor and wit.

Believing that the single common denominator to solid creative ideas is their "unexpectedness," the agency set out to stir the reader's involvement and imagination. This could be achieved by means of participation and surprise. The idea would stimulate the audience to do something with the ad. And once done, that something would lead to surprise.

At one time, the agency executed a dealer piece that made use of a riffle book. That's a book where you riffle or flip the pages and get a sequence of pictures creating a sense of motion or action. Why couldn't that be applied to a magazine spread ad? What would happen if the meaning of your ad idea depended on the audience turning the page? There would certainly be an element of suspense before the page was turned. There would also be an element of surprise after the page was turned. The inspiration struck, and the idea was created.

Once again, for Rubin Postaer and Associates, as inspirational as the creative idea was, there were a number of realities and concepts connected along the way in order to generate that idea. Riffle books. Audience involvement and participation. Excitement. Wit. And, of course, openness allowing the creative idea to enter in the first place.

There can be no doubt that the Honda Prelude ad idea is unique. Its uniqueness grabs the attention of the audience. It does more, however. It holds that attention steadfast because the audience is absorbed into the ad through participation. In turning the page (turning it quickly, by the way), and then having to re-create the fast movement of the car, the audience is involved. That involvement, however, is centered on the theme of excitement coming to life in the form of a Honda Prelude. Again, the product becomes the hero. And, once again, the creative idea carries the theme. Its tone is exciting. The audience action is exciting. The entire imaginary re-creation of car movement in the audience's mind is exciting.

PORSCHE

We've identified the Porsche television ad idea (see Figure 9–10) as a projection. At the start of the commercial, the audience is invited to become a Porsche. For the remainder of the ad, the viewing audience is the car.

Much like the Honda Prelude ad idea, the Porsche idea uses a closure technique to stimulate audience involvement. Unlike the Honda idea, the Porsche idea is aimed at a different target audience. For the Porsche models 944, 911, and 928, the audience is upscale, mostly male, and clearly high income earners.

In positioning the car, both the Chiat/Day and Fallon McElligott advertising agencies rely on the demographic, psychographic, and behavioristic profiles of the target audience. For example, potential Porsche owners tend to be classified psychographically as "successfuls, speed demons, or enthusiasts." Some perceive the Porsche as a status item. Others perceive it as representative of the good things in life. Most perceive it as exciting and exhilarating.

One of the common denominators to positioning the Porsche line of cars favorably in the audience's mind is how well the audience can vicariously experience the car and its exhilaration. Because of the potential pride, pleasure, and prestige of Porsche ownership, there's also that tendency for the audience to become highly involved with the car. In many ways, the car becomes an image of the audience's self. Consequently, if the advertising for Porsche can make the audience feel like the car, then the audience will feel exhilarated and prestigious. A kind of symbolic association can be made between what a Porsche is and what the audience perceives itself to be. Since the car is exciting, the audience will be exciting. Since the car is prestigious, the audience will be prestigious.

You can easily see this kind of connection between the audience and the car in the Porsche television commercial. The reason it's so easy to see is because the car and the audience are unified. One becomes the other. Of course, this is the basis of the projection technique. With Porsche, it's particularly appropriate since the audience's connection and involvement with the car are central to how the audience views itself and its choice of automobile.

PRICE PFISTER

We've identified the Price Pfister television ad idea (see Figure 10–7) as a verbal play with more specific reference to alliteration. The commercial uses "pf" words such as pfancy, pfabulous, and pfaucets in connection with the Pfister name.

As with Maxell, Price Pfister faced a similar problem of having devoted itself to trade advertising over the years. When the reality of a strong primary demand trend existed among consumers, Price Pfister saw an opportunity to target its advertising to a new audience of homeowners, slightly skewed toward men in the 25–54 age bracket. As with Maxell again, the problem for Price Pfister was the lack of an image in the minds of that audience. Even more so, however, preresearch focus group results indicated confusion over the Price Pfister name. Was it Fisher-Price toys? Was it the Pfizer Corporation? It semed that the target audience of homeowners didn't know who the real Price Pfister was. This led the Price Pfister agency, Eisaman, Johns & Laws, to brainstorm for a creative idea based on an objective of having the audience "do nothing other than to recognize and remember the name."

In addition to the objective of increasing name recognition and memorability, the agency believed it should connect the name with some of the positive product selling points such as competitive prices and quality fixtures. Obviously, the creative task wasn't easy given the need to reach several goals. Still, during brainstorming sessions, creative director Jim Benson and copy supervisor Andrea Jamboni began to play with words. The first word was faucet. They connected the word with Pfister. They superimposed the Pfister "Pf" onto faucet. The result was pfaucet. And from there the creative possibilities for the idea took off.

While exploring the possibility of verbal plays, it became clear to Jim Benson that the graphics of the idea would have to be simple, while at the same time suggesting the high quality of the fixtures. The reason for the simplicity of the graphic approach was one of not upstaging the theme of the name and its easy recognition and memorability. As a kind of subtheme, product affordability could be embedded into the voice-over announcer's script.

The Price Pfister creative idea is an example of how something so simple can be so effective. Tested with great success in the Phoenix and Atlanta markets, the creative idea is targeted for eventual nationwide exposure. It's one of those rare creative ideas that gets talked about. Even within the Price Pfister company, memos and communiqués are written with references to "f" words spelled "pf."

SIX CREATIVE IDEAS IN REVIEW

We've discussed the actual planning, strategies, and seeds of six creative ideas. Despite the differences in these ideas, they are similar in many respects. Let's note their similarities, since they exemplify as a group what constitutes an advertising creative idea.

Notice, for example, how the themes and ideas are tightly connected and unified. A company is innovative. It has an innovative headquarters building. The ad idea is innovative. It relies on the innovative headquarters building.

A watch is tough. The ad idea conveys toughness, but it does it with an association to something considered tough.

An audio tape has long-lasting power, enough to blow away a new, young audience. The ad idea shows how the audience can feel the power.

A car excites. The ad idea swoops into the head of the audience, generating involvement and excitement along the way.

Another car exhilarates and thrills. The ad idea projects the audience into an exhilarating, thrilling experience in connection with the car.

A faucet company has a funny, confusing, and unrecognizable name. The ad idea uses the funny name as the essence in making the name memorable.

Notice, too, how the ideas are new and different. Pick up a magazine, any magazine. How many pop-ups do you see? And if you do see them, how many of the ideas are tightly coiled around key advertiser features, selling points, or benefits? When was the last time you saw a watch being slapped by a hockey player into a goalie's glove? When was the last time you saw sound in an ad? The last time a car actually zipped along in your mind after you turned a page? Or, for that matter, the last time you were invited to be a car? Or the last time you saw faucet spelled pfaucet?

Plus, notice how the ideas are relevant. They key into important advertiser features, selling points, and benefits or problem solutions. As such, they key into themes and the advertiser as the hero. But they do so in connection with what makes the advertiser important and involving to specific audiences. When you want innovativeness with your insurance company, Transamerica will give it to you, just like they do with a pop-up ad. When you're a tough-minded sports fan and you're sitting in front of the television watching a hockey game on a cold, wintry night, guess what Casio will give you? When you want to get blown away again and again by the sound from your audio tape, try sitting in front of your stereo system with a Maxell tape inside it. When you want to feel excitement with your car, then QUICK, turn the page. When you want the car and you to be one, then why not become the car? When you can't remember the name of a faucet company, then just remember "pf."

You can even notice how the ideas connect with their audiences as forms of communication and persuasion. Because they're different, they grab attention and stimulate involvement. Because they're relevant, they're understood by their respective audiences. They talk the language and show the pictures the audiences want to hear and see. In such ways, they break through the clutter of multiple senders, noises, and screens.

Finally, notice how the ideas stem from the creative mind's ability to think by connections. Often these connections are between realities that seem at opposite ends from one another. For the creative mind, however, they're not. For the creative mind, there are no opposite ends. There are no hard and fast realities. There are only possibilities of new realities. But, you have to be open, alert, ready, willing, and able to see them. This means you can't be afraid to play or be different. This means you have to believe, believe in yourself and your own creativity, especially. As a small help in these respects, treat this book as a kind of guide to creative playfulness—a guide for actualizing your own creative powers to connect what's outside and inside together into new and relevant creative ideas.

NOTES

CHAPTER 1

1. Graham Wallas, "Stages in the Creative Process," in *The Creativity Quest*, eds. Albert Rothenberg and Carl R. Hausman (Durham, NC: Duke University Press, 1976), pp. 69–73.
2. Alex F. Osborn, *Applied Imagination: Principles and Procedures of Creative Thinking*, rev. ed. (New York: Charles Scribner's Sons, 1957), pp. 114–16.
3. James Webb Young, *A Technique for Producing Ideas* (Lincolnwood, IL: NTC Business Books, 1975).
4. Rollo May, "The Nature of Creativity," in *Creativity and Its Cultivation: Addresses Presented at The Interdisciplinary Symposia on Creativity, Michigan State University*, ed. Harold H. Anderson. (New York: Harper & Row, 1959), pp. 58–59.
5. Young, *A Technique*, p. 52.
6. Katherine Kuh, ed., *The Artist's Voice: Talks with Seventeen Artists* (New York: Harper & Row, 1962), p. 190.
7. Olivia Bertagnolli and Jeff Rackham, eds., *Creativity and the Writing Process* (New York: John Wiley & Sons), pp. 2–3.
8. Stanley Rosner and Lawrence E. Abt, eds., *The Creative Experience* (New York: Grossman, 1970), pp. 358–59.
9. John Haefele, *Creativity and Innovation* (New York: Reinhold Publishing Corp., 1962), p. 90.
10. Ibid., p. 98.

11. Arthur Koestler, *The Act of Creation* (New York: The Macmillan Co., 1964), p. 210.

12. Ibid., p. 211.

13. See David Douglas Duncan, *Viva Picasso: A Centennial Celebration, 1881–1981* (New York. The Viking Press, n.d.), p. 15, and *Gertrude Stein on Picasso,* ed. Edward Burns (New York: Liveright Publishing Corporation, 1970), p. 108.

14. Marco Vassi, *Lying Down: A Horizontal Worldview* (Santa Barbara, CA: Cabra Press, 1984).

15. Koestler, *The Act,* p. 211.

16. Haefele, *Creativity,* p. 90.

17. Ibid., p. 90.

18. Morris I. Stein, *Stimulating Creativity,* Vol. I (New York: Academic Press, 1974), p. 20.

19. Ibid., pp. 20–21.

20. All of the foregoing anecdotes pertaining to composers and musicians were derived from Ann F. Isaacs, "Creativity in Musical Composition: How Does the Composer Work?", *The Creative Child and Adult Quarterly* (Autumn, 1979), 152–71.

21. Koestler, *The Act,* p. 225.

22. Haefele, *Creativity,* p. 63.

23. Stein, *Stimulating Creativity,* pp. 231–32.

24. Samuel Taylor Coleridge, *Biographia Literaria,* Vol. I (London: William Pickering, 1847), p. 28.

25. Jean H. Hagstrum, *William Blake: Poet and Painter* (Chicago: The University of Chicago Press, 1964), pp. 17–19.

26. Koestler, *The Act,* pp. 202–4.

27. Gary K. Himes, "Developing Your Creative Ideas." *Supervision,* Vol. 44 (October, 1982), 14–15, 23–26.

CHAPTER 2

1. Niles Howard, "Business Probes the Creative Spark." *Dun's Review,* Vol. 115, 1 (January, 1980), 32–33, 36, 38.

2. Charles H. Clark, *Idea Management: How to Motivate Creativity and Innovation* (New York: Amacom, 1980), pp. 18–19.

3. Ted Pollock, "Mind Your Own Business," *Supervision,* Vol. 40, 7 (July, 1978), 17–19.

4. In the interest of clustering notes for easier reference, see Jere W. Clark and Juanita Stone Clark, "The Art of Soaring," *The Journal of Creative Behavior,* Vol. 13, 2 (1979), 110–118 for Einstein and Edison; Francoise Gilot and Carlton Lake, *Life with Picasso* (New York: McGraw-Hill, Inc., 1964) for Picasso; Philip Norman, *Shout: The Beatles and Their Generation* (New York: Simon and Schuster, 1981) for Lennon.

5. Stewart Alter, "New York Ad Club Hears Agency Creatives," *Advertising Age,* (September, 1985), 86.

6. For a thorough review of the workings of Synectics, see William J. J. Gordon, *Synectics: The Development of Creative Capacity* (New York: Collier Books, 1968).

7. Several studies have been completed on the effectiveness of Purdue's program.

For example, see Penny Britton Kollof and John F. Feldhusen, "The Effects of Enrichment on Self-Concept and Creative Thinking," *Gifted Child Quarterly*, Vol. 28, 2 (Spring, 1984), 53–57, and Twila H, Jaben, "Effects of Instruction on Elementary-Age Students' Productive Thinking," *Psychological Reports*, Vol. 57 (1985), 900–902.

8. Howard, "Business Probes," p. 36.
9. Ibid., p. 37.

CHAPTER 3

1. William C. Cowan, "How Agencies Are Most Likely to Win Accounts," *Advertising Age* (November 17, 1986), 18.
2. For example, see Thomas Duncan and Linda Lazier Smith, "Ad Agencies Get Yeas, Nays," *Advertising Age* (October 27, 1986), 50.
3. "Execs Analyze Creativity," *Advertising Age* (June 17, 1985), 42.
4. David Ogilvy, *Ogilvy on Advertising* (London: Pan Books, 1983), p. 205.
5. Michael L. Ray, *Advertising and Communication Management* (Englewood Cliffs, NJ: Prentice-Hall, Inc., 1982), p. 288.
6. Stewart Alter, "New York Ad Club Hears Agency Creatives," *Advertising Age* (September 30, 1985), 86.
7. Jerry Della Femina, *From Those Wonderful Folks Who Gave You Pearl Harbor*, ed. Charles Sopkin (New York: Pocket Books, 1971), p. 108.
8. Ibid., pp. 250–53.
9. Niles Howard, "Madison Avenue Rediscovers Creativity," *Dun's Review*, Vol. 115, 5 (May, 1980), 82–83, 85, 89–90.
10. Ogilvy, *Ogilvy*, pp. 16–17.
11. For Hopkins, see Claude Hopkins, *Scientific Advertising* (New York: Crown Publishers, [1923] 1966), p. 83. For Reeves, see Rosser Reeves, *Reality in Advertising* (New York: Alfred A. Knopf, 1961), pp. 46–49. For Burnett, see Ray, *Advertising and Communication*, p. 277.
12. Ogilvy, *Ogilvy*, p. 201.
13. Roy Paul Nelson, *The Design of Advertising*, 3rd ed. (Dubuque, Iowa: Wm. C. Brown Publishers, 1977), p. 156.
14. "Teachers, Agency Execs Trade Barbs," *Advertising Age* (September 15, 1986), 94.
15. John Sweeney, "Making the Breakthrough—Be Daring Yet Personal," *Advertising Age* (November 2, 1987), 64.
16. Peter Cornish, "Advertising That Gets Talked About," *Advertising Age* (November 16, 1987), 18.

CHAPTER 4

1. Rosser Reeves, *Reality in Advertising* (New York: Alfred A. Knopf, 1961), p. 46.
2. Al Reis and Jack Trout, *Positioning: The Battle for Your Mind* (New York: Warner Bros. Books, 1981).

3. Ibid.
4. "Right on, Ron," *Advertising Age* (March 26, 1987), 56.
5. Adam Knowles, "That Creative Spark," *Industrial Management and Data Systems* January (1981), pp. 17–18.
6. All three authors take exception to unbridled creativity, many times because it gets in the way of the "product-as-hero" approach. See Reeves, *Reality*, p. 117, David Ogilvy, *Ogilvy on Advertising* (London: Pan Books, 1983), p. 18, and Hank Seiden, *Advertising Pure and Simple* (New York: Amacom, 1976), p. 71.
7. Ogilvy, *Ogilvy*, p. 16.
8. Ibid., p. 14.
9. Ibid., p. 16.
10. Steuart Henderson Britt, "How Advertising Can Use Psychology's Rules of Learning," *Printer's Ink* 252 (September, 1955), 74, 77, 80.
11. David Ogilvy, *Confessions of an Advertising Man* (New York: Dell Publishing Co., 1964), p. 130.
12. Marvin Bell, "The Technique of the Right Attitude," In *Creativity and the Writing Process*, eds. Olivia Bertagnolli and Jeff Rackham (New York: John Wiley & Sons), pp. 181–82.

CHAPTER 5

1. Rosser Reeves, *Reality in Advertising* (New York: Alfred A. Knopf, 1961), p. 27.
2. Herbert W. Simons, *Persuasion: Understanding, Practice, and Analysis* (Reading, MA: Addison-Wesley, 1976), p. 174.
3. Albert C. Book and C. Dennis Schick, *Fundamentals of Copy and Layout: A Manual for Advertising Copy and Layout* (Chicago: Crain Books, 1984), p. 4.
4. For an overview of the topic, see Alexis S. Tan, *Mass Communication Theories and Research* (Columbus, OH: Grid Publishing, 1981), pp. 106–9, or James T. Tedeschi, "Attributions, Liking, and Power," in *Foundations of Interpersonal Attraction*, ed. Ted L. Huston (New York: Academic Press, 1974), pp. 193–215.
5. Sanford L. Braver and others, "Some Conditions That Affect Admissions of Atitude Change," *Journal of Experimental Social Psychology*, 13 (1977), 565–76.
6. Zick Rubin, "From Liking to Loving: Patterns of Attraction in Dating Relationships," in *Foundations of Interpersonal Attraction*, ed. Ted L. Huston (New York: Academic Press, 1974), pp. 383–402.
7. H. Cantril, "Perception and Interpersonal Relations," *American Journal of Psychiatry*, 114 (1957), 119–26.
8. Herbert Krugman, "The Impact of Television Advertising: Learning Without Involvement," *Public Opinion Quarterly*, 29 (1965), 349–56.
9. Don E. Schultz, *Essentials of Advertising Strategy* (Lincolnwood, IL. NTC Business Books, 1986), pp. 34–38.
10. Wilbur Schramm, "How Communication Works," in *The Process and Effects of Mass Communications*, ed. Wilbur Schramm (Urbana, IL: University of Illinois Press, 1954), pp. 3–26.
11. W. Keith Hafer and Gordon E. White, *Advertising Writing: Putting Creative Strategy to Work*, 3rd ed. (St. Paul: West Publishing Co., 1989), p. 99.

CHAPTER 6

1. Sandra E. Moriarty, *Creativity Advertising: Theory and Practice* (Englewood Cliffs, NJ: Prentice-Hall, 1986), pp. 54–55.
2. Ibid., p. 57.
3. For a full discussion of the buying process beyond the simplistic impulsive, habitual, and extended buy as presented in this chapter, see Michael L. Rothschild, *Advertising: From Fundamentals to Strategies* (Lexington, MA: D.C. Heath and Company, 1987), pp. 70–72.
4. W. Keith Hafer and Gordon E. White, *Advertising Writing: Putting Creative Strategy to Work*, 2nd ed. (St. Paul, MN.: West Publishing Company, 1982), p. 5.

CHAPTER 7

1. Reconciliation of opposites, or creating harmony out of apparent discordant qualities, has been given considerable attention in a variety of areas of creativity research. For example, see William J. Gordon, *Synectics: The Development of Creative Capacity* (New York: Collier Books, 1968), p. 3; Albert Rothenberg, "Creative Contradictions," *Psychology Today* (June, 1979), 55–62; and Albert Rothenberg, *The Emerging Goddess: The Creative Process in Art, Science, and Other Fields* (Chicago: University of Chicago Press, 1979), pp. 139–40.
2. Vincent J. Blasko and Michael P. Mokwa, "Creativity in Advertising: A Janusian Perspective," *Journal of Advertising*, Vol. 15, 2 (1986), 43–50, 72.
3. Ibid., p. 47.
4. John W. Haefele, *Creativity and Innovation* (New York: Reinhold Publishing Corp., 1962), p. 66.
5. William C. Miller, *The Creative Edge: Fostering Innovation Where You Work* (Reading, MA: Addison-Wesley Publishing Co., Inc., 1987), p. 41.
6. John M. Kiel, *The Creative Mystique: How to Manage It, Nuture It, and Make It Pay* (New York: John Wiley & Sons, 1985), p. 25.
7. Richard S. Crutchfield, "Conformity and Creative Thinking," in *Contemporary Approaches to Creative Thinking: A Symposium Held at The University of Colorado*, eds. Howard E. Gruber, Glenn Terrell, and Michael Wertheimer (New York: Atherton Press, 1964), pp. 120–40.
8. Charlan Jeanne Nemeth and Julianne L. Kwan, "Originality of Word Associations as a Function of Majority vs. Minority Influence," *Social Psychology Quarterly*, Vol. 48, 3 (1985), 277–82.
9. J. P. Guilford, "A Psychometric Approach to Creativity," in *Creativity in Childhood and Adolescence: A Diversity of Approaches*, ed. Harold H. Anderson (Palo Alto, CA: Science and Behavior Books, Inc., 1965), pp. 1–19.
10. Joseph McGrath, *Groups: Interaction and Performance* (Englewood Cliffs, NJ: Prentice-Hall, Inc., 1984), p. 131.
11. David Ogilvy, *Ogilvy on Advertising* (London: Pan Books, 1983), p. 20.
12. Much has been discussed in the area of positive reinforcement as a means for stimulating creativity. For example, see Alex F. Osborn, *Applied Imagination: Principles and Procedures of Creative Thinking*, rev. ed. (New York: Charles Scribner's

Sons, 1957), 31–37; Kimberly A. Daubman and Gary P. Nowicki, "Positive Affect Facilitates Creative Problem Solving," *Journal of Personality and Social Psychology,* Vol. 52, 6 (1987), 1122–31.

13. Osborn, *Applied,* p. 12. Many others have reached similar conclusions regarding deferring judgment. For example, see Gordon, *Synectics,* p. 27, and Michael Ray and Rochelle Myers, *Creativity in Business* (Garden City, NY: Doubleday & Co., Inc., 1986), pp. 39–43.

14. Again, many researchers and theorists have reached a similar conclusion regarding quantity leading to quality. For example, see Osborn, *Applied,* pp. 149–151, and Charles H. Clark, *Idea Management: How to Motivate Creativity and Innovation* (New York, Amacom, 1980), p. 44, and Bruce G. Vanden Bergh, Leonard N. Reid, and Gerald A. Schorin, "How Many Creative Alternatives To Generate?," *Journal of Advertising,* Vol. 12, 4 (1983), 46–49.

15. Edward de Bono, *Lateral Thinking: Creativity Step by Step* (New York: Harper Colophon Books, 1973), pp. 13, 39–45.

16. Marco Vassi, *Lying Down: A Horizontal Worldview* (Santa Barbara, CA: Cabra Press, 1984), p. 56.

17. John Keats, "Letter to George and Thomas Keats, December 21 or 27, 1817," in *The Norton Anthology of English Literature,* Vol. 2, ed. M. H. Abrams (New York: W. W. Norton & Co., 1962), pp. 398–399.

18. "Messages from Manning," *Advertising Age* (March 26, 1987), 72.

19. Erich Fromm, "The Creative Attitude," in *Creativity and Its Cultivation: Addresses Presented at The Interdisciplinary Symposia on Creativity, Michigan State University* ed. Harold H. Anderson (New York: Harper & Row, Publishers, 1959), pp. 44–54.

20. Gordon, *Synectics,* p. 41.

21. Ray and Myers, *Creativity,* p. 67.

22. E. Paul Torrance, *The Search for Satori & Creativity* (Buffalo, NY: The Creative Education Foundation, Inc. in association with Creative Synergetic Association, Ltd., 1979), pp. 2–3.

23. Arthur Koestler, *The Act of Creation* (New York: The Macmillan Co., 1964), p. 119.

24. Timothy A. Bengston, "Creativity's Paradoxical Character: A Postscript to James Webb Young's *A Technique for Producing Ideas,*" *Journal of Advertising,* Vol. 11, 1 (1982), 3–9.

25. Stephen Spender, "The Obsession of Writers With The Act of Writing," *Michigan Quarterly Review,* Vol. 21, 1 (Winter, 1982), 553–60.

26. Eugene Raudsepp, "Nurturing Managerial Creativity," *Administrative Management,* 41, 10 (October, 1980), pp. 32–33; 55–56.

27. Mary Henle, "The Birth and Death of Ideas," in *Contemporary Approaches to Creative Thinking: A Symposium Held at The University of Colorado,* eds. Howard E. Gruber, Glenn Terrell, and Michael Wertheimer (New York: Atherton Press, 1964), pp. 31–62.

28. Gordon, *Synectics,* p. 121.

29. Susanna Miller, *The Psychology of Play* (Middlesex, England: Penguin Books, 1968), pp. 60–83.

30. Haefele, *Creativity,* pp. 57–58.

31. For example, see Joe Khatena, Neha Sharad, and Anjoo Sikka, "A Study in India of Originality and Repeated Presentation of Sound Stimuli," *Perceptual and Motor Skills,* 61 (1985), 754, and William G. Masten, Joe Khatena, and David Morse,

"Originality and Repeated Presentation of Sound Stimuli in Intellectually Superior Adolescents," *Perceptual and Motor Skills*, 6 (1986), 709–10.

32. Joan C. Gondola, "Effects of a Systematic Program of Exercise on Selected Measures of Creativity," *Perceptual and Motor Skills*, 60 (1985), 53–54.

33. Ray and Myers, *Creativity*, pp. 15–19, 34.

34. Ruth E. Hartley, Lawrence K. Frank, and Robert M. Goldenson, *Understanding Children's Play* (New York: Columbia University Press, 1952), pp. 159–67.

35. Ray and Myers, *Creativity*, p. 37.

36. Lenore Skenazy, "Who: Agency Creative. Where: Improv.," *Advertising Age* (January 16, 1986), 50. Others recommend role playing or dramatic exercises to stimulate creativity. For example, see E. Paul Torrance, *The Search*, pp. 33–34.

37. Eugene S. Ferguson, "The Mind's Eye: Nonverbal Thought in Technology," *Science*, Vol. 197, 4306 (August 26, 1977), 827–63.

38. Koestler, *The Act*, p. 171.

39. Rosemary D. Gaymer, "You Are a Camera . . . Some Aspects of Observation," *The Journal of Creative Behavior*, Vol. 19, 1 (1985), 67–75.

40. Albert Rothenberg, "Artistic Creation as Stimulated by Superimposed Versus Combined-Composite Visual Images," *Journal of Personality and Social Psychology*, Vol. 50, 2 (1986), 370–381.

41. Miller, *The Creative Edge*, p. 42.

42. Koestler, *The Act*, p. 174.

43. Eugene K. von Fange, *Professional Creativity* (Englewood Cliffs, NJ: Prentice-Hall, Inc., 1959), p. 57.

INDEX